Preface books

A series of scholarly and critical studies of major writers intended for those needing modern and authoritative guidance through the characteristic difficulties of their work to reach an intelligent understanding and enjoyment of it.

General Editor: MAURICE HUSSEY

Available now:

A Preface to Wordsworth   JOHN PURKIS
A Preface to Donne   JAMES WINNY
A Preface to Milton   LOIS POTTER

Other titles in preparation:

A Preface to Pope   IAN GORDON
A Preface to Shelley   VALERIE PITT
A Preface to Spenser   HELENA SHIRE
A Preface to Jane Austen   CHRISTOPHER GILLIE
A Preface to Dryden   DAVID WYKES

Coleridge by Washington Allston, 1814

A Preface to Coleridge

Allan Grant

Longman

LONGMAN GROUP LIMITED

London

*Associated companies, branches and
representatives throughout the world*

First published 1972

ISBN o 582 31515 8 Cased
      31516 6 Paper

Printed in Great Britain by Lowe and Brydone (Printers) Ltd

ALLAN GRANT is lecturer in English in the Humanities Department of
Chelsea College of Science, in the University of London. His primary
interest is in the aesthetics of literature of the nineteenth and twentieth
centuries and he teaches mainly in the area of modern cultural studies.
He has edited *The City and the Court*, an anthology of five Jacobean
Comedies of London Life.

Contents

List of Illustrations

Acknowledgements

This book owes much to the generous advice and inexhaustible patience of the General Editor, Maurice Hussey. Every student of Coleridge owes an immeasurable debt of gratitude to those scholars, such as Kathleen Coburn and Earl Leslie Griggs, who are engaged in making available the whole of Coleridge's work. In writing this book I have also drawn heavily on the sympathy and resources of my wife and friends, of colleagues and students in the Department of Humanities at Chelsea College.

The author and publisher are grateful to the following for permission to reproduce photographs: British Museum, pages 37 and 44; Lord Clark, page 117 *bottom*; Country Life, page 25 *bottom*; Fogg Art Museum, Harvard University, Loan—The Washington Allston Trust, page 178; Glasgow Art Gallery and Museum, page 25 *top*; M. H. Hole Williton, page 65 *bottom*; Horniman Museum, page 101; Laing Art Gallery, page 26; Leeds City Art Galleries, page 171 *bottom*; Mansell Collection, pages 71 and 117 *top*; Museum Folkwan Essen, page xi; National Gallery, page 111; National Monuments Record, page 12; National Portrait Gallery, pages 59 *both* 107 and *frontispiece*; J. C. D. Smith, page 65 top; Victoria and Albert Museum, pages 135 and 173 *both*.

They are grateful also to the Clarendon Press for permission to quote extracts from *Collected Letters of Samuel Taylor Coleridge*, edited by Earl Leslie Griggs *vol. 1 1785–1800* (1956).

Foreword

This present volume is the fourth in the series, and complements the first, *A Preface to Wordsworth* by John Purkis. In the valuable concise argument that follows, the present author characterises and compares our two senior Romantics who were inextricably related in an artistic friendship. To emphasise the exceptional range of Coleridge's mind, Allan Grant uses the analogy of the open circle as a way of contrasting it with the more self-contained though no less penetrating intelligence of the other poet. As we read them side by side each reveals to the other different facets of the outer and inner landscapes that make up his individual creative work. In this respect they resemble quite closely the two figures in the picture 'Kindred Spirits' by Asher B. Durand which forms the cover of this book.

In 1972, as we write, Coleridge attains his bicentenary, but still resists too strenuous attempts to pigeonhole him. Like Francis Bacon he might well have claimed 'all knowledge as [his] province.' In Part One of this book Mr Grant makes it clear that the philosophic roots out of which Coleridge grew were firmly set in an eighteenth-century soil, even though the esotericism and mystery that we find in most of his output proclaims the outgrowth of Romantic exuberance. Jorge Luis Borges expresses the opinion that 'every writer creates his own precursors. His work modifies our conception of the past'. Chapter Two of the present volume offers genuine illumination of this principle.

The development of Victorian thought may be said to have created a still more significant view of Coleridge. In spite of the fragmentary nature of his later work the transmission of ideas took place. Those numerous lectures in London, said to be so pleasant or stirring to the auditors but in the end apparently so unintelligible, would appear to have possessed a form of communication through which the influence of the Sage of Highgate travelled: a subliminal one even. To assess as much of this inspiration as has reached the later twentieth century is the task of the present-day Coleridgeans and Mr Grant's sensitive commentaries will put many aspirants in his debt.

A Note on the Illustrations

The arts of painting and language were close neighbours in the Romantic period. It would require a gallery to do justice to the pictorial representations of Nature imbued with the same pantheistic feelings as those expressed by Coleridge in 1795:

And what if all of animated nature
Be but organic Harps diversely framed,
That tremble into thought?

(Eolian Harp)

Our illustrations, from the cover-picture inwards, are viewed as close adjuncts to the text and as further ways of grasping the aesthetic principles of the Romantic period.

As will be seen hereafter, Coleridge was intent on revealing a world of landscape in poetry which was associated in his mind with the limitless horizons of some contemporary painters. To look at the two poets in a slightly different light, Wordsworth admitted to a complete ignorance of the more exotic mysticism of the German metaphysicians, and chose, as a fully congenial artist, the English painter John Constable. True to the nature of his own insights on the other hand, Coleridge, the metaphysician, preferred as his painterly counterpart the more sublime and pantheistic German artist, Caspar David Friedrich, who lived in Pomerania between 1774 and 1840. It was with the voice of so many Romantics that Friedrich stated: 'I have to be united with my clouds and rocks'. In this yearning fashion he expresses the affinity existing between the artist and such typical symbols as moon, clouds or rainbow (see p. x) with their luminosity and spaciousness, while acknowledging such features as the forests as symbols of social restrictions placed upon the artist's creative freedom. We have Weber's opera *Der Freischutz* of 1821 to remind us that forests contained in similar fashion the spirit of German Romanticism and there seems little doubt that Coleridge absorbed something of that same quality from the Harz Mountains in the course of his travels in Germany. No doubt at times Wordsworth possessed the same ability to identify himself completely with those images drawn from his own closeness to the English landscape which recur most consistently in his poems: I mean the cloud and the grey stone.

Throughout his career Coleridge chose abstraction and mysticism, speaking of the 'tyranny of the eye' as if the concrete or the specific were something restricting to be guarded against. The student of either poet, then, will find considerable enjoyment and profit in collections or discussions of the landscape art of the period. Rather in the prefatory manner of this book as a whole, the illustrations that we have included are intended only as a preface to further and later discoveries for the reader. The objective of the present book is to bring closer to the eye some of the foreground and major peaks of Coleridge's art and thought, and to enable the modern reader to judge their quality and significance in spite of the multiplicity of obscuring trees that Coleridge seemed intent on cultivating in his own inner landscape.

MAURICE HUSSEY
General Editor

Introduction

Coleridge's younger contemporaries William Hazlitt and Thomas Carlyle put at the centre of their descriptions of him the complaint that he never walked in a straight line, and felt that his habit of lurching from side to side as he walked was symptomatic of his whole character and thought. His young admirer Thomas De Quincey asserted to the contrary that Coleridge's whole mode of peripatetic conversation was governed by the severest logical continuity. This book does not go about its subject in a straight line and, if it contains any logical continuity at all, that derives from a half-submerged thesis concerning the entire argument about the relationship between an individual writer and what is often casually described as the 'spirit of the age'. Carlyle complained of Coleridge because he was looking for a particular kind of guidance; the kind that would unravel for him some of his puzzles about the mysteries of the world. Neither the study of Coleridge nor a reading of this book will offer that kind of guidance. As far as possible I have tried to present throughout Coleridge's own writings and those of others, especially those of his contemporaries, in such a way as to allow them to speak for themselves without interposing my own view. The effect of the attempt may be kaleidoscopic and sometimes contradictory. It is an effect not unlike that of Coleridge himself on the reader or student.

As my purpose is introductory, so I have kept my major argument about Coleridge outside the main body of the text, although as I present different aspects of him as poet and critic, I have produced the evidence in such a way as to suggest that he is a certain kind of poet and that he is a critic of a very high order who obliges us to question our assumptions as to what kind of thing literature is. Alongside these views and the evidence I set the major social, intellectual and political currents of his age of which he was very much aware. A primary function of this book, therefore, is a backwards and forwards reference between individual works, the man in his society, against it or even out of it altogether, and the background of intellectual, aesthetic and political affairs. At the centre of the book is Part Two, a critical survey of Coleridge's major poetry. Part One is a series of studies of Coleridge's beginnings as a poet and his development as a thinker. It also provides a biographical and chronological skeleton. Part Three is designed to fulfil two functions, the first of which is to give information about people and places relevant to Coleridge's life and work. The second function of Part Three is to invite the reader to be tempted further into the arena of Coleridge studies by providing some of the equipment required for such an enterprise. The study of

Coleridge or the reading of this book by way of introduction is not an undertaking that I would recommend to those who think they prefer to walk in a straight line.

A Note on the State of the Texts

Rather than have to apologize every time for a fidelity to the punctuation of the original texts, I have preferred to alter spellings and punctuation marks as unobtrusively as possible so that the reader will not confuse early nineteenth-century eccentricity with a twentieth-century commentator's errors.

A.G.

Mountain Landscape with Rainbow *by Caspar David Friedrich*

The Argument

The comment is that of Professor Kathleen Coburn who is perhaps the foremost Coleridge scholar of our day. In her use of the word 'almost' she acknowledges all the hopes and frustrations of the Coleridge commentator. There is always something to be discovered that sheds further light on the subject, yet, at the same time, the student experiences the certainty that there is still more to be known and that the subject is finally inexhaustible. It is like the words of the Duke in John Webster's play *The Duchess of Malfi*:

> He who has compassed me and knows my drift
> May say he has put a girdle 'bout the world
> And sounded all her quicksands.   (Act III scene i)

No other English poet seems so effectively to have engineered the defeat of his self-appointed tasks while able simultaneously to observe the details of the drama of that defeat. Yet it would be false to impose on Coleridge the modern myth of the attractiveness of failure. If we prefer to see the man as a bundle of fragments then we shall not feel compelled to make the effort to follow the movements of his convoluted mind to see where they lead us. If so much of Coleridge's career appears to be strewn with false hopes, false beginnings and large failures, the appearance is misleading. A further distortion of what lies behind the appearance grows out of the fact that so much of his *ephemera* and *marginalia* have come down to us, so that our perspective on his work is like a view of broken country as we pass through it on a journey. The grander peaks are obscured by the nearer, lesser ranges. It is also the case that only in our own time is the exhaustive task of publishing and annotating *all* of his known writings being undertaken. If for that reason alone, our view of him is bound to be incomplete. Again, if the many contemporary accounts of him are to be believed, and even when they are sometimes hostile they are extraordinarily persuasive, a large part of Coleridge's fascination for his friends and patrons lay in the quality of his talk. He talked at least as much as he wrote, more in his last years at Highgate, and the atmosphere created by his often brilliant extemporizations in public or in private is something that can only be elusively recaptured through those baffling accounts of such occasions that others have left for us.

It is possible to pay so much attention to what Coleridge did not do, and to seek to know what can never be known again, that we miss the point of what he did achieve. In the publishers' booklists of the middle of the nineteenth century Coleridge appears as a very substantial author. Edward Moxon's list for 1852 includes ten works by Coleridge in seventeen volumes as well as three editions by Hartley Coleridge, of his father's works, each in seven volumes. Perhaps the identification of Coleridge with the myth of the *poète maudit*, the poet born under a curse, is of a later date; he may even have helped to create the myth, so powerful has been the effect on later readers of *The Ancient Mariner*. Virginia Woolf has likened his self-absorption to that of Mr Micawber in Charles Dickens's *David Copperfield* with a touch of Mr Pecksniff, and the grain of truth in her perception marks an important premise of Coleridge's whole mode of enquiry.

For Coleridge, to know the human mind was an essential task of the philosopher. Nearest to hand for observation was his own mind, and what he felt in his own mind was his test of any systematic philosophical explanation of mind. What he did feel most powerfully and describe continually in his notebooks, letters and poetry, was *process*. 'The very process of life and consciousness', as he called it. It followed, therefore, that there could be no final account of the human mind and its relations with the knowable world which did not acknowledge this sense of process and the uncloseable circle of experience. His self-analysis led him to try to account for the unaccountable in himself. The contrast with the career and character of William Wordsworth in this, as in so many other respects, is illuminating. As poets they are marvellously complementary to each other, but it is as though each drew apart from the other after a period of close and creative collaboration. Wordsworth suffered the consequences of cutting himself off, of contributing to the myth of what he was, while Coleridge, on the other hand, suffered for his vulnerability, for his very refusal to close the circle. Like 'the never-bloomless furze' of the Quantock Hills, his work abounds with reference to change within continuity, to renewal and persistence. Coleridge also suffered long spells of appalling ill-health which were neither merely imagined nor induced by his long and wearying addiction to opium. While it is true that in his letters he sometimes pleads his miseries in extenuation of his failure to fulfill the highest expectations that he and others entertained of him, it is also true that he was able to confront his miseries and inspect them as experiences. He considered that they were as much a part of him as his more hopeful and successful self. And he was surely right. Not only that: he did more with them in that he made out of them poetry that is among the greatest, not only of the Romantic period, but of the whole range of poetry written in the English language.

In coming to his poetry, I come to the core of my argument. This book is only incidentally about Coleridge the man. Neither is it a book intended to pursue his philosophy in any detail, if only because our main business is with the poetry and the criticism, and that the status of Coleridge's philosophy is a matter of sharp dispute among those more qualified than I to deal with it. But some effort must be made: some understanding of his philosophical position is necessary to our understanding of his poetry and criticism. Eighteenth-century philosophers in England had approached the perennial problem of the constitution of the human mind and knowledge in a new way. They considered the human mind to be nothing more than an accumulation and combination of experiences or sensations. One part of Coleridge's argument against this 'modern' view was poetry. At an early date he saw clearly that the general tendency of such sensationalist philosophies was to endanger the notions of free will, human choice and man's moral life. He held and developed afresh the notion that the moral life, from which all great poetry flows, is independent of the facts of experience and their causes, even if it is in continuous relations with them. This belief is a belief in the freedom and creativity of the human spirit, the source of which spirit he located in the faculty of imagination. It is on the area of these relations that the argument of this book is concentrated.

While preparing the book I have noticed two unexpected side effects. One is the impression which has forced itself on me of just how modern a figure is Coleridge as poet and thinker, and what a particularly brilliant light he throws on the human condition in our own time. The other is the way in which he forces his reader to look beyond the period in which he grew up and wrote to the whole preceding history of man's thought and creative endeavour from Plato onwards. He said that he disliked history and yet in himself resumes all history. His personality leaps at us from almost every page he wrote. It is a modern one and we cannot ignore it. He is a witness to the fragmentation of life that is the modern experience, to which others such as Matthew Arnold, W. B. Yeats and T. S. Eliot have been later witnesses, and he bent his whole energy to its repair. Who shall say whether this was success or failure?

Part One

The Poet and Critic in his Setting

The Coleridge Family

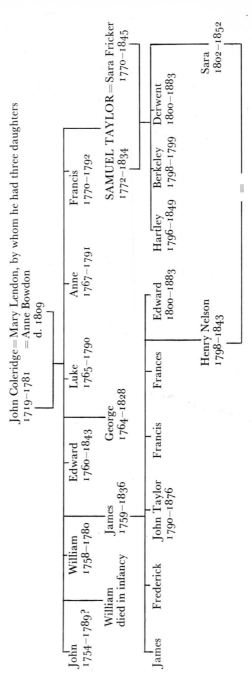

John Coleridge = Mary Lendon, by whom he had three daughters
1719–1781　　　= Anne Bowdon
　　　　　　　　　　d. 1809

John
1754–1789?

William
1758–1780

William
died in infancy

Edward
1760–1843

James
1759–1836

Luke
1765–1790

George
1764–1828

Anne
1767–1791

Francis
1770–1792

SAMUEL TAYLOR = Sara Fricker
1772–1834　　　　　1770–1845

Frederick

James

John Taylor
1790–1876

Francis

Frances

Edward
1800–1883

Henry Nelson
1798–1843

Hartley
1796–1849

Berkeley
1798–1799

Derwent
1800–1883

Sara
1802–1852

1 Biographical summaries

Chronological table

	LITERARY EVENTS	HISTORICAL & RELATED EVENTS
1770	William Wordsworth born. Joseph Cottle born. Thomas Chatterton dies.	Ludwig van Beethoven born.
1771	First edition of the *Encyclopaedia Britannica*. Beattie's *The Minstrel*. Walter Scott born. Dorothy Wordsworth born.	
1772	S. T. Coleridge born. *The Morning Post* founded.	
1774	Robert Southey born. First British Copyright Act.	Accession of Louis XVI of France.
1775	Charles Lamb born.	American War of Independence begins. James Watt perfects the steam engine.
1776	Adam Smith's *The Wealth of Nations*.	American Declaration of Independence. John Constable born.
1778	William Hazlitt born. Jean-Jacques Rousseau dies.	Humphry Davy born.
1780		The Gordon Riots in London against Catholic emancipation.
1781	Coleridge's father dies. Kant's *Critique of Pure Reason*. Jean-Jacques Rousseau's *Confessions*.	
1782	William Cowper's *Table Talk*.	

1783	William Blake's *Poetical Sketches*.	Peace of Versailles signed between Britain, France and America. William Pitt Prime Minister at 24.
1784	Samuel Johnson dies.	
1785	Thomas De Quincey born.	
1788	Kant's *Critique of Practical Reason*. George (later Lord) Byron born.	
1789	William Blake's *Songs of Innocence*. William Lisle Bowles's *Fourteen Sonnets written chiefly on picturesque spots*.	The French Revolution begins.
1790	William Blake engraves *The Marriage of Heaven and Hell*. Edmund Burke's *Reflections on the Revolution in France*.	
1791	Coleridge enters Jesus College, Cambridge Thomas Paine's *Rights of Man* published: 1,500,000 copies sold in the next five years.	
1792	Percy Bysshe Shelley born.	
1793	William Godwin's *The Inquiry Concerning Political Justice*. Wordsworth's *Descriptive Sketches*.	France declares war on Britain. In France Louis XVI is executed, Jean Marat is murdered and Christianity 'abolished'.
1794	William Blake's *Songs of Innocence and Experience*. Meeting at Oxford of Coleridge and Southey. *The Fall of Robespierre*	Robespierre executed in Paris.

1794 (*cont.*)	published in Coleridge's name. In December Coleridge leaves Cambridge to pursue the scheme of Pantisocracy.	
1795	John Keats born. The Wordsworths stay at Racedown in Dorset and William meets Coleridge in Bristol. Coleridge marries Sara Fricker of Bristol. They settle at Clevedon, Somerset.	In France, the Directory is established following the Terror. Pitt's Treasonable Practices Bill and Seditious Meetings Bill.
1796	Southey's *Joan of Arc*. Hartley Coleridge born. *Poems* by S. T. Coleridge published. Coleridge edits *The Watchman*. The Coleridge family move on the last day of the year to Nether Stowey.	Napoleon Bonaparte's Italian Campaign.
1797	Southey's *Poems*. Edmund Burke dies. Franz Schubert born. The Wordsworths move to Alfoxden to be near Coleridge. Coleridge publishes *Poems* by himself, Lamb and Charles Lloyd.	
1798	T. R. Malthus's *Essay on the Principle of Population*. A second son, Berkeley, born who dies during Coleridge's German tour. The younger Wedgwoods, Josiah and Thomas, settle an annuity of £150 on Coleridge for life. First edition of *Lyrical Ballads* published at Bristol by Cottle.	

1798 (cont.)	Coleridge and the Wordsworths sail for Germany.	
1799	Returning from Goslar, the Wordsworths settle at Dove Cottage, Grasmere. Coleridge, on his return from Germany, contributes to the *Morning Post*.	Napoleon established as First Consul for ten years.
1800	F. W. von Schelling's *System of Transcendental Idealism*. William Cowper dies. The Coleridges settle at Greta Hall, Keswick, where Derwent is born. Second edition of *Lyrical Ballads* with a Preface by Wordsworth.	Humphry Davy's *Researches, Chiefly Concerning Nitrous Oxides* published. Pitt's Combination Acts forbid trade associations.
1802	Wordsworth marries Mary Hutchinson. The Southeys move permanently to Greta Hall. The *Edinburgh Review* founded. Sara, a daughter, born to Coleridge. Coleridge addresses *Dejection: an Ode* to Sara Hutchinson. Third edition of *Lyrical Ballads*.	Thomas Wedgwood makes the first photograph on glass.
1803	Coleridge abandons a tour of Scotland with William and Dorothy Wordsworth.	
1804	Having decided to separate from his wife, Coleridge sails for Malta, hoping that a warmer climate will improve his health.	
1805	Southey's *Madoc*. Walter Scott's *The Lay of*	The Battles of Trafalgar and Austerlitz.

1805 (*cont*).	*the last Minstrel.*	Thomas Wedgwood dies.
1806	John Stuart Mill born. Coleridge returns to London by way of Italy.	William Pitt dies.
1807	Charles and Mary Lamb *Tales from Shakespeare.* De Quincey meets Coleridge at Bridgewater in Somerset. Wordsworth's *Poems in Two Volumes.*	
1808	Charles Lamb's *Specimens of English Dramatic Poets Contemporary with Shakespeare.* Walter Scott's *Marmion.* Coleridge gives his first series of lectures at the Royal Institution in London. Later in the year he stays with the Wordsworths at Grasmere, where De Quincey is also a guest.	
1809	Walter Scott founds the *Quarterly Review.* Alfred (later Lord) Tennyson born. Coleridge edits *The Friend* until March 1810.	
1810	Walter Scott's *The Lady of the Lake.* Coleridge leaves the Lake District for London and breaks with Wordsworth.	
1811	Coleridge lectures in London on the English poets. Josiah Wedgwood withdraws his half of the legacy.	The Prince of Wales becomes Regent in the place of his father George III and gives the name to the literary and cultural period of the Regency. An immediate expression of the period is the rebuilding of

1811 *(cont.)*		Regent Street in the centre of London by John Nash.
1812	Byron's *Childe Harold's Pilgrimage.* Charles Dickens born. Coleridge continues to lecture sporadically in London and Bristol.	Napoleon retreats from Moscow.
1813	Southey's *Life of Nelson.* Shelley's *Queen Mab.* Coleridge's early play *Osorio,* revised as *Remorse,* runs for 20 nights at Drury Lane theatre, London.	
1814	Wordsworth's *Excursion.* Walter Scott's *Waverley.* Coleridge stays with his friend John Morgan, first at Hammersmith, London, and then at Calne, Wiltshire.	George Stephenson constructs a working steam locomotive.
1815	At Calne, Coleridge begins dictating *Biographia Literaria.*	Napoleon defeated at Waterloo.
1816	Coleridge goes to stay at Highgate, London, as a patient of Dr James Gillman. *Christabel* and *Kubla Khan.* Coleridge's *The Statesman's Manual: or The Bible the best Guide to Political Skill and Foresight.*	
1817	*Poems* by John Keats. *Blackwood's Magazine* founded. Jane Austen dies. Coleridge publishes *Biographia Literaria, Sybilline Leaves* and his two *Lay Sermons.*	

1818	Coleridge lectures on Philosophy and on Shakespeare. He publishes an edited selection from *The Friend* and *On Method*, a preliminary treatise to the *Encyclopaedia Metropolitana*.	
1819	'George Eliot' born.	A large crowd, gathered in Manchester at Peterloo Fields to promote Parliamentary reform and the repeal of the Corn Laws, is charged at by the Militia and fired upon.
1820	Wordworth's poetry published in four volumes. Shelley's *Prometheus Unbound*. Keats' *Lamia, Isabella, Hyperion*. Hartley Coleridge loses his fellowship at Oriel College, Oxford.	
1821	De Quincey's *Confessions of an English Opium Eater*. John Keats dies and Shelley writes *Adonais*.	Napoleon dies. George III dies and his son is crowned George IV.
1822	Matthew Arnold born. Shelley dies.	
1824	Byron dies in Greece. Jeremy Bentham founds the *Westminster Review*. At the founding of the Royal Society for Literature under the patronage of George IV Coleridge is made one of the first ten associates with a pension of £100 a year.	
1825	William Hazlitt's *The Spirit of the Age; or Contemporary Portraits*. Coleridge's *Aids to Reflection*	The Stockton to Darlington Railway opened. Beethoven's 9th Symphony performed in England by the

1825 (*cont.*)	*in the Formation of a Manly Character* published	Philharmonic Society who originally commissioned the work.
1827	Wordsworth's third collected edition published in five volumes, including *The Excursion*. Sir George Beaumont dies.	University College London, founded. Beethoven dies.
1828	Coleridge's *Poetical Works* published. He and Wordsworth spend a fortnight in Germany touring the River Rhine together	Franz Schubert dies. The Test and Corporation Acts repealed by Parliament so that Catholic and Protestant Nonconformists in Britain are allowed to hold public office.
1829		Sir Humphry Davy dies. Roman Catholic Relief Bill passes through the House of Lords, giving them right of suffrage and the right to sit and vote in Parliament.
1830	Tennyson's *Poems Chiefly Lyrical*. William Hazlitt dies. Coleridge's *On the Constitution of Church and State* published and reprinted.	Paris revolts against the repressive ordinances of Charles X; Louis Philippe elected first Lieutenant General and then constitutional monarch.
1831		Third Reform Bill introduced into the House of Commons. Charles Darwin voyages to the Pacific in the *Beagle*.
1832	The fourth edition of Wordsworth's poetry published (in four volumes). George Crabbe dies. Sir Walter Scott dies. Jeremy Bentham dies. Goethe dies.	The Reform Bill becomes law; over 140 parliamentary seats redistributed and the franchise reformed and extended to include leaseholders paying a minimum of £10 annual rent.

1833	*Poems* by Hartley Coleridge appears.	The first state grant for education in England. The British Factory Act passed prohibiting the employment of children under the age of nine, and establishing a system of Factory Inspectors.
1834	Coleridge dies on 25 July. Charles Lamb dies on 27 December.	A Grand National Consolidated Trades Union formed in Britain; at Tolpuddle in Dorset, labourers are transported for taking an illegal oath in forming a lodge of the Union. The Poor Law Amendment Act establishing workhouses throughout England. Slavery abolished throughout the British Empire.
1836	Henry Nelson Coleridge edits four volumes of Coleridge's *Literary Remains*.	
1840	He publishes Coleridge's *Confessions of an Enquiring Spirit*.	

Biographical sketch

Samuel Taylor Coleridge, poet, literary critic and religious philosopher, was born on 21 October 1772, the tenth and youngest child by his second wife, of the vicar and schoolmaster of Ottery St Mary in Devon. At the age of eight, according to his own account, he ran away from home after a quarrel with his brother who had provoked him, and slept that night on the bank of a stream, an adventure which he dated as the beginning of his continuous later ill-health. Following the death of his father two years later in 1782, a place was found for him at Christ's Hospital, the London charity school, where Charles Lamb was his junior. In October 1791 he entered Jesus College, Cambridge. Perhaps because he had been disappointed in love, certainly because he was in debt, he disappeared in December 1793 and enlisted in the Light Dragoons at Reading under the name of Silas Tomkyns Comberbache. (Note the initials S.T.C. He refused to submerge himself completely.) He had also told some of the boys

St Mary's Church, Ottery

from Christ's Hospital whom he met at the Angel Inn on his way through London of his intention to enlist. Discharged in April 1794 after the intervention of family and friends, he returned to Cambridge. On a vacation walking tour, he met Robert Southey, poet and 'sturdy Republican', at Oxford in June, with whom during the following three weeks or so he outlined a plan to establish (in a remote part of America) an ideal community which Coleridge called Pantisocracy.

Coleridge went down from Cambridge in December 1794 without a degree and settled for a time with Southey in Bristol, where he delivered a series of subscription lectures on contemporary political themes. By this time, several poems and sonnets by Coleridge had been published in local and national newspapers. The only practical consequence of the Utopian American scheme was Coleridge's marriage on 4 October at Bristol to Sara, sister of Edith Fricker, whom Robert Southey was to marry. The Coleridges settled in a cottage in Clevedon in Somerset, where Coleridge wrote and studied and produced ten numbers of a magazine, *The Watchman*, a political and literary periodical. There also in September 1796 their first child Hartley was born. In December of this year the family moved to Nether Stowey. In 1795 Coleridge met William Wordsworth, whose poetry he had already read; and in July two years later Wordsworth and his sister rented Alfoxden, a large house in the district, so as to be near Coleridge. In the next year, 1798, they wrote *Lyrical Ballads* and, immediately following its publication, embarked for Germany to learn the language and study contemporary philosophy and science. On his return from Göttingen University Coleridge visited the Wordsworths and Hutchinsons near Durham. When Wordsworth married and settled at Grasmere in the Lake District, Coleridge and his family followed in July 1800, where they, in turn, were followed by the Southeys who shared their house, Greta Hall near Keswick. Coleridge's health was not good at this time and he began taking opium. Relations with his wife grew even more difficult than they had been before he left for Germany and he imagined himself, whether he in fact was or not, to be in love with Wordsworth's sister-in-law Sara Hutchinson. He was encouraged to talk of separating from his wife and so left for Malta in June 1804, where he held the post of temporary secretary to the governor Sir Alexander Ball. From this time, Southey took more or less full responsibility for maintaining Coleridge's family. He returned two years later via Rome in no better health and suffering the effects of separation from his friends.

After a short period in London during which he wrote to no one, he returned for two years to live with the Wordsworths and produced another periodical, *The Friend*, his second venture into periodical editing, of which twenty-seven numbers appeared. Sara Hutchinson, who had copied the manuscripts for the printer, left to live with a brother in Wales and Coleridge, his life and work in pieces, left for

13

London where the breach with Wordsworth opened and was never again completely healed. In London and Bristol Coleridge continued sporadically to write and lecture at a time when for nearly ten years his life and health were in almost continual crisis. In 1816 he went to live for a short time, as he thought, as a patient in the house at Highgate of James Gillman, a physician. He never moved again. He became the sage of Highgate, and the house a place of pilgrimage for writers and thinkers. Here Carlyle came, and William Blake. Walking on Hampstead Heath he met the young John Keats. In these last calm years he completed, even though his health was never fully restored, *Biographia Literaria* and the Lay Sermons in 1817, *Aids to Reflection* in 1825, an edition of his poems in 1828, and two years later, *On the Constitution of Church and State*. He died on 25 July 1834 and was buried in Highgate Churchyard. A few months previously he had composed his own epitaph.

> Stop, Christian passer-by!—Stop, child of God,
> And read with gentle breast. Beneath this sod
> A poet lies, or that which once seem'd he.
> O, lift one thought in prayer for S.T.C.;
> That he who many a year with toil of breath
> Found death in life, may here find life in death!
> Mercy for praise—to be forgiven for fame
> He ask'd, and hoped, through Christ. Do
>   thou the same!

Sketches from life

Even in his own time Coleridge was much written about by both friends and enemies and I have selected the following descriptions for the particular light each throws on this many-faceted character.

1. Coleridge wrote a series of autobiographical letters to Thomas Poole in 1797 and 1798. He describes his early childhood:

From October 1775 to October 1778
These three years I continued at the reading-school—because I was too little to be trusted among my Father's School-boys—. After breakfast I had a halfpenny given me, with which I bought three cakes at the Baker's close by the school of my old mistress—& these were my dinner on every day except Saturday & Sunday—when I used to dine at home, and wallowed in a beef & pudding dinner.—I am remarkably fond of Beans & Bacon—and this fondness I attribute to my father's having given me a penny for having eat a large quantity of beans, one Saturday—for the other boys did not like them, and as it was an economic food, my father thought, that my attachment & penchant for it ought to be encouraged.—My Father was very fond of me, and I was my mother's darling—in

consequence, I was very miserable. For Molly, who had nursed my Brother Francis, and was immoderately fond of him, hated me because my mother took more notice of me than of Frank —and Frank hated me, because my mother gave me now & then a bit of cake, when he had none—quite forgetting that for one bit of cake which I had & he had not, he had twenty sops in the pan & pieces of bread & butter with sugar on them from Molly, from whom I received only thumps & ill names.—So I became fretful, & timorous, & a tell-tale—& the School-boys drove me from play, & were always tormenting me—& hence I took no pleasure in boyish sports—but read incessantly. My Father's Sister kept an *every-thing* Shop at Crediton—and there I read thro' all the gilt-cover little books that could be had at that time, & likewise all the uncovered tales of Tom Hickathrift, Jack the Giant-killer, &c & &c &c &c—and I used to lie by the wall, and *mope*—and my spirits used to come upon me suddenly, & in a flood—& then I was accustomed to run up and down the church-yard, and act over all I had been reading on the docks, the nettles, and the rank-grass. —At six years old I remember to have read Belisarius, Robinson Crusoe, & Philip Quarll—and then I found the Arabian Nights' entertainments—one tale of which (the tale of a man who was compelled to seek for a pure virgin) made so deep an impression on me (I had read it in the evening while my mother was mending stockings) that I was haunted by spectres, whenever I was in the dark—and I distinctly remember the anxious & fearful eagerness, with which I used to watch the window, in which the books lay— & whenever the Sun lay upon them, I would seize it, carry it by the wall, & bask, & read—. My Father found out the effect, which these books had produced—and burnt them.—So I became a *dreamer*—and acquired an indisposition to all bodily activity—and I was fretful, and inordinately passionate, and as I could not play at any thing, and was slothful, I was despised & hated by the boys; and because I could read & spell, & had, I may truly say, a memory & understanding forced into almost an unnatural ripeness, I was flattered & wondered at by all the old women—& so I became very vain, and despised most of the boys, that were at all near my own age—and before I was eight years old, I was a *character*—sensibility, imagination, vanity, sloth, & feelings of deep & bitter contempt for almost all who traversed the orbit of my understanding, were even then prominent & manifest.

2. Charles Lamb was Coleridge's junior at Christ's Hospital and his lifelong admirer. The following extract comes from one of Lamb's many nostalgic essays about childhood, *Christ's Hospital Thirty-five years ago.*

Come back into memory, like as thou wert in the day-spring of thy fancies, with hope like a fiery column before thee—the dark pillar not yet turned—Samuel Taylor Coleridge—Logician, Metaphysician, Bard!—How have I seen the casual passer through the Cloisters stand still, entranced with admiration (while he weighed the disproportion between the *speech* and the *garb* of the young Mirandula), to hear thee unfold, in thy deep and sweet intonations, the mysteries of Jamblichus, or Plotinus (for even in those years thou waxedst not pale at such philosophic draughts), or reciting Homer in his Greek, or Pindar—while the walls of the old Grey Friars re-echoed to the accents of the *inspired charity-boy*! Many were the 'wit-combats' (to dally awhile with the words of old Fuller) between him and C. V. Le G——, 'which two I behold like a Spanish great gallion, and an English man-of-war; Master Coleridge, like the former, was built far higher in learning, solid, but slow in his performances. C.V.L., with the English man-of-war, lesser in bulk, but lighter in sailing, could turn with all tides, tack about, and take advantage of all winds, by the quickness of his wit and invention.'

3. Dorothy Wordsworth first described Coleridge (in a letter of 1797) not long after his first visit to Racedown.

You had a great loss in not seeing Coleridge. He is a wonderful man. His conversation teems with soul, mind and spirit. At first I thought him very plain, that is for about three minutes. He is pale, thin, has a wide mouth, thick lips, not very good teeth, longish loose-growing half-curling rough black hair. But, if you hear him speak for five minutes, you think no more of them. His eye is large and full, and not very dark, but grey, such an eye as would receive from a heavy soul the dullest expression; but it speaks every emotion of his animated mind. It has more of the poetic eye in a fine frenzy rolling, than I ever witnessed. He has fine dark eyebrows, and an overhanging forehead.

4. William Hazlitt's essay *My First Acquaintance among Poets* is a splendid memorial to Coleridge's influence. After this first meeting, Hazlitt stayed with Coleridge and Wordsworth on a number of occasions.

Coleridge had agreed to come over and see my father, according to the courtesy of the country, as Mr Rowe's probable successor; but in the meantime I had gone to hear him preach the Sunday after his arrival. A poet and a philosopher getting up into a Unitarian pulpit to preach the Gospel, was a romance in these degenerate days, a sort of revival of the primitive spirit of Christianity, which was not to be resisted.

It was in January, 1798, that I rose one morning before daylight, to walk ten miles in the mud, and went to hear this celebrated person preach. Never, the longest day I have to live, shall I have

such another walk as this cold, raw comfortless one, in the winter of the year 1798. . . . When I got there, the organ was playing the 100th Psalm, and when it was done, Mr Coleridge rose and gave out his text, 'And he went up into the mountain to pray, HIMSELF, ALONE.' As he gave out this text, his voice 'rose like a steam of rich distilled perfumes,' and when he came to the two last words, which he pronounced loud, deep, and distinct, it seemed to me, who was then young, as if the sounds had echoed from the bottom of the human heart, and as if that prayer might have floated in solemn silence through the universe. The idea of St John came into my mind, 'of one crying in the wilderness, who had his loins girt about, and whose food was locusts and wild honey.' The preacher then launched into his subject, like an eagle dallying with the wind. The sermon was upon peace and war; upon church and state—not their alliance but their separation—on the spirit of the world and the spirit of Christianity, not as the same, but as opposed to one another. He talked of those who had 'inscribed the cross of Christ on banners dripping with human gore.' He made a poetical and pastoral excursion—and to show the fatal effects of war, drew a striking contrast between the simple shepherd-boy, driving his team afield, or sitting under the hawthorn, piping to his flock, 'as though he should never be old,' and the same poor country lad, crimped, kidnapped, brought into town, made drunk at an alehouse, turned into a wretched drummer-boy, with his hair sticking on end with powder and pomatum, a long cue at his back, and tricked out in the loathsome finery of the profession of blood:

Such were the notes our once-lov'd poet sung.

And for myself, I could not have been more delighted if I had heard the music of the spheres. Poetry and Philosophy had met together. Truth and Genius had embraced, under the eye and with the sanction of Religion. This was even beyond my hopes. I returned home well satisfied. The sun that was still labouring pale and wan through the sky, obscured by thick mists, seemed an emblem of the *good cause*; and the cold dank drops of dew, that hung half melted on the beard of the thistle, had something genial and refreshing in them; for there was a spirit of hope and youth in all nature, that turned everything into good. The face of nature had not then the brand of JUS DIVINUM on it:

Like to that sanguine flower inscribed with woe.

On the Tuesday following, the half-inspired speaker came. I was called down into the room where he was, and went half-hoping, half-afraid. He received me very graciously, and I listened for a long time without uttering a word. I did not suffer in his opinion by my silence. 'For those two hours,' he afterwards was pleased to say, 'he was conversing with W.H.'s forehead!' His appearance was different from what I had anticipated from seeing him before. At a distance, and in the dim light of the chapel, there was to me a strange wildness in his aspect, a dusky obscurity, and I thought him pitted with the small-pox. His complexion was at that time clear, and even bright—

As are the children of yon azure sheen.

His forehead was broad and high, light as if built of ivory, with large projecting eyebrows, and his eyes rolling beneath them, like a sea with darkened lustre. 'A certain tender bloom his face o'erspread,' a purple tinge as we see it in the pale thoughtful complexions of the Spanish portrait-painters, Murillo and Velasquez. His mouth was gross, voluptuous, open, eloquent; his chin good-humoured and round; but his nose, the rudder of the face, the index of the will, was small, feeble, nothing—like what he has done. It might seem that the genius of his face as from a height surveyed and projected him (with sufficient capacity and huge aspiration) into the world unknown of thought and imagination, with nothing to support or guide his veering purpose, as if Columbus had launched his adventurous course for the New World in a scallop, without oars or compass. So, at least, I comment on it after the event. Coleridge, in his person, was rather above the common size, inclining to the corpulent, or like Lord Hamlet, 'somewhat fat and pursy.' His hair (now, alas! grey) was then black and glossy as the raven's and fell in smooth masses over his forehead. This long pendulous hair is peculiar to enthusiasts, to those whose minds tend heavenward; and is traditionally inseparable (though of a different colour) from the picture of Christ. It ought to belong, as a character, to all who preach *Christ crucified*, and Coleridge was at that time one of those! . . .

. . . the next morning Mr Coleridge was to return to Shrewsbury. When I came down to breakfast, I found that he had just received a letter from his friend, T. Wedgwood, making him an offer of £150 a year if he chose to waive his present pursuit, and devote himself entirely to the study of poetry and philosophy. Coleridge seemed to make up his mind to close with this proposal in the act of tying on one of his shoes. It threw an additional damp on his departure. It took the wayward enthusiast quite from us to cast him into Deva's winding vales, or by the shores of old romance. Instead of living at ten miles' distance, of being the pastor of a Dissenting congregation at Shrewsbury, he was henceforth to inhabit the Hill of Parnassus, to be a Shepherd on the Delectable Mountains. Alas! I knew not the way thither, and felt very little gratitude for Mr Wedgwood's bounty. I was presently relieved from this dilemma; for Mr Coleridge, asking for a pen and ink, and going to a table to write something on a bit of card, advanced towards me with undulating step, and giving me the precious document, said that that was his address, *Mr Coleridge, Nether-Stowey, Somersetshire*; and that he should be glad to see me there in a few weeks' time, and, if I chose, would come half-way to meet me. I was not less surprised than the shepherd boy (this simile is to be found in "Cassandra"), when he sees a thunderbolt fall close at his feet. I stammered out my acknowledgments and acceptance of this offer (I thought Mr Wedgwood's annuity a trifle to it) as well as I could; and this mighty business being settled, the poet preacher took leave, and I accompanied him six miles on the road. It was a fine morning in the middle of winter, and he talked the whole way. The scholar in Chaucer is described as going

—Sounding on his way.

So Coleridge went on his. In digressing, in dilating, in passing from subject to subject, he appeared to me to float in air, to slide on ice. He told me in confidence (going along) that he should have preached two sermons before he accepted the situation at Shrewsbury, one on Infant Baptism, the other on the Lord's Supper, showing that he could not administer either, which would have effectually disqualified him for the object in view. I observed that he continually crossed me on the way by shifting from one side of the footpath to the other. This struck me as an odd movement; but I did not at that time connect it with any instability of purpose or involuntary change of principle, as I have done since. He seemed unable to keep on in a straight line.

5. Thomas De Quincey had read *Lyrical Ballads* as a young boy, and was particularly impressed with *The Ancient Mariner* which, he learned later, was by Coleridge. As an Oxford undergraduate he determined to get to know Coleridge who, as he had heard, was now studying philosophy and psychology. On a visit to Bristol in the summer of 1807 he happened to discover that Coleridge was at Nether Stowey when he thought that the poet must still be in Malta. As a result of this meeting, De Quincey accompanied Mrs Coleridge and the children back to Keswick and became closely identified with the 'Lake Poets'. From the chapter on Coleridge in *Recollections of the Lake Poets*:

I had received directions for finding out the house where Coleridge was visiting; and, in riding down a main street of Bridgewater, I noticed a gateway corresponding to the description given me. Under this was standing, and gazing about him, a man whom I will describe. In height he might seem to be about five feet eight (he was, in reality, about an inch and a half taller, but his figure was of an order which drowns the height); his person was broad and full, and tended even to corpulence; his complexion was fair, though not what painters technically style fair, because it was associated with black hair; his eyes were large, and soft in their expression; and it was from the peculiar appearance of haze or dreaminess which mixed with their light that I recognized my object. This was Coleridge. I examined him steadfastly for a minute or more; and It struck me that he saw neither myself nor any other object in the street. He was in a deep reverie; for I had dismounted, made two or three trifling arrangements at an inn-door, and advanced close to him, before he had apparently become conscious of my presence. The sound of my voice, announcing my own name, first awoke him; he started, and for a moment seemed at a loss to understand my purpose or his own situation; for he repeated rapidly a number of words which had no relation to either of us. There was no *mauvaise honte* in his manner, but simple perplexity, and an apparent difficulty in recovering his position amongst day-light realities. This little scene over, he received me with a kindness of manner so marked that it might be called gracious. The hospitable family with whom he was domesticated were distinguished for their amiable manners and enlightened understandings: they were descendants from Chubb, the philosophic writer, and bore the same name. For Coleridge they all testified deep affection and esteem—sentiments in which the whole town of Bridgwater seemed to share; for in the evening, when the heat of the day had declined, I walked out with him; and rarely, perhaps never, have I seen a person so much interrupted in one hour's space as Coleridge, on this occasion, by the courteous attentions of young and old.

All the people of station and weight in the place, and apparently all the ladies, were abroad to enjoy the lovely summer evening; and not a party passed without some mark of smiling recognition; and the majority stopping to make personal inquiries about his health, and to express their anxiety that he should make a lengthened stay amongst them. . . .

. . . Coleridge led me to a drawing room, rang the bell for refreshments, and omitted no point of a courteous reception. He told me that there would be a very large dinner party on that day, which, perhaps, might be disagreeable to a perfect stranger; but, if not, he could assure me of a most hospitable welcome from the family. I was too anxious to see him under all aspects to think of declining this invitation. That point being settled, Coleridge, like some great river, the Orellana, or the St Lawrence, that, having been checked and fretted by rocks or thwarting islands, suddenly recovers its volume of waters and its mighty music, swept at once, as if returning to his natural business, into a continuous strain of eloquent dissertation, certainly the most novel, the most finely illustrated, and traversing the most spacious fields of thought by transitions the most just and logical, that it was possible to conceive. What I mean by saying that his transitions were 'just' is by way of contradistinction to that mode of conversation which courts variety through links of *verbal* connexions. Coleridge, to many people, and often I have heard the complaint, seemed to wander; and he seemed then to wander the most when, in fact, his resistance to the wandering instinct was greatest—viz., when the compass and huge circuit by which his illustrations moved travelled farthest into remote regions before they began to revolve. Long before this coming round commenced, most people had lost him, and naturally enough supposed that he had lost himself. They continued to admire the separate beauty of the thoughts, but did not see their relations to the dominant theme. . . .

. . . However, I can assert, upon my long and intimate knowledge of Coleridge's mind, that logic the most severe was as inalienable from his modes of thinking as grammar from his language.

6. In 1819 when Coleridge had settled at Highgate with the Gillmans, Keats was living on the other side of Hampstead Heath. J. H. Green, who became Coleridge's literary executor, was at this time still a teaching professor of anatomy, whom Keats would have known from his year of medical studies. Shortly after this encounter outside the park of Kenwood, as the great house standing at the top of the heath had come to be called, Keats wrote his *Ode to a Nightingale*. Keats is writing to his brother.

Last Sunday I took a Walk towards Highgate and in the lane that winds by the side of Lord Mansfield's park I met Mr Green our Demonstrator at Guy's in conversation with Coleridge—I joined them, after enquiring by a look whether it would be agreeable—I walked with him at his alderman-after-dinner pace for near two miles I suppose. In those two Miles he broached a thousand things —let me see if I can give you a list—Nightingales, Poetry—on Poetical Sensation—Metaphysics—Different genera and species of Dreams—Nightmare—a dream accompanied by a sense of touch— single and double touch—A dream related—First and second consciousness—the difference explained between will and Volition —so many metaphysicians from a want of smoking the second consciousness—Monsters—the Kraken—Mermaids—Southey believes in them—Southey's belief too much diluted—a Ghost story— Good morning—I heard his voice as he came towards me—I heard it as he moved away—I had heard it all the interval—if it may be called so. He was civil enough to ask me to call on him at Highgate. Goodnight!

7. Thomas Carlyle's ambiguous portrait of Coleridge dates from the last years at Highgate. It appears in a study of the life of a little known writer, John Sterling, a fellow-countryman of Carlyle's, whose work

was influenced by Coleridge but which remained utterly neglected when it appeared. Carlyle clearly considered Coleridge's reputation inflated and undeserved, but the particular animosity owes as much to his sense of Sterling's unmerited failure as to that of Coleridge's success. In any case, Carlyle is writing years after the event.

Coleridge sat on the brow of Highgate Hill, in those years, looking down on London and its smoke-tumult, like a sage escaped from the inanity of life's battle; attracting towards him the thoughts of innumerable brave souls still engaged there. His express contributions to poetry, philosophy, or any specific province of human literature or enlightenment, had been small and sadly intermittent; but he had, especially among young inquiring men, a higher than literary, a kind of prophetic or magician character. He was thought to hold, he alone in England, the key of German and other Transcendentalisms; knew the sublime secret of believing by 'the reason' what 'the understanding' had been obliged to fling out as incredible; and could still, after Hume and Voltaire had done their best and worst with him, profess himself an orthodox Christian, and say and print to the Church of England, with its singular old rubrics and surplices at Allhallowtide, *Esto perpetua*. A sublime man; who, alone in those dark days, had saved his crown of spiritual manhood; escaping from the black materialisms, and revolutionary deluges, with 'God, Freedom, Immortality' still his: a king of men. The practical intellects of the world did not much heed him, or carelessly reckoned him a metaphysical dreamer: but to the rising spirits of the young generation he had this dusky sublime character; and sat there as a kind of *Magus*, girt in mystery and enigma; his Dodona oak-grove (Mr Gillman's house at Highgate) whispering strange things, uncertain whether oracles or jargon.

The Gillmans did not encourage much company, or excitation of any sort, round their sage; nevertheless access to him, if a youth did reverently wish it, was not difficult. He would stroll about the pleasant garden with you, sit in the pleasant rooms of the place, — perhaps take you to his own peculiar room, high up, with a rearward view, which was the chief view of all. A really charming outlook, in fine weather. Close at hand, wide sweep of flowery leafy gardens, their few houses mostly hidden, the very chimney-pots veiled under blossomy umbrage, flowed gloriously down hill; gloriously issuing in wide-tufted undulating plain-country, rich in all charms of field and town. Waving blooming country of the brightest green; dotted all over with handsome villas, handsome groves; crossed by roads and human traffic, here inaudible or heard only as a musical hum: and behind all swam, under olive-tinted haze, the illimitable limitary ocean of London, with its domes and steeples definite in the sun, big Paul's and the many memories attached to it hanging high over all. Nowhere, of its kind, could you see a grander prospect on a bright summer day, with the set of the air going southward,—southward, and so draping with the city-smoke not *you* but the city. Here for hours would Coleridge talk, concerning all conceivable or inconceivable things; and liked nothing better than to have an intelligent, or failing that, even a silent and patient human listener. He distinguished himself to all that ever heard him as at least the most surprising talker extant in this world,—and to some small minority, by no means to all, as the most excellent.

The good man, he was now getting old, towards sixty perhaps; and gave you the idea of a life that had been full of sufferings; a life heavy-laden, half-vanquished, still swimming painfully in seas of manifold physical and other bewilderment. Brow and head were round, and of massive weight, but the face was flabby and irresolute. The deep eyes, of a light hazel, were as full of sorrow as of inspiration; confused pain looked mildly from them, as in a kind of mild astonishment. The whole figure and air, good and amiable other-wise, might be called flabby and irresolute; expressive of weakness under possibility of strength. He hung loosely on his limbs, with knees bent, and stooping attitude; in walking, he rather shuffled than decisively stept; and a lady once remarked, he never could fix which side of the garden walk would suit him best, but continually shifted, in corkscrew fashion, and kept trying both. A heavy-laden, high-aspiring and surely much-suffering man. His voice, naturally soft and good, had contracted itself into a plaintive snuffle and singsong; he spoke as if preaching,—you would have said, preaching earnestly and also hopelessly the weightiest things. I still recollect his 'object' and 'subject,' terms of continual recurrence in the Kantean province; and how he sang and snuffled them into 'om-m-mject' and 'sum-m-mject,' with a kind of solemn shake or quaver, as he rolled along. No talk, in his century or in any other, could be more surprising. . . .

. . . Nothing could be more copious than his talk; and furthermore it was always, virtually or literally, of the nature of a monologue; suffering no interruption, however reverent; hastily putting aside all foreign additions, annotations, or most ingenious desires for elucidation, as well-meant superfluities which would never do. Besides, it was talk not flowing anywhither like a river, but spread-ing everywhither in inextricable currents and regurgitations like a lake or sea; terribly deficient in definite goal or aim, nay often in logical intelligibility; *what* you were to believe or do, on any earthly or heavenly thing, obstinately refusing to appear from it. So that, most times, you felt logically lost; swamped near to drowning in this tide of ingenious vocables, spreading out boundless as if to submerge the world. . . . In close colloquy, flowing within narrower banks, I suppose he was more definite and apprehensible; Sterling in aftertimes did not complain of his unintelligibility, or imputed it only to the abstruse high nature of the topics handled. Let us hope so, let us try to believe so! There is no doubt but Coleridge could speak plain words on things plain: his observations and responses on the trivial matters that occurred were as simple as the commonest man's or were even distinguished by superior simplicity as well as pertinency. 'Ah, your tea is too cold, Mr Coleridge!' mourned the good Mrs Gillman once, in her kind, reverential and yet protective manner, handing him a very tolerable though belated cup.—'It's better than I deserve!' snuffled he, in a low hoarse murmur, partly courteous, chiefly pious, the tone of which still abides with me: 'It's better than I deserve!' . . .

. . . The truth is, I now see, Coleridge's talk and speculation was the emblem of himself: in it as in him, a ray of heavenly inspiration struggled, in a tragically ineffectual degree, with the weakness of flesh and blood. He says once, he 'had skirted the howling deserts of Infidelity;' this was evident enough: but he had not had the courage, in defiance of pain and terror, to press resolutely across said deserts to the new firm lands of Faith beyond; he preferred to create logical fatamorganas for himself on this hither side, and laboriously solace himself with these.

8. We catch a glimpse of a very different, but still recognizable Coleridge of this time in *Theodore Hook. A Sketch*, by J. G. Lockhart, Sir Walter Scott's biographer.

The first time I ever witnessed Hook's improvisation was at a gay young bachelor's villa near Highgate, when the other lion was one of a very different breed, Mr Coleridge. Much claret had been shed before the *Ancient Mariner* proclaimed that he could swallow no more of anything, unless it were punch. The materials were forthwith produced; the bowl was planted before the poet, and as he proceeded in his concoction, Hook, unbidden, took his place at the piano. He burst into a bacchanal of egregious luxury, every line of which had a reference to the author of the *Lay Sermons* and the *Aids to Reflection*. The room was becoming excessively hot: the first specimen of the new compound was handed to Hook, who paused to quaff it, and then, exclaiming that he was stifled, flung his glass through the window. Coleridge rose with the aspect of a benignant patriarch and demolished another pane—the example was followed generally—the window was a sieve in an instant—the kind host was furthest from the mark, and his goblet made havoc of the chandelier. The roar of laughter was drowned in Theodore's resumption of the song—and window and chandelier and the peculiar shot of each individual destroyer had apt, in many cases exquisitely witty, commemoration. In walking home with Mr

Coleridge, he entertained—and me with a most excellent lecture on the distinction between talent and genius, and declared that Hook was as true a genius as Dante—*that* was his example.

Hampstead Heath by John Constable

3, The Grove, Highgate, Coleridge's house from 1816

The Sublime in Art: The Bard *by John Martin*

2   Coleridge as Romantic Poet

I feel strongly, and I think strongly, but I seldom feel without thinking, think without feeling. Hence tho' my poetry has in general a *hue* of tenderness, or Passion over it, yet it seldom exhibits unmixed & simple tenderness or Passion. My philosophical opinions are blended with, or deduced from, my feelings: & this, I think, peculiarizes my style of Writing. And like everything else, it is sometimes a beauty, and sometimes a fault. But do not let us introduce an act of Uniformity against Poets—I have room enough in *my* brain to admire, aye & almost equally, the *head* and fancy of Akenside, and the *heart* and fancy of Bowles, the solemn Lordliness of Milton, & the divine Chit Chat of Cowper: and whatever a man's excellence is, that will be likewise his fault.

Letter to John Thelwall, 17 December 1796

The roots of Coleridge's Romanticism

It has been well written that a great writer chooses his precursors. We often think that Romantic poetry represents an entirely new beginning, a 'spontaneous overflow of powerful feelings' in Wordsworth's famous phrase, but every poet makes use of those earlier poets he admires until he finds his own voice, and when we look at his early work we do so with two perspectives in mind. We want to know the nature and extent of the debt and also to catch the particular accent of the fully individualised tones yet to come. About his debts as a poet Coleridge is, in other respects, quite explicit, peculiarly conscious of his role as mediator between the old and the new, tradition and novelty. At a very early age he had read astonishingly widely in English and classical poetry and so, like almost all English poets of the eighteenth century, could scarcely have avoided the influence of the lordliness of Milton. Every poet writing in English must, sooner or later, come to terms with the achievements of Milton and Shakespeare. But there were particular pressures in the age in which Coleridge began writing which forced him constantly to choose Milton as a model. If Milton's influence appears dominant in the eighteenth century and even clearly in the exalted moods of the poetry of Wordsworth and Coleridge, then it is largely owing to Coleridge's critical placing of Shakespeare's poetry that Shakespeare's has come to supplant Milton's in modern ears as the type of English poetry. If we can pause to make a rough and ready distinction between the two achievements, they can appear to be mutually exclusive. In Shakespeare's work the poet is absent and, over the whole range of experience, the language recreates life as the thing itself. In Milton's verse, on the other hand, we are immediately aware of the voice, the solemnity that supports the dignity of the intention and the system of belief. The exalted language celebrates and illustrates the belief in such a way that the *separation* between language and belief is very firmly sustained. Now, even before he met Wordsworth in 1795, Coleridge saw poetry as an instrument of propaganda on behalf of Christian belief in religion, democratic principles in politics and freedom of expression.

> Yet is the day of Retribution nigh:
> The Lamb of God hath opened the fifth seal:
> And upward rush on swiftest wing of fire
> The innumerable multitude of wrongs
> By man on man inflicted! Rest awhile,
> Children of Wretchedness! The hour is nigh
> And lo! the Great, the Rich, the Mighty Men,
> The Kings and the Chief Captains of the World,
> With all that fixed on high like stars of Heaven

Shot baleful influence, shall be cast to earth,
Vile and down-trodden, as the untimely fruit
Shook from the fig-tree by a sudden storm.
Even now the storm begins: each gentle name,
Faith and meek Piety, with fearful joy
Tremble far-off—for lo! the Giant Frenzy
Uprooting empires with his whirlwind arm
Mocketh high Heaven; burst hideous from the cell
Where the old Hag, unconquerable, huge,
Creation's eyeless drudge, black Ruin, sits
Nursing the impatient earthquake.
Religious Musings, lines 302–322

The Sublime

From my early readings of Faery Tales, & Genii &c &c—my mind had
been habituated *to the Vast*—& I never regarded *my senses* in any way
as the criteria of my belief.

Letter to Poole, 16 October 1797

For poets of the later part of the eighteenth century, Milton was the
type of the sublime poet. His epic *Paradise Lost* in particular displayed
a grandeur of scale and conception and expressed a range of emotion
of which many poets and their readers seemed to feel the lack in the
poetry of the early eighteenth century. Ideas of the vast, the horrific,
the irregular and the solitary find only an occasional, almost, as it
were, covert place in the precise and balanced intensity of Alexander
Pope's verse. At best the 'peace of the Augustans' was a precariously
balanced arrangement. It was as though in the continual process of
discovery that is art, other worlds than that of the manners and
thoughts of London society challenged man's power to respond to
them. What, in the Augustan scheme of things, was man's experience
of nature? In October 1739 Thomas Gray wrote a letter to his mother
during his tour in Europe with Horace Walpole.

It is a fortnight since we set out . . . upon a little excursion to Geneva.
We took the longest road, which lies through Savoy, on purpose to
see a famous monastery, called the Grande Chartreuse, and had no
reason to think our time lost. After having travelled seven days very
slow (for we did not change horses, it being impossible for a chaise
to go post in these roads) we arrived at a little village among the
mountains of Savoy, called Echelles; from thence we proceeded on
horses, who are used to the way, to the mountain of the Chartreuse:
it is six miles to the top; the road runs winding up it, commonly not

six feet broad; on one hand is the rock with woods of pine trees hanging over head; on the other, a monstrous precipice, almost perpendicular, at the bottom of which rolls a torrent, that sometimes tumbling among the fragments of stone that have fallen from on high, and sometimes precipitating itself down vast descents with a noise like thunder, which is still made greater by the echo from the mountains on each side, concurs to form one of the most solemn, the most romantic, and the most astonishing scenes I have ever beheld. Add to this the strange views made by the crags and cliffs on the other hand; the cascades that throw themselves from the very summit down into the vale, and the river below; and many other particulars impossible to describe; you will conclude we had no occasion to repent our pains.

A consciousness of difficulty and a sense of continuous danger are essential elements of Gray's enjoyment of the experience as he describes it. An illuminating comparison can be made between Gray's description and Wordsworth's in Book Six of *The Prelude*, from which I can quote only an example:

> The melancholy slackening that ensued
> Upon those tidings by the peasant given
> Was soon dislodged. Downwards we hurried fast,
> And, with the half-shaped road which we had missed,
> Entered a narrow chasm. The brook and road
> Were fellow-travellers in this gloomy strait,
> And with them did we journey several hours
> At a slow pace. The immeasurable height
> Of woods decaying, never to be decayed,
> The stationary blasts of waterfalls,
> And in the narrow rent at every turn
> Winds thwarting winds, bewildered and forlorn,
> The torrents shooting from the clear blue sky,
> The rocks that muttered close upon our ears,
> Black drizzling crags that spake by the way-side
> As if a voice were in them, the sick sight
> And giddy prospect of the raving stream,
> The unfettered clouds and region of the Heavens,
> Tumult and peace, the darkness and the light—
> Were all like workings of one mind, the features
> Of the same face, blossoms upon one tree;
> Characters of the great Apocalypse,
> The types and symbols of Eternity,
> Of first, and last, and midst, and without end.

Gray's letter is, after all, a private communication and the aesthetic experience it recreates is one which finds no place in his poetry. For

Wordsworth the experience is a moral one, not only because he moralizes it (which he does), but because the scene imposes on him an awe and a sense of the endurance of the place over against his sense of his own transitoriness and solitude. He wishes Coleridge had been there, not to *share* the experience, but to have it for himself and so be equally impressed. For Coleridge's response to a very similar situation, we must turn to his walk with Charles Lamb to Moss Force near Keswick in August 1802.

All night it rained incessantly—& in a hard storm of Rain this morning, at ½ past 10, I set off, & drove away toward Newlands— there is a Waterfall that divides Great Robinson from Buttermere Halse Fell, which when Mary & Tom [Hutchinson], & I passed, we stopped & said—what a wonderful Creature it would be in a hard Rain—dear Mary was especially struck with its latent Great-ness—& since that time I have never passed it without a haunting wish to see it in its fury—it is just 8 miles from Keswick. I had a glorious Walk—the rain sailing along those black Crags & green Steeps, white as the wooly Down on the under side of a Willow Leaf, & soft as Floss Silk, & silver Fillets of Water down every mountain from top to bottom that were as fine as Bridegrooms. I soon arrived at the Halse—& climbed up by the waterfall as near as I could, to the very top of the Fell—but it was so craggy—the Crags covered with spongy soaky Moss, and when bare so jagged as to wound one's hands fearfully—and the Gusts came so very sudden & strong, that the going up was slow, & difficult & earnest—& the coming down, not only all that, but likewise extremely dangerous. However, I have always found this *stretched & anxious* state of mind favorable to depth of pleasurable Impression, in the resting Places & *lownding* Coves. The Thing repaid me amply, it is a great Torrent from the Top of the Mountain to the Bottom. The lower part of it is not the least Interesting, where it is beginning to slope to a level—the mad water rushes thro' its *sinuous* Bed, or rather prison of Rock, with such rapid Curves, as if it turned the Corners not from the mechanic force, but with foreknowledge, like a fierce & skilful Driver. Great Masses of Water, one after the other, that in twilight one might have feelingly compared them to a vast crowd of huge white Bears, rushing, one over the other, against the wind—their long white hair shattering abroad in the wind. The remainder of the Torrent is marked out by three great Waterfalls—the lowermost apron-shaped, & though the Rock down which it rushes is an inclined Plane, it shoots off in such an independence of the Rock as shews that its direction was given it by the force of the water from above. The middle, which in peaceable times would be two tinkling Falls, formed in this furious Rain one great *Water-wheel* endlessly revolving & double the size & height of the lowest—the third & highest is a mighty one indeed, it is twice the height of both the others added together, nearly as high as Scale Force, but it rushes down an inclined Plane—and does not *fall*, like Scale Force. However, if the Plane had been smooth, it is so near a Perpendicular that it would have *appeared* to fall—but it is indeed so fearfully savage, & black, & jagged, that it tears the flood to pieces—and one great black Outjutment divides the water, & overbrows & keeps uncovered a long slip of jagged black Rock beneath, which gives a marked *character* to the whole force. What a sight it is to look down on such a Cataract!—the wheels, that circumvolve in it—the leaping up & plunging forward of that infinity of Pearls & Glass Bulbs—the continual *change* of the *Matter*, the perpetual *Sameness* of the *Form*—it is an awful Image & Shadow of God & the World.

The most celebrated theoretical expression of the sublime in eighteenth-century aesthetics is Edmund Burke's *Enquiry into the Origin of our Ideas of the Sublime and the Beautiful*, first published in 1757. Section VII opens as follows:

> Whatever is fitted in any sort to excite, the idea of pain, and danger, that is to say, whatever is in any sort terrible, or is conversant about terrible objects, or operates in a manner analogous to terror, is a source of the *sublime*; that is, it is productive of the strongest emotion which the mind is capable of feeling.

Burke, like almost all eighteenth-century writers on aesthetics, takes as his starting point John Locke's theory of knowledge: that is, that all knowledge begins in impressions received through the senses. But Burke fails to discriminate that which distinguishes ordinary experience from *aesthetic* experience and confuses sense data (which are, admittedly, the raw material of the aesthetic experience) with the aesthetic perception. He fails to see that art and life are different. For those eighteenth-century empirical philosophers and psychologists interested in aesthetics, the perception of beauty was only a special case of a more general theory of perception. Burke's *Enquiry* is a characteristic and influential example of this particular tradition and, although Coleridge in his *Table Talk* late in life dismissed Burke's contribution to aesthetics as worthless, we shall see when we come to consider Coleridge's literary criticism that his own work grew out of the earlier tradition and that his theory of literature is an integral part of his more general enquiries into psychology and the philosophy of mind. Furthermore, it is clear that in questions of taste, Coleridge still entertained some notion of the sublime after he had worked out his philosophical rejection of the eighteenth-century tradition. I shall have more to say about Coleridge's notion of the sublime when I come to the discussion of *Kubla Khan* in Part Two, but I should like to indicate here by two references my feeling that for Coleridge, the sublime was an important and essentially religious notion centred on his perception of the Godhead. The first reference comes from his notebook of 1795–96 which seems to refer to the writings of Thomas Burnet, the seventeenth-century religious philosopher. Coleridge's entry reads: 'Love transforms the souls into a conformity with the object loved.' The gloss in Professor Coburn's edition of the Notebooks refers these words to Burnet's *Sacred Theory of the Earth*: 'An *Immense Being* does strangely fill the soul: and Omnipotency, Omnisciency, and Infinite Goodness do enlarge and dilate the Spirit, while it fixtly looks upon them. They raise strong Passions of Love and Admiration, which melt as Nature, and transform it into the mould and image of that we contemplate.' The second reference I want to make in this connection is to a letter which Coleridge wrote to John Thelwall on 14 October 1797.

> —I can *at times* feel strongly the beauties, you describe, in themselves & for themselves—but more frequently *all things* appear little —all the knowledge, that can be acquired, child's play—the universe itself—what but an immense heap of *little* things?—I can contemplate nothing but parts, & parts are all *little*—!—My mind feels as if it ached to behold & know something *great*—something *one* & *indivisible*—and it is only in the faith of this that rocks or waterfalls, mountains or caverns give me the sense of sublimity or majesty!—But in this faith *all things* counterfeit infinity!—

The letter continues with a quotation from *This Lime Tree Bower My Prison* (see Part Two, p. 108 lines 38–43) and Coleridge comments:

> It is but seldom that I raise & spiritualise my intellect to this height —& at other times I adopt the Brahman Creed, & say—It is better to sit than to stand, it is better to lie than to sit, it is better to sleep than to wake—but Death is the best of All!

If we recall Gray's thrill before the Grande Chartreuse and compare that moment with these two references, it is as though we can read Coleridge's intention as an attempt to spiritualize the aesthetic of the sublime, to transform and recreate it as a religious expression of his intuition that all things are reconciled in the immensity of God's presence. And again in this kind of ambition, one detects the presence of Milton's epic example.

Gilpin and the Picturesque

Burke's *Enquiry* also had more immediately palpable and influential consequences. In making his basic distinction between beauty and sublimity his basic idea was psychological. He was more interested in the effect on the observer than in the constituents of a sublime representation. When, on those occasions he does try to exemplify the 'sublime', he chooses, from poetry, Milton as his supreme example. These elements were soon supplied, however, by William Gilpin, the priest of a country parish in the New Forest in Hampshire, who published his *Picturesque Remarks on the River Wye* in 1782. To Burke's two categories, Gilpin adds a third, that of the picturesque out of which he makes a philosophy of scenery. Influenced by the great European landscape painters of the previous century, especially Ruysdael from Holland and Claude and Poussin from France, Gilpin evolved a mechanical formula for discerning the picturesque landscape. His *Observations on a Picturesque Tour of the Lake District made in 1772* appeared in 1786 and there is no doubt that, despite the limitations of his methods and the easily parodied content, he did much to popularize the scenic tour in Britain, especially of those regions of lake and mountain. Occasionally he makes a valuable remark, such as the following from the Preface:

> Lake-scenery, it is true, is less subject to change. The broader the features are, the less they will vary. Water which makes the grand part of this scenery, remains unaltered by time: and the rocks, and mountains, which environ the lake, are as little subject to Variation, as any of the materials of landscape can be.

Neither Coleridge nor Wordsworth, since he was brought up in the Lake District of the north-west of England, needed Gilpin to remind them that the significance of lakes and mountains was the image of permanence that they present, but Gilpin was very much a part of the aesthetic climate of the time towards the end of the eighteenth century in England to which these young men were so acutely attuned.

Percy's 'Reliques' and Thomas Chatterton

Just as the Romantic poets did not discover the association between landscape and certain emotional states, so, already in the second half of the eighteenth century the recreation of the medieval world had been seriously begun. Bishop Percy published his *Reliques of Ancient English Poetry* in 1765. He drew his collection from a seventeenth-century manuscript, altering and adding as he saw fit. The description 'ancient' here is liberally interpreted as, among Elizabethan and later poems, few of which are songs or ballads, Percy included songs and poems that were current in his own day. Of greater interest to the next generation of poets were the traditional ballads, *Chevy Chace*, *Sir Patrick Spens* (see the opening lines of *Dejection: an Ode* p. 136 passim and Appendix C), *Sir Cauline* and *Robin Hood*. Sometimes he prints earlier and later versions of the same poem and shows a preference for the older, grander verse even where it might sound crude and primitive to 'modern' ears. The work found a readymade audience and did much to free the appreciation of older English poetry from the atmosphere of uninspired antiquarianism in which such studies had grown up during this period. What Percy meant to the Romantic poets is acknowledged by Wordsworth writing in the 1815 Preface to his poems: 'I do not think that there is an able writer in verse of the present day who would not be proud to acknowledge his obligations to the *Reliques*; I know that it is so with my friends; and for myself I am happy on this occasion to make a public avowal of my own.'

Coleridge follows Burke's observation in his *Enquiry* that the ballad style has had a great influence on popular poetry. Burke's point is that the passions of the common people are very strongly roused by ballads and 'by other little popular poems and tales that are current in that rank of life'. The point would not be lost on the authors of *Lyrical Ballads*, who shared an ambition to write poetry that would illustrate their thesis that the imagination was the prime human faculty, but that would at the same time reflect and appeal to the consciousness of ordinary people.

It is not, however, solely on account of the popularity of traditional ballad metres and subjects that poets of the Romantic age turned their attention to the literature of the medieval world. They had before them the example of Thomas Chatterton, the Bristol poet, who died before his eighteenth birthday in 1770. From some old manuscripts he found in the church of St Mary Redcliffe in Bristol where his forebears had been sextons for several generations, Chatterton created his own medieval world in poetry. It was a fiction of pure imagination evoked in an archaizing language which owed more to Edmund Spenser, the Elizabethan poet, than to any earlier English poetry. Nevertheless it was an extraordinary enterprise which was crushed by the near total lack of sympathy for any such undertaking. What defeated Chatterton was the early success of his subterfuge, the pretence that he had discovered the literary output of a fifteenth-century Bristol monk Thomas Rowley and, following not long after a famous earlier deception in which a Scotsman, Macpherson, had claimed to have discovered and translated the poems of the Gaelic bard Ossian, the argument over the 'Rowley manuscripts' raged round its authenticity as a fifteenth-century manuscript. It was pronounced a fake by Horace Walpole, who in the earlier controversy had been persuaded that the Ossian poems were genuine. Chatterton's bitter disappointment led him to commit suicide soon after his arrival in London.

It can be said with confidence, as of so few innovators, that he was genuinely ahead of his time because his influence on the next two generations of poets was quite unexpected. It was an influence exerted in two ways. The importance of his language and subject matter for the work of John Keats cannot be discussed here, but Chatterton's life was an important example of the rejected poet for both Coleridge and Wordsworth. Wordsworth refers to 'the marvellous boy' in *Resolution and Independence*, a poem in which reflecting dejectedly on the fate of poets and on his own in particular, he is cheered by the old leech-gatherer who must, like the poet, endure the dwindling of his life's resources (see Appendix B). Coleridge knew about Chatterton early in life. Whilst still at Christ's Hospital he wrote his *Monody on the Death of Chatterton* in which he laments the death of the young poet and expresses the hope that he, who will also be a poet, will be better able to resist the pains of neglect.

> Grant me, like thee, the lyre to sound,
> Like thee, with fire divine to glow—
> But Ah! when rage the Waves of Woe,
> Grant me with firmer breast t'oppose their hate,
> And soar beyond the storms with upright eye elate.

The poem was recorded in Bowyer's *Golden Book* in this first version but Coleridge returned to it and revised it at various times during his poetic career. He contributed a version to an edition of the Rowley Poems which was made in Cambridge in 1794; and a version of the monody was printed in the subscription edition prepared on behalf of Chatterton's family by Robert Southey and Joseph Cottle at Bristol. The edition finally appeared in 1803, but in July 1797 Coleridge wrote to Southey that he would prefer to write an essay for the occasion and that the monody '*must not be reprinted*' for 'on a life & death so full of heart-giving *realities*, as poor Chatterton's to find such shadowy nobodies, as cherub-winged Death, Trees of Hope, bare-bosom'd Affection, & simpering Peace—makes one's blood circulate like ipecacuanha'. Coleridge is rejecting a whole poetic mode of abstraction and personification which appeared in his earlier poetry, but uses the occasion to discuss further the place of 'feelings' in the work of a young poet.

> .--But so it is. A young man by strong feelings is impelled to write on a particular subject—and this is all his feelings do for him. They set him upon the business & then they leave him.—He has such a high idea of what poetry ought to be, that he cannot conceive that such things as his natural emotions may be allowed to find a place in it—his learning therefore, his fancy or rather conceit, and all his powers of buckram are put on the stretch—. It appears to me, that strong feeling is not *so* requisite to an Author's being profoundly pathetic, as taste and good sense.

Such words, of course, could only come from the mature poet who has found his own voice. He wrote them in 1797 when he was probably at the height of his poetic powers during his intimate collaboration with Wordsworth. The discovery of his own voice was not a result of that friendship so much as a confirmation and strengthening of it. Coleridge's mature poetry and sensibility grow out of his early imitations.

36

Chatterton accepting Poison from Despair *by John Flaxman*

Bowles and Cowper

Recalling his literary education at Christ's Hospital in the first chapter of *Biographia Literaria*, Coleridge moves from the recollection of his teacher Dr James Bowyer and his insistence on a plain and direct style of composition to single out the Reverend William Lisle Bowles and William Cowper as the two modern poets who had achieved a combination of natural thoughts and natural diction, a reconciliation of the head and heart. Coleridge maintains that his early enthusiasm for Bowles was comparative in that his *Sonnets* which appeared in 1789 seemed to owe nothing to the formal, social mode of Augustan poetry. They were written mainly on particular places which are celebrated for their picturesque beauty and for the emotions which they arouse. Wordsworth stood on Westminster bridge and read Bowles's volume through during a walk with his brother. Coleridge copied out more than forty transcriptions to distribute among his friends. He also wrote in imitation of Bowles's style.

In 1793 he reworked Bowles's *The River Itchin* as an address to the River Otter which flows through his birth place Ottery St Mary. Both sonnets associate loss of childhood with memories of the river. First the original:

> Itchin! when I behold thy banks again,
>   Thy crumbling margin, and thy silver breast,
>   On which the self-same tints still seem to rest,
> Why feels my heart a shivering sense of pain!
> Is it, that many a summer's day has past
>   Since, in life's morn, I carolled on thy side!
>   Is it, that oft since then my heart has sighed,
> As Youth, and Hope's delusive gleams, flew fast!
>   Is it, that those who gathered on thy shore,
>   Companions of my youth, now meet no more!
> Whate'er the cause, upon thy banks I bend,
>   Sorrowing; yet feel such solace at my heart,
> As at the meeting of some long-lost friend,
> From whom, in happier hours, we wept to part.

And now Coleridge's version:

> Dear native Brook! wild Streamlet of the West!
>   How many various-fated years have past,
>   What happy and what mournful hours, since last
> I skimm'd the smooth thin stone along thy breast,
> Numbering its light leaps! yet so deep imprest
> Sink the sweet scenes of childhood, that mine eyes
>   I never shut amid the sunny ray,
> But straight with all their tints thy waters rise,

> Thy crossing plank, thy marge with willows grey,
> And bedded sand that vein'd with various dyes
> Gleam'd through thy bright transparence! On my way,
>   Visions of Childhood! oft have ye beguil'd
> Lone manhood's cares, yet waking fondest sighs:
>   Ah! that once more I were a careless Child!

A comparison perhaps tells us immediately that the later sonnet is more richly charged with energy. The Bowles sonnet seems to sit placidly and contentedly within the form. The formal arrangement supports what the poem has to say. On the contrary the rhythm of Coleridge's poem cuts right across the formal structure of the sonnet. Furthermore, first the child and then the river are each more concretely realized in the imitation. The child remembered is caught in a typical action, skimming a flat stone over the water, and the language and rhythm trace the rhythm of the stone as it skims along.

Again, 'Thy crumbling margin, and thy silver breast' strikes me as a very conventional rendering of a river scene, compromised perhaps by echoes of both earlier streams described in poetry and traditional pictorial representations, whereas:

> Thy crossing plank, thy marge with willows grey,
> And bedded sand that vein'd with various dyes
> Gleamed through thy bright transparence!

is not only more concretely remembered and evoked, but makes us pause over the resonances that the description of the river bed seems to offer. The whole picture is suffused with light and life and energy. And not remembered life only, as we feel the adult poet to be alive now in the act of writing the poem and recollecting. As he shuts his eyes his mind is immediately and involuntarily filled with this scene of childhood, so deeply *impressed* in his mind are such early memories. The poet also sees their double nature: memories of childhood beguile or soothe the cares of the adult, but at the same time they make him wish to be a child again. We never feel, in the Bowles sonnet, this kind of commitment to the poem. He is content to turn aside from the memory in order to look for an answer to the question of what has become of his companions.

> Whate'er the cause, upon thy banks I bend,
> Sorrowing . . .

'Bend' seems very formal and distant at the end of the line, cut off from 'Sorrowing' at the beginning of the next. The sonnet moves consciously to a close; a rounding off of the impression and its significance that we feel is too conventional, too complacently settled in the movement of the iambic really to impress on the reader's mind any sense of an experience. Bowles's sonnet is a formal address of praise. Coleridge's imitation grasps successfully at that most congenial of Romantic subjects, the poet's own childhood.

The two poets met in later life, but, in trying to offer friendly criticism of his later work, Coleridge offended the older man by the telling and damning accuracy of his remarks. In a letter of 1794, however, he called Bowles's works 'descriptive, dignified, tender, sublime', and in the same year addressed the following sonnet to him.

> My heart has thank'd thee, BOWLES! for those soft strains
>   Whose sadness soothes me, like the murmuring
>   Of wild bees in the sunny showers of spring!
> For hence not callous to the mourner's pains
>
> Through Youth's gay prime and thornless paths I went:
>   And when the mightier Throes of mind began,
>   And drove me forth, a thought-bewilder'd man,
> Their mild and manliest melancholy lent
>
> A mingled charm, such as the pang consign'd
>   To slumber, though the big tear it renew'd;
>   Bidding a strange mysterious PLEASURE brood
> Over the wavy and tumultuous mind,
>
> As the great SPIRIT erst with plastic sweep
> Mov'd on the darkness of the unform'd deep.

But what Coleridge found of central importance to him in Bowles's verse is stated in a letter to Robert Southey: 'It is among the chief excellences of Bowles that his imagery appears almost always prompted by the surrounding scenery.' The remark seems more readily applicable to his own verse.

Coleridge's debt to Cowper is another matter. *The Task*, published in 1785, is 'chit-chat'; a long anecdotal blank verse poem in six books, notable for its occasional portrayals of intimate rural scenes and sounds and the delight Cowper took in minute and exact descriptions.

> No noise is here, or none that hinders thought.
> The redbreast warbles still, but is content
> With slender notes, and more than half suppressed:
> Pleas'd with his solitude, and flitting light
> From spray to spray, where'er he rests he shakes
> From many a twig the pendant drops of ice,
> That tinkle in the wither'd leaves below.
> Stillness, accompanied with sounds so soft,
> Charms more than silence.
>   From Book VI, *The Winter Walk at Noon*

What Coleridge notes in Cowper's verse is chastity of diction and the harmony of blank verse; to which one might add that the musing tone that Cowper achieves here matches exactly the delicate quality and scale of the scene he is describing. But it is more than a useful conversational tone and handling of a domestic scale that Coleridge takes from *The Task*. From the following passage, Coleridge seems to have seized on the mood and the movement of the mind through the scene during a long moment of *decreation* which both Coleridge and Wordsworth saw as an essential moment in the act of poetic creation.

> Just when our drawing-rooms begin to blaze
> With lights, by clear reflection multiplied
> From many a mirror, in which he of Gath,
> Goliath, might have seen his giant bulk
> Whole, without stooping, tow'ring crest and all,
> My pleasures, too, begin. But me, perhaps,
> The glowing hearth may satisfy awhile
> With faint illumination, that uplifts
> The shadow to the ceiling, there by fits
> Dancing uncouthly to the quiv'ring flame.
> Not undelightful is an hour to me
> So spent in parlour twilight; such a gloom
> Suits well the thoughtful or unthinking mind,
> The mind contemplative, with some new theme
> Pregnant, or indispos'd alike to all.
> Laugh ye, who boast your more mercurial pow'rs,
> That never feel a stupor, know no pause,
> Nor need one; I am conscious, and confess,
> Fearless, a soul that does not always think.
> Me oft has fancy, ludicrous and wild,
> Sooth'd with a waking dream of houses, tow'rs,
> Trees, churches, and strange visages, express'd
> In the red cinders, while with poring eye
> I gaz'd, myself creating what I saw.
> Nor less amus'd have I quiescent watch'd
> The sooty films that play upon the bars,
> Pendulous, and foreboding, in the view
> Of superstition, prophesying still,
> Though still deceiv'd, some stranger's near approach.
> 'Tis thus the understanding takes repose
> In indolent vacuity of thought,
> And sleeps and is refresh'd. Meanwhile the face
> Conceals the mood lethargic with a mask
> Of deep deliberation, as the man
> Were task'd to his full strength, absorb'd and lost.
> Thus oft, reclin'd at ease, I lose an hour
> At ev'ning, till at length the freezing blast,
> That sweeps the bolted shutter, summons home

41

The recollected pow'rs; and, snapping short
The glassy threads, with which the fancy weaves
Her brittle toys, restores me to myself.
How calm is my recess; and how the frost,
Raging abroad, and the rough wind, endear
The silence and the warmth enjoy'd within!
From Book IV, *The Winter Evening*

Coleridge almost certainly had these lines in mind when writing *Frost at Midnight* (see Page Two, p. 112). It is not merely the striking similar use of the folk superstition of the smoky film of gas that refuses to ignite announcing the arrival of a stranger. Coleridge's poem also shares with this description a number of features that seem very characteristically Coleridgean. For example the reverie or waking dream in which one *creates* fancies out of what one can see.

It is this quality, the approximation of fancy, creation and perception that surely Coleridge read in the poem and retained in order to recreate it in a similarly solitary mood and situation. There is also a considerable degree of similarity between chit-chat and the voice of Coleridge's so called 'conversational' poems to a number of which he fixed the motto *Sermoni propriòr*—'more fitted for speech'. None of the foregoing, however, could allow one to confuse the two poets. Similarities there are, but they do not make of Cowper a Romantic poet before his time. As he wrote of his own verse:

But no prophetic fires to me belong;
I play with syllables and sport in song.

The differences are more important to us. If Coleridge's borrowings from Cowper strike us as more interesting than those he made from Bowles, it is nevertheless quite clear in how many ways Coleridge enriches those materials and qualities found in the work of his immediate predecessors. Milton, Cowper and Bowles come together with other lesser figures to show Coleridge a way, or while we are still dealing with his beginnings, several ways, of making poetry, both public and private. Milton's is the voice we hear behind the *Sonnets on Eminent Characters* of 1794 and 1795 which he contributed to the *Morning Chronicle*. It is also Milton who stands behind the ambition, which he at the same time urged on Wordsworth, to write a great philosophical poem. My feeling is that Milton comes at him in yet another way, quite apart from the continuous and conscious references to and echoes of him throughout Coleridge's poetry, and that is by way of the eighteenth-century tradition of the ode, the poem of formal address to an abstraction. The ode is a form that Coleridge employs throughout his career as a poet, especially the later Pindaric, irregular or 'sublime' ode of his eighteenth-century forerunners such as Collins and Gray in whose work we hear repeated echoes of Milton. Good examples of the *genre* are Gray's *The Progress of Poesy* and Collins's *Ode on the Poetical Character*; both would be well known to Coleridge.

From Cowper, Coleridge seems to have taken an informal, intimate tone and to have invented a form based on this; that is, the 'effusion' or conversation poem. What I am getting at is my view that Coleridge inherited a notion of poetic *genres* from Milton and the eighteenth-century Miltonic poets which he never lost sight of. A particular form suits a particular kind of subject matter and mood, so that the choice of the ballad form is as conscious an act as the choice of a monody in the manner of Milton's *Lycidas* to lament the death of a young poet. The preface to *Christabel*, however, should remind us what is the proper relation of a poet to his predecessors.

> For there is amongst us a set of critics who seem to hold that every possible thought and image is traditional; who have no notions that there are such things as fountains in the world, small as well as great; and who would therefore charitably derive every rill they behold flowing, from a perforation made in some other man's tank.

Coleridge's most original contribution to the forms of poetry is the conversation poem but, like all poets, he began by taking his materials where he found them. It would be to misconceive the originality of the poet to look only at that which distinguishes him from his predecessors and to deny important influences. It is a characteristic of Coleridge's intelligence that he was able to assimilate so many influences and, as he gained mastery, to make them entirely his own creation, as I hope my reading of his major poems in Part Two will show.

The GIANT-FACTOTUM amusing himself.

A Gillray cartoon of Pitt crushing the Opposition

3 Poetry and Radicalism: Coleridge's Bristol circle

'Ah me! literary *Adventure* is but bread and cheese *by chance*!

Letter to Thelwall, November 1796

Coleridge and Southey

Coleridge's connection with Bristol, his marriage there and the friendship with Wordsworth, was a result of making the acquaintance of Robert Southey in June 1794 at Oxford. Coleridge and a companion, Joseph Huck, were setting out on a walking tour of the Wye Valley and Wales, as Wordsworth had done three years previously, in the spirit of Gilpin's *Picturesque Remarks on the River Wye*. Intending only to call on an acquaintance, Robert Allen, in the university, the young men stayed three weeks after Allen had introduced them to Southey. Huck later published an account of the tour, but more important for our purposes, is the fact that Coleridge again stayed with Southey on the return journey. For young men of modern and democratic views 1794 was a stirring year. Both Coleridge and Southey called themselves Republicans in sympathy with the aspirations of the French Revolution. It is clear that, in his first two years at Cambridge, Coleridge had not merely got himself into scrapes between bouts of work, but had spent a great deal of his time in religious and political discussion. He seems to have been influenced towards republicanism in politics and unitarianism in religion by a Fellow of Jesus College, William Frend. In 1788 Frend's tutorship was removed by the college authorities on account of his religious views. In 1793 after he had published a pamphlet entitled *Peace and Union recommended to the associated bodies of republicans and anti-republicans*, he was tried and sentenced to be banished from the university. The undergraduates apparently were unanimous in support of Frend's position. His case is an example of a growing alarm on the part of authority in England at this time at any expression of democratic feeling. The event which polarized the feeling of all sections of the politically minded community was, of course, the revolution in France of 1789.

English Politics and the French Revolution

When in December 1783 William Pitt the Younger was invited by George III to become prime minister, it was generally assumed that he was the one man who would accommodate the pressures for parliamentary reform which had been growing through the previous decade and, at the same time, increase the authority and autonomy of Parliament against the king's declared intention of increasing his own political influence. Certainly, for a time at least it looked as though under Pitt's leadership, Parliament had at last embarked on the enormous task of reforming its own structures and practices. Pitt was, after all, a friend of William Wilberforce, who was soon to accomplish the abolition of slavery in England, and had read Adam Smith's *The Wealth of Nations*, while still an undergraduate at Cambridge. Pressure for reform was exerted from several quarters.

Firstly there was the need expressed in Parliament itself to define and limit the extent of the king's personal intervention in affairs of state. There was also the need to make good the appalling inefficiencies in government that the loss of the American colonies had brought forcibly to light. Considerable pressure came from the need to reform the rotten and pocket boroughs. Parliament was still divided into the constituencies suitable for a landowning society and in the uncontrolled development of towns and industry in the provinces, many interests, groups and sources of political power were not represented in Parliament at all. Further pressure was exerted by those religious groups, the Catholics and dissenters, who were disqualified from holding public office by reason of their religious affiliation. Mild attempts at reform in this direction in 1778 had produced a violent reaction from the London mob led by Lord George Gordon, who attempted in 1780 to have the Act for the Relief of Roman Catholics repealed. London was looted and burned for several days and there was much destruction. These riots were not wholly inspired by religious fervour. Other kinds of discontent were expressed in the anarchic savagery of the event. But the riots were an invitation to caution on the part of intending reformers.

At a moment when, to all appearances, the British Parliament was poised, under Pitt, to reform its own structures and procedures in response to at least some of these pressures, the series of upheavals in France put a firm stop to such intentions.

The events of the French Revolution

The need to reform government was much more acute in France at this time than in England which had had a form of rule by parliament for over a hundred years. It was the calling together of the French Estates in parliament in May 1789 and its attempts to force a constitution on an unwilling and incompetent king that sparked off the great fires of political emotion that burned in France until the moment when they were diverted, if not extinguished, in 1795 by a young artillery officer, Napoleon Bonaparte.

The storming of the Bastille on 14 July 1789 brought a powerful and unpredictable new force into the French political arena. The Paris mob often, in the course of the next few years, took affairs into its own hands. The constitutional phase of the Revolution ended with the attempted flight from Paris of King Louis XVI and the rise of the party of Republicanism under Danton. In August 1792 the revolutionary Commune established itself in Paris, the mob invaded the Tuileries, the Legislative Assembly was suspended and the king and his family imprisoned. It was at this moment that the new Convention offered assistance to all people in other countries who wished to overthrow their governments. Also growing in power during this year was another political group not yet represented in the Assembly. These were the Jacobins, a group of extreme radicals who were making forceful propaganda on behalf of absolute equality. The Jacobins were so called because they established themselves as a political club in the old buildings of the Convent of the Jacobin order of monks, but the word Jacobinism, especially in England, came rapidly to be associated with anarchy and political terrorism. Any expression of reforming opinion in England came to be associated indiscriminately with Jacobinism.

The leaders of the provincial, or Girondin, party of the Assembly executed the king in January, but were themselves overthrown by the Jacobins in June 1793. The setting up of the Committee of Public Safety, with Danton as its virtual dictator, inaugurated the Reign of Terror. Danton himself was executed in April 1794 having been ousted by Robespierre, who was himself defeated by the moderates and executed only three months later. His death marked the end of the Terror and the establishment of the Directory. Work on a new constitution was begun, but meanwhile the fact that France was almost continuously at war with her European neighbours produced its own effects inside France. What finally emerged from the years of revolutionary fervour and violent upheavals was a military dictatorship.

Reactions in England 1789–94

The most important consequence of the events in France for England was the postponement for another forty years of any attempt to reform Parliament or of any reordering of the relations between government and the governed. Pitt embarked on a series of measures intended to stifle reformist opinion and the expression of republican sympathy in England. These measures grew in severity until the execution of Louis XVI and the declaration of war by France provoked the Traitorous Correspondence Act. As a result writers and journalists were tried on charges of sedition and Pitt ordered the suspension of the *Habeas Corpus* Act. This ancient law that the accused person must be presented before a judge to decide the lawfulness of the accusation was a cornerstone of the English legal system, and its suspension appeared to present a serious threat to personal liberty and the whole notion of English justice. Coleridge wrote the following vehement sonnet on Pitt for the *Morning Chronicle* in December 1794. In it he compares Pitt's behaviour with that of Judas Iscariot, crucifying liberty, while Justice is unaccountably disabled.

> Not always should the Tear's ambrosial dew
>   Roll its soft anguish down thy furrow'd cheek!
> Not always heaven-breath'd tones of Suppliance meek
>   Beseem thee, Mercy! Yon dark Scowler view,

Who with proud words of dear-lov'd Freedom came—
   More blasting than the mildew from the South!
And kiss'd his country with Iscariot mouth
(Ah! foul apostate from his Father's fame!)
Then fix'd her on the Cross of deep distress,
   And at safe distance marks the thirsty Lance
   Pierce her big side! But O! if some strange trance
The eye-lids of thy stern-brow'd Sister press,
Seize, Mercy! thou more terrible the brand,
And hurl her thunderbolts with fiercer hand!

The first important intellectual response came from Edmund Burke.
Burke had supported the American cause during the War of Independence and had lost his seat as Member of Parliament for Bristol in 1780
after making a speech in which he advocated a degree of emancipation
for the Roman Catholics in England. He had also been brilliantly
successful as a crusading reformer of governmental abuses.

His *Reflections on the Revolution in France* appeared in 1791 and
argued, eloquently, against the abstract ideas of Revolution, 'rights'
and 'reason', in favour of those institutions which he considered to
have *grown* among a people. 'Politics', Burke argued, 'ought to be
adjusted, not to human reasonings, but to human nature; of which the
reason is but a part, and by no means the greatest part.' He asserted
further that those who argued in favour of revolution were 'so taken
up with their theories about the rights of man, that they have totally
forgotten his nature'. Burke saw that man's social relations were
intricate and complex, not to be settled once and for all by any simple
disposition or direction of power. Human society in its historical
development was of natural growth, a part of human nature not a
corruption of it as revolutionary opinion asserted.

His general conclusion that the old order in France could have been
reformed and should not have been destroyed, brought him into
favour with the king but caused the breach within the liberal, or Whig
party in Parliament, which resulted in the muffling of the voice of
opposition to the repressive policies of William Pitt.

Burke's political prescriptions in his *Reflections* were roundly
contested in Part I of Thomas Paine's *Rights of Man* published later in
this year. Paine asserted the right of a people to constitute a
government and that, in the absence of a written constitution, all
government is tyranny. Part Two, which appeared in 1792, is made up
of a comparison of the American and French constitutions with those
of British institutions to the grave disadvantage of the British model,
and of a series of positive 'proposals for improving the condition of
Europe'. Paine's works were both banned and widely read in England.
He was forced to flee to France to escape prosecution, but once there
opposed the royal execution and narrowly escaped guillotining.

In the following year·William Godwin wrote his *Enquiry Concerning Political Justice*. Pitt did not think it worth prosecuting so expensive a book but its influence, even if it was very shortlived, was immediate and powerful among young intellectuals of the time. Coleridge wrote in his sonnet *To William Godwin* of 1795:

> Nor will I not thy holy guidance bless,
> And hymn thee, GODWIN! with an ardent lay;
> For that thy voice, in Passion's stormy day,
> When wild I roam'd the bleak Heath of Distress,
> Bade the bright form of Justice meet my way—
> And told me that her name was HAPPINESS.

The work was also written in response to Burke's *Reflections* and provides the most extreme expression of pure rationalism found in England at this time. Godwin was in no sense a systematic thinker, and in his book he tries to hold together several incompatible notions, borrowed from writers such as Burke, Priestley and Rousseau. The first of these is that man is rational and perfectible and that all forms of government are a constraint on man's free rationality. 'The uncontrolled exercise of private judgement' was his central idea but to it he attached a view of moral necessity that declared that 'in the life of every human being there is a chain of events, generated in the lapse of ages which preceded his birth, and going on in regular procession through the whole period of his existence, in consequence of which it was impossible for him to act in any instance otherwise than he has acted'. If this were the case, then it would also be the case that governments and institutions could not be other than what, of necessity, they had become. But I am less concerned here with the nature of Godwin's arguments than with their effects. They were revolutionary, optimistic and, in appearance at least, humane.

Many of his suggestions for the reform of penal practices, for example, were extremely enlightened, but it was his doctrine of moral necessity that came to be attacked, directly by Coleridge in several issues of *The Watchman* and indirectly by Wordsworth in his poems of beggars, peasants and simple country folk. Were it the case that circumstances make human beings what they are, then many of these figures simply could not have endured so much adversity as Wordsworth ascribes to them. The characters of Wordsworth's ballads do not only endure stoically whatever happens to them, they are also often depicted as possessing strong bonds of affection and feelings which could have no place in Godwin's scheme as he developed it in the *Enquiry*. But Godwin is an influential figure who provides some of the background to the poetry that Coleridge and Wordsworth wrote over the next few years. Although he escaped prosecution, in 1794 there took place a number of notable trials of writers and teachers of reformist views. Horne Tooke and John Thelwall, who later became a close friend and correspondent of Coleridge, were acquitted on a charge of sedition by a London jury following severe sentences of transportation for other victims tried in Edinburgh on similar offences. Opposition to any expression of reforming or liberal views was further strengthened by the formation up and down the country in this year of Loyalist societies. All such expression was treated as a seditious mixture of Jacobinism, Godwinian anarchy and the republicanism of Tom Paine.

It was in this atmosphere of upheaval and repression that the friendship of the two undergraduates developed quickly during the summer of 1794. Their response to the political situation and the cross-currents of ideas was to plan an emigration to America, the land of new beginnings. They called their scheme 'pantocracy' or, more often, 'pantisocracy'—rule by all who are all equal. It was to be a combination of Godwinism, democracy and religion. Although, as we shall see, the plan was never tested in practice, it exerted a considerable fascination and was the forerunner of a number of attempts made, right up to our own time, to establish ideal intellectual communities in the new world.

An immediate precedent was the example of Joseph Priestley, the Birmingham Unitarian minister, whose house had been sacked and burned by the mob following his enthusiastic welcome of the fall of the Bastille which announced the French Revolution. Like other Dissenters, Priestley had thought that Parliamentary reform constituted the sure road to eventual religious equality, but finding life in England intolerable, he emigrated to America in this year. It was a sermon preached by an associate of Priestley's that provoked Burke into writing his *Reflections*.

Pantisocracy

Events of our own time bear witness to the continued vitality of the myth of 'the American dream'. Columbus, as much as the Pilgrim Fathers or the leaders of the revolutionary War of Independence, was aware of the fundamentally religious significance of the discovery of a new land. Each restatement of the myth has been accompanied by the conviction that the old world has now become irredeemably corrupted and materialistic. Pantisocracy is just such a response and an attempt at the renewal of the shared life on a religious basis. The clearest statement of pantisocratic principles and intentions is made in a letter written by Thomas Poole to an enquirer who had expressed interest in the scheme.

Dear Sir,
I received your obliging letter a day or two ago, and will with pleasure give you all the information I can respecting the emigration

to America to which you allude. But first, perhaps, you would like to have some idea of the character of the projectors of the scheme. Out of eight whom they informed me were engaged, I have seen but two, and only spent part of one day with them; their names are Coleridge and Southey.

Coleridge, whom I consider the Principal in the undertaking, and of whom I had heard much before I saw him, is about five and twenty, belongs to the University of Cambridge, possesses splendid abilities—he is, I understand, a shining scholar, gained the prize for the Greek verses the first or second year he entered the University, and is now engaged in publishing a selection of the best modern Latin poems with a poetical translation. He speaks with much elegance and energy, and with uncommon facility, but he, as it generally happens to men of his class, feels the justice of Providence in the want of those inferior abilities which are necessary to the rational discharge of the common duties of life. His aberrations from prudence, to use his own expression, have been great; but he now promises to be as sober and rational as his most sober friends could wish. In religion he is a Unitarian, if not a Deist; in politicks a Democrat, to the utmost extent of the word.

Southey, who was with him, is of the University of Oxford, a younger man, without the splendid abilities of Coleridge, though possessing much information, particularly metaphysical, and is more violent in his principles than even Coleridge himself. In Religion, shocking to say in a mere Boy as he is, I fear he wavers between Deism and Atheism.

Thus much for the characters of two of the Emigrators. Their plan is as follows:—

Twelve gentlemen of good education and liberal principles are to embark with twelve ladies in April next. Previous to their leaving this country they are to have as much intercourse as possible, in order to ascertain each other's dispositions, and firmly to settle every regulation for the government of their future conduct. Their opinion was that they should fix themselves at—I do not recollect the place, but somewhere in a delightful part of the new back settlements; that each man should labour two or three hours in a day, the produce of which labour would, they imagine, be more than sufficient to support the colony. As Adam Smith observes that there is not above one productive man in twenty, they argue that if each laboured the twentieth part of their time, it would produce enough to satisfy their wants. The produce of their industry is to be laid up in common for the use of all; and a good library of books is to be collected, and their leisure hours to be spent in study, liberal discussions, and the education of their children. A system for the education of their children is laid down, for which, if this plan at all suits you, I must refer you to the authors of it. The regulations relating to the females strike them as the most difficult; whether the marriage contract shall be dissolved if agreeable to one or both parties, and many other circumstances, are not yet determined. The employments of the women are to be the care of infant children, and other occupations suited to their strength; at the same time the greatest attention is to be paid to the cultivation of their minds. Every one is to enjoy his own religious and political opinions, provided they do not encroach on the rules previously made, which rules, it is unnecessary to add, must in some measure be regulated by the laws of the state which includes the district in which they settle. They calculate that each gentleman providing £125 will be sufficient to carry the scheme into execution. Finally, every individual is at liberty, whenever he pleases, to withdraw from the society.

These are the outlines of their plan, and such are their ideas. Could they realize them they would, indeed, realize the age of reason; but, however perfectible human nature may be, I fear it is not yet perfect enough to exist long under the regulations of such a system, particularly when the Executors of the plan are taken from a society in a high degree civilized and corrupted. America is certainly a desirable country, so desirable in my eye that, were it not for some insuperable reasons, I would certainly settle there. At some future period I perhaps may. But I think a man would do well first to see the country and his future hopes, before he removes his connections or any large portion of his property there. I could live, I think, in America, much to my satisfaction and credit, without joining such a scheme as I have been describing, though I should like well to accompany them, and see what progress they make. . . . I shall be happy to hear from you soon, and to learn your opinion of this scheme. Should you wish for further information, I will get you Coleridge's address, and pave the way for your writing to him. . . .

Whether in this spirit, or because he had recently been rejected by Mary Evans whom he had known and to whom he had addressed verses while still at Christ's Hospital, or whether he was genuinely attracted to her, Coleridge had during this stay in Bristol paid court to the youngest Fricker sister Sara, and in August they became engaged. During the course of the next twelve months or so all his actions and movements seem to have been dedicated to the realization of the idea of Pantisocracy. He and Southey busied themselves attempting to gain support and recruits in the surrounding district. It is probable that Coleridge first met Thomas Poole of Nether Stowey on such an occasion. Poole owned a tannery in the village and was known locally as a good employer, concerned for the welfare of his workers and for terms of trade for the local tanning industry. It followed that he was also actively sympathetic to liberal ideas and therefore likely to be interested in the scheme. It may even have been at Poole's house that the two young men first heard the news of the execution of Robespierre, the leader of the extreme revolutionary party in France and, until the moment of his downfall, virtual dictator of the country.

Coleridge and Southey immediately set about writing a drama on the subject, dividing the three acts between them, and *The Fall of Robespierre* was published by Benjamin Flower, editor of the *Cambridge Intelligencer*, under Coleridge's name in September 1794. Meanwhile he was writing letters and meeting people in a continuous effort to publicise the grand project. The following letter to Charles Heath, the brother of a Bristol apothecary who was already committed to the plan, is characteristic of his efforts at this time.

Jesus College, Cambridge, 29th August, 1794

Sir,

Your brother has introduced my name to you; I shall therefore offer no apology for this letter. A small but liberalized party have formed a scheme of emigration on the principles of an abolition of individual property. Of their political creed, and the arguments by which they support and elucidate it, they are preparing a few copies—not as meaning to publish them, but for private distribution. In this work they will have endeavoured to prove the exclusive justice of the system and its practicability; nor will they have omitted to sketch out the code of contracts necessary for the internal regulation of the society; all of which will of course be submitted to the improvements and approbation of each component member. As soon as the work is printed, one or more copies shall be transmitted to you. Of the characters of the individuals who compose the party, I find it embarrassing to speak; yet, vanity apart, I may assert with truth, that they have each a sufficient strength of head to make the virtues of the heart respectable; and that they are all highly charged with that enthusiasm which results from strong perceptions of moral rectitude, called into life and action by ardent feelings. With regard to pecuniary matters it is found necessary, if twelve men with their families emigrate on this system, that 2000£ should be the aggregate of their contributions; but infer not from hence that each man's quota is to be settled with the littleness of arithmetical accuracy. No; *all* will strain *every* nerve, and then I trust the surplus money of some will supply the deficiencies of others. The minutiae of topographical information we are daily endeavouring to acquire; at present our plan is, to settle at a distance, but at a convenient distance, from Cooper's Town on the banks of the Susquehannah. This, however, will be the object of future investigation. For the time of emigration we have fixed on next March. In the course of the winter those of us whose bodies, from habits of sedentary study or academic indolence, have not acquired their full tone and strength, intend to learn the theory and practice of agriculture and carpentry, according as situation and circumstances make one or the other convenient.

Your fellow Citizen,
S. T. Coleridge.

He returned to Cambridge at the end of August and filled university society with enthusiasm for Pantisocracy, but by the end of the year he was impatient to be active and, despite his family's conviction that he must be deranged, he went down in December 1794 without waiting to take his degree.

Coleridge had scarcely gone back to Cambridge before a hint of querulousness enters his correspondence with Bristol. Southey appears to have taken it upon himself to oblige Coleridge to keep faith with Sara Fricker and he reacted sharply to any suspicion he had of the other's weakening intention. Meanwhile Coleridge who was attempting to look up to Southey was beginning to find him precipitate and morally inflexible. His continuous changes of mind about the emigration and Pantisocracy were also a shock to Coleridge's ardour. Southey wanted a preliminary attempt to be made on a farm in Wales, which Coleridge thought would merely delay the scheme and waste money. Then he wanted the servants and their children who were to accompany the party to remain a servant class. It was Southey's vacillations and increasing preoccupation with the need to reconcile himself to his family and choose a career they would approve which rendered even the Welsh scheme finally impossible. He continued to make difficulties during the early months of 1795 and outraged Coleridge by, at one moment, contemplating going into the Church. The one design with which Southey persisted forcibly however, was to marry Coleridge off to his younger prospective sister-in-law. When he went down from Cambridge, Coleridge went first, not to Bristol, but to London. He was obviously unhappy and had confessed to Southey that he had difficulty in forgetting Mary Evans who had written to him condemning the Pantisocratic scheme and was about to marry, and that he did not feel that he was in love with Sara Fricker.

> To lose her [*Mary Evans*]! I can rise above that selfish Pang. But to marry another—O Southey! bear with my weakness, Love makes all things pure and heavenly like itself:— but to marry a woman whom I do *not* love—to degrade her, whom I call my Wife, by making her the Instrument of low Desires—and on the removal of a desultory appetite, to be perhaps not displeased with her absence! —Enough!—These Refinements are the wildering Fires, that lead me into Vice. Mark you Southey!—*I will do my Duty.*

In order to ensure that Coleridge did do his duty, Southey fetched him from London to Bristol early in January 1795 and settled him in his own lodging.

It is clear that Coleridge already enjoyed a reputation as thinker and talker in liberal and dissenting circles in and around Bristol, where he was plunged immediately into political controversy. He delivered a *Moral and Political Lecture* to a paying audience which aroused considerable enthusiasm and branded him as a 'damn'd Jacobin'. Looking back a few years later, Coleridge made light of his democratic leanings, but, from all reports, in 1795 they were serious. Southey and Coleridge were working closely together through the early months of the year and Southey gave a series of public lectures on historical subjects to which Coleridge contributed.

Coleridge also gave a number of lectures throughout this year: on revealed religion, on the slave trade and the corn laws. He contemplated giving others, including a comparison of the English and French revolutions. But even if his sympathies were ardently democratic, the range of reference, the combination of religion and political thought and, above all, his declaration of 'the necessity of *bottoming* on fixed Principles' show that he carried certain profoundly characteristic qualities from the beginning to the end of his career as a political and religious thinker. Nor was he at this time tempted to identify with any particular political organization. He felt that clubs and associations were 'wicked Conspiracies' but it seems equally clear that he instinctively clung to the independence of his thought.

In his relationships with his friends it may have been a very different matter in that this whole period of his life is marked by a series of friendships which were decisive in making him what he became and in which he always appears to take the dependent role. Southey was of great importance to him in that he needed always someone to look up to and before whom he could appear to be the weaker vessel. Most of Coleridge's important friendships were of this kind, necessary but ambiguous, fruitful but marred by destructive quarrels. Southey's friendship was important for other, more practical reasons. He introduced Coleridge to his friends and circle of intellectual acquaintances and put him in touch with Joseph Cottle the Bristol bookseller and publisher. Although in these years neither Coleridge nor Wordsworth broke free of occasional patronage, they mark the beginnings in the history of English literature of the establishment of direct and often close relations between writer and publisher that are such a striking feature of literature in England in the nineteenth century. It was in great part owing to Cottle's backing that none of the Bristol group was finally obliged to take up the career, whether in the Church or a profession, that their families expected of them. The career of Coleridge in these Bristol years and a little later at Keswick in Cumberland is an interesting moment in the history of the struggle to liberate the writer as an independent professional. Many of the admired figures of the previous generation; Bowles, Priestley and Godwin had been Churchmen. Cowper, until his recurrent depressive illness overtook him, was a solicitor and House of Commons Clerk.

It is remarkable how already in these early months of 1795 Coleridge had established, in outline at least, his areas of concern, and his reputation. His brilliance was immediately recognized and he formed a number of connections and friendships that, despite difficulties often of his own making, were to last throughout his life. He was often in desperate financial straits during this period, but events moved as though inevitably towards his marriage to Sara Fricker. His correspondence just before and after the wedding on 4 October is full of notes to Cottle requesting small sums of money in advance. In August he leased a small cottage at Clevedon-on-the-Sea at some distance from the town and settled there immediately after the marriage.

The major element to enter his poetry at this period is the theme of domestic retirement and happiness. Perhaps the first note of his great poetry is struck in *The Æolian Harp* (see p. 103) but the poem which refers in detail to the Clevedon cottage and the mood he chose to write about at this time is *Reflections on having left a place of retirement* which appeared in the *Monthly Magazine* of October 1796.

> Low was our pretty Cot: our tallest Rose
> Peep'd at the chamber-window. We could hear
> At silent noon, and eve, and early morn,
> The Sea's faint murmur. In the open air
> Our Myrtles blossom'd; and across the porch
> Thick Jasmins twined: the little landscape round
> Was green and woody, and refresh'd the eye.
> It was a spot which you might aptly call
> The Valley of Seclusion! Once I saw
> (Hallowing his Sabbath-day by quietness)
> A wealthy son of Commerce saunter by,
> Bristowa's citizen: methought, it calm'd
> His thirst of idle gold, and made him muse
> With wiser feelings: for he paus'd, and look'd
> With a pleas'd sadness, and gaz'd all around,
> Then eyed our Cottage, and gaz'd round again,
> And sigh'd, and said, it was a Blessèd Place.
> And we *were* bless'd. Oft with patient ear
> Long-listening to the viewless sky-lark's note
> (Viewless, or haply for a moment seen
> Gleaming on sunny wings) in whisper'd tones
> I've said to my Belovèd, 'Such, sweet Girl!
> The inobtrusive song of Happiness,

Unearthly minstrelsy! then only heard
When the Soul seeks to hear; when all is hush'd,
And the Heart listens!'
                    But the time, when first
From that low Dell, steep up the stony Mount
I climb'd with perilous toil and reach'd the top,
Oh! what a goodly scene! *Here* the bleak mount,
The bare bleak mountain speckled thin with sheep;
Grey clouds, that shadowing spot the sunny fields;
And river, now with bushy rocks o'er-brow'd,
Now winding bright and full, with naked banks;
And seats, and lawns, the Abbey and the wood,
And cots, and hamlets, and faint city-spire;
The Channel *there*, the Islands and white sails,
Dim coasts, and cloud-like hills, and shoreless Ocean—
It seem'd like Omnipresence! God, methought,
Had built him there a Temple: the whole World
Seem'd *imag'd* in its vast circumference:
No *wish* profan'd my overwhelmèd heart.
Blest hour! It was a luxury,—to be!
        Ah! quiet Dell! dear Cot, and Mount sublime!
I was constrained to quit you. Was it right,
While my unnumber'd brethren toil'd and bled,
That I should dream away the entrusted hours
On rose-leaf beds, pampering the coward heart
With feelings all too delicate for use?
Sweet is the tear that from some Howard's eye
Drops on the cheek of one he lifts from earth:
And he that works me good with unmov'd face,
Does it but half: he chills me while he aids,
My benefactor, not my brother man!
Yet even this, this cold beneficence
Praise, praise it, O my Soul! oft as thou scann'st
The sluggard Pity's vision-weaving tribe!
Who sigh for Wretchedness, yet shun the Wretched,
Nursing in some delicious solitude
Their slothful loves and dainty sympathies!
I therefore go, and join head, heart, and hand,
Active and firm, to fight the bloodless fight
Of Science, Freedom, and the Truth in Christ.

Yet oft when after honourable toil
Rests the tir'd mind, and waking loves to dream,
My spirit shall revisit thee, dear Cot!
Thy Jasmin and thy window-peeping Rose,
And Myrtles fearless of the mild sea-air.

Portraits of Coleridge and Southey in 1796 by Peter Van Dyke

And I shall sigh fond wishes—sweet Abode!
Ah!—had none greater! And that all had such!
It might be so—but the time is not yet.
Speed it, O Father! Let thy Kingdom come!

The 'return' at the end of the poem to the 'window-peeping Rose' is a marvellously fresh invention which gives shape to the poem of private reflection and solves the problem of shapelessness that Coleridge saw in Cowper's *The Task*. He used it many times in his great conversational poems of this most remarkable period.

But, as *Reflections* announces, marriage could not mean for Coleridge, this most active and restless thinker, a complete retirement. He was soon called on to respond to a further tightening of Pitt's repressive measures designed to deal with growing unrest and discontent at the inflationary pressures of the war with France.

On his way to the state opening of Parliament on 29 October the king was attacked and his carriage jostled by the crowd. The authorities immediately connected the outrage to a mass meeting three days previously of the London Corresponding Society, at which universal suffrage, annual parliaments and an end to the war were all demanded. The war was the major cause of the rapid inflation and increasing rural poverty of the period. A Royal Proclamation offered £1000 reward for the capture of the assailants, and Pitt introduced in the House of Commons an Act for the More Effective Preventing of Seditious Meetings and Assemblies. Central to the Bill was the clause prohibiting meetings of more than fifty persons without the permission of a magistrate. At the same time an Act against Treasonable and Seditious Practices and Attempts was put to the House of Lords. A meeting was called at Bristol by the mayor to propose a vote of thanks for the safe delivery of His Majesty from the Assault, to which Coleridge and his friends tried to move an amendment. This was refused, and on 28 November Coleridge delivered his lecture on the two Bills. The lecture, which was printed immediately afterwards, is a mixture of serious analysis of despotism, Godwinian enthusiasm and virulent polemic. Similar protest meetings were held in many parts of the country, but the Act quickly became law.

Coleridge's first periodical: 'The Watchman'

Coleridge was not finished with politics; the subject occupied him intensely throughout his life. He only changed direction, withdrawing from the activities of petitioning and speech-making to the more characteristic enquiry into principles and the moral and religious foundations of politics in its relation to society. Persuaded by his circle of friends he immediately set about planning a provincial magazine which he called *The Watchman*. Prominent among the supporters of the venture was Dr Joseph Beddoes, who not only conducted private research in medical chemistry at his institute at Clifton, near Bristol, but was also a convinced radical who had written anti-Pitt pamphlets on several occasions. With such support behind him Coleridge set out on 9 February 1796 on a tour of dissenting and liberal circles in the Midlands to advertise the project and drum up a list of potential subscribers. He lectured and preached all the way, returning to Bristol on 13 February. The first issue appeared two weeks later on 1st March with the motto 'THAT ALL MAY KNOW THE TRUTH: AND THAT THE TRUTH MAY MAKE US FREE!' The miscellany failed quickly and the last, the tenth issue of 13 May closed with the words: 'O Watchman! thou hast watched in vain!' On the whole his readers, those who remained faithful that is, seemed to prefer the poetry which Coleridge included to the political commentary which, though lively and occasionally satirical, carried its load of bombast. Notable among the verse contributions are the lines in the second number on *The Present State of Society*, an extract from a much longer poem, *Religious Musings* begun two years earlier.

The difficulties of the editor were threefold. His wife's mother and brother-in-law died at this time. Coleridge also thought his wife was about to miscarry and he himself suffered from an eye infection and other complaints so that, in a letter to a Birmingham correspondent, he wrote that he was 'obliged to take laudanum every night'. This is the first reference to the lifelong habit of taking opium (laudanum is an alcoholic tincture of opium), which he was never able to break completely. Then, despite considerable practical financial help from Cottle, the arrangements for getting money back from distributors did not exist and, thirdly, working to an eight-day deadline was uncongenial to Coleridge's temperament. That the paper appeared every eighth day was an awkward part of the effort to keep down costs. Had it appeared regularly every week it would have been liable to the tax designed to exert some control over printed and published matter. Many friends considered the chief cause of failure was its editor's 'indolence', a sin of which Coleridge was always the first to accuse himself. It may also have been the case that Coleridge attempted too much too soon, but paved the way for the great period of intellectual miscellanies that were central to the artistic and cultural life of the nineteenth century. At the same time as undertaking all this editorial activity, he was engaged on preparing a volume of his poems for Cottle, and *Poems on Various Subjects* appeared in April.

Having given up the magazine, Coleridge immediately began planning to study German in order to write philosophy, and to become a dissenting parson as an alternative to 'remaining in neediness and uncertainty'. He also considered starting a small school. Thomas Poole's response to the letter mentioning these schemes was to set up a small subscription fund among Coleridge's intellectual and religious friends which gave him a little money, less than £100 over the next two years. For the remainder of 1796 Coleridge corresponded frequently with Poole and, at considerable length on political and literary matters, with John Thelwall. His first child was born on 19 September, while he was absent in Birmingham.

> The baby seems strong, & the old Nurse has overpersuaded my Wife to discover a Likeness of me in its face—no great Compliment to me—for in truth I have seen handsomer Babies in my Life time.— Its name is DAVID HARTLEY COLERIDGE.—I hope, that ere he be a man, if God destine him for continuance in this life, his head will be convinced of, & his heart saturated with, the truths so ably supported by that great master of *Christian* Philosophy.

The honeymoon cottage was now too small and Coleridge and his family moved, at the very end of the year, to Nether Stowey, to a cottage backing on to the garden of Thomas Poole's house in the centre of the village.

Domestic cares and concerns that no idealistic scheme of emigration could have removed, continued to multiply for him. After their disagreements over the scheme of Pantisocracy, Southey had finally gone off to Portugal to write and study. Their dream had come to nothing; it did not even produce any very satisfactory poetry. The following sonnet, usually attributed to Coleridge, is a most unmemorable memorial.

On the Prospect of Establishing A Pantisocracy in America

Whilst pale Anxiety, corrosive Care,
The tear of Woe, the gloom of sad Despair,
  And deepen'd Anguish generous bosoms rend;—
Whilst patriot souls their country's fate lament;
Whilst mad with rage demoniac, foul intent,
  Embattled legions Despots vainly send
To arrest the immortal mind's expanding ray
  Of everlasting Truth;—I other climes
Where dawns, with hope serene, a brighter day
  Than e'er saw Albion in her happiest times,
With mental eye exulting now explore,
  And soon with kindred minds shall haste to enjoy
(Free from the ills which here our peace destroy)
Content and Bliss on Transatlantic shore.

4 Poetry and Philosophy: Coleridge and Wordsworth in Somerset

Indeed, if I live in cities, my children . . . will necessarily become acquainted with politicians and politics—a set of men and a kind of study which I deem highly unfavourable to all Christian graces. I have myself erred greatly in this respect; but I trust, I have now seen my error. I have accordingly snapped my squeaking baby-trumpet of sedition, and have hung up its fragments in the chamber of Penitences.

Letter to Charles Lloyd's father, 15 October 1796

Early meetings

Coleridge's plan to settle in the country as a smallholder dates from the last months in 1796. He was looking for a large home for his family and wanted to take in as a lodger the young Charles Lloyd, whose father Coleridge had met in Birmingham on his advertising tour for *The Watchman*. It was Poole who finally procured the cottage behind his house in Nether Stowey to which the family moved on the last day of the year. A path with a gate was made between the houses so that Coleridge could walk in Poole's orchard and garden. Here his attention turned again to poetry. He had been writing on poetry and thought to John Thelwall. Southey, as a gesture of reconciliation, had sent him his new poems to criticize. Coleridge wrote *Ode on the Departing Year*, and R. B. Sheridan, the playwright, who was now owner and manager of the Drury Lane theatre in London, had sent him an invitation through Bowles to write a tragedy on a popular subject.

But this retirement, however long it might have lasted had Coleridge (as seems unlikely) been left to his own devices, was given new meaning and impetus following a visit from Wordsworth in early April 1797. The two poets had met previously in Bristol in 1795, probably at the end of September. It is also possible that Wordsworth had heard Coleridge speaking in public on an earlier occasion. He and his sister Dorothy were living at Racedown, in the neighbouring county of Dorset, at the invitation of the Pinneys, a Bristol family. In October 1796, he wrote: 'Coleridge was at Bristol part of the time I was there, I saw but little of him. I wished indeed to have seen more—his talent appears to me very great.' After the April visit to Stowey Coleridge paid a return visit to Racedown in June, from where he wrote to Cottle: 'I speak with heart-felt sincerity & (I think) unblinded judgment, when I tell you, that I feel myself *a little man by his side*; & yet I do not think myself the less man, than I formerly thought myself.' He was as much struck with Dorothy—'her eye watchful in minutest observation of nature—and her taste a perfect electrometer'.

At the same time as he was preparing a new edition of his poems for Cottle to which were to be added poems by Charles Lloyd and Charles Lamb, Coleridge went backwards and forwards to Racedown until he was able to write to Southey (on 17 July):

I had been on a visit to Wordsworth at Racedown near Crewkerne —and brought him & his sister back with me & here I have settled *them*. By a combination of curious circumstances a gentleman's seat, with park and woods, elegantly and completely *furnished* with 9 *lodging rooms*, three parlours & a Hall—in a most beautiful & romantic situation by the sea side—4 miles from Stowey—this we have got for Wordsworth at the rent of 23£ *a year, taxes included*!!...

Coleridge's Cottage, Nether Stowey, now a National Trust Museum

Alfoxton, Wordsworth's house in Somerset and the Quantock Hills

Charles Lamb has been with me for a week—he left me Friday morning.

This was the occasion of *This Lime Tree Bower My Prison* (see Part Two, p. 107) and the establishment of Poole's 'poor man's Club', for Poole was their backer and supporter in all their dealings with the locality. They must all have sometimes appeared inexplicable and outlandish to Poole's more settled neighbours. Not only were a brother and sister who were friends of Poole's Jacobin acquaintances to take Alfoxton (or, as Dorothy transcribes it, Alfoxden) House together, they also had with them a child born of neither of them who lived with them. The likeliest explanation was that they were all French spies. Coleridge's account of the spying affair in Chapter 10 of *Biographia Literaria* was thought for a long time to have been an invention, or at best, a gross exaggeration. But certainly a government agent was sent to Stowey to observe the group in their walks after gossip among the villagers was reported to a local landowner. The spy even thought he had been discovered when he distinctly overheard the name *Spy nosy* repeatedly used by Coleridge. The reference was, of course, to Spinoza, the Dutch seventeenth-century philosopher. The affair came to nothing although the local residents seemed never to lose their uneasiness before the extraordinary ways of these intruders, their eccentric talk and their stream of mysterious visitors, among whom came the notorious Jacobin Thelwall.

Still, the memorable year had begun which was to culminate in the publication of *Lyrical Ballads* just over a year later. Living next to Tom Poole and among friends and visitors, Coleridge, despite continued financial anxieties, must have felt as settled as he was ever able to do.

The shared intellectual background

The most important legacy that Dorothy Wordsworth has left is the journal she kept of her life and journeys with her brother. Her *Alfoxden Journal*, which covers the early months of 1798, is full of details of their life with Coleridge at this time: the talk, the walks and the simple meals, the storms, stick-gathering, baking and the appearance of the landscape in different lights. What is lacking is any indication whatsoever of the content of the poets' yearlong discussion. I have already adverted to their reaction to Godwin's thought. Neither considered that man was a purely rational being obstructed and corrupted by external restraints; both were deeply interested in what Coleridge calls 'facts of the mind' and the springs of man's moral life. It was probably Coleridge who led the discussion in this direction but Wordsworth was also (from before their meeting) engaged in the immensely difficult task of reconstructing himself after the loss of Annette Vallon and his daughter Caroline, from whom the war with

France had quite cut him off. Both, like Milton, had dedicated themselves to poetry and both had in mind a particular kind of poetry. Each had admired, for example, James Beattie's *The Minstrel*, a long poem in Spenserian stanzas, of which the first book appeared in 1770 and the second in 1774. Beattie's design was, as he declares in the Preface, 'to trace the progress of a Poetical Genius, born in a rude age, from the first dawning of fancy and reason, till that period at which he may be supposed capable of appearing in the world as a MINSTREL, that is, as a poet and musician :– a character which, according to the notions of our forefathers, was not only respectable, but sacred'. Baldly told, the plot consists of the education in poetry of Edwin, a shepherd boy, by way of the simplicity and sublimity of Nature, his young fancy stocked with medieval ballads and tales of the marvellous. In a wild valley he overhears the song of a Sage mourning for man ruined by pride, selfishness and lust. The Sage instructs him to avoid despair by cultivating philosophy. But Beattie cannot follow the renewed song of Edwin. He breaks off with a lament for a dead friend.

Few would now read Beattie's stanzas with much pleasure, and I only note the poem here, not merely because both poets shared an enthusiasm for it, but because, behind the gothic and pastoral apparatus, its subject matter is discernibly that of the education of the poet in Nature, and because, no matter how dimly the idea is expressed, the poem does celebrate the poet as a special kind of human being.

A poem that interested Coleridge particularly at this time was Akenside's *The Pleasures of the Imagination*. Having first appeared in 1744 and again, rewritten, in 1757, a new edition had just been published in 1796. Coleridge as we have already read, admired Akenside for his *head* and fancy, and *The Pleasures of the Imagination* is a long philosophical and didactic poem in three books of which the object was:

> To pierce divine Philosophy's retreats,
> And teach the muse her lore.

For Akenside the imagination is a faculty of the human mind which, in the poem, he seeks 'to enlarge and harmonize', 'by exhibiting the most engaging prospects of nature . . . and by that means insensibly dispose the minds of men to a similar taste and habit of thinking in religion, morals and civil life'.

I shall leave discussion of the central place of imagination in Coleridge's developed critical theory to the next section, but it is important to notice the link that Akenside assumes between the operation of the imagination and its influence on the mind generally. The notion of 'insensibly disposing the mind' implies a philosophy of how the mind works the central notion of which, in the middle of the eighteenth century, is that of the association of ideas.

David Hartley and Associationism

Hartley was an important reference for the two poets at this time. Many of the *Lyrical Ballads* which have as their subject what we can know assume Hartley's theory of knowledge. Hartley seemed an obvious step on from dissatisfaction with Godwin, to whom we referred in the previous section. Godwin admired Hartley's *Observations on Man, His Frame, His Duty and His Expectations*, when it appeared first in 1749, took over his theory of knowledge and developed from it the view of education which is such an important aspect of *Political Justice*. Hartley's most important contribution to eighteenth-century discussion of the relation of sensations and ideas, feelings and reason, is his elaboration of the theory of the association of ideas. From this beginning he attempts to build up morality and religion on the solid physical foundation of perceptions received through the senses, in opposition to that school of philosophers who, in the earlier years of the century, had posited an *innate* moral sense. Although Hartley is, finally, more important to an understanding of Wordsworth's philosophy as it is displayed in *The Prelude*, there is no doubt of Coleridge's assent to the doctrine at this stage of his development. Hartley's theory is praised in *Religious Musings* and Coleridge had recently called his first son after the philosopher.

Hartley's mood is characteristic of its age. He is at once empirical, optimistic and religious. The basic principle of associationism as Hartley develops it is a mechanical one. The nervous system vibrates when an object is perceived through the senses. Sense perceptions that usually accompany one another are always recalled together when, on any future occasion, only one is stimulated: 'All reasoning, as well as attention, is the mere result of association.' All responses, even the highest kind of reasoning, derive ultimately from the association of original primitive sensations and impulses. Or, as a critic writing in the twentieth century summarized the position, 'man is a kind of barrel organ set in motion by the external forces of the world'. Such a doctrine has two consequences. It makes of the mind a passive instrument of perception, and it automatically implies the doctrine of necessity, as there would appear to be no way in which the sensory system could reject sensations or even choose among them. This, in fact, was already Coleridge's position in 1794 while still at Jesus College where Hartley had been a student earlier in the century. 'I am a complete Necessitarian—and understand the subject as well almost as Hartley himself—but I go farther than Hartley and believe the corporeality of *thought*.'

This was a philosophical step, fraught as it is with difficulties, that Hartley refused to take. He was content to assume merely a parallelism between matter and mind. Certain actions are associated with pleasure, others with pain, until, by repeated associations, preferred actions become habitual and the mind progresses, from the pleasures of the senses by way of the pleasures of the imagination, to the final stage of the pleasure of the law of God. It seemed an attractive doctrine and gave an important, if only temporary place to the imagination, which Hartley considered to be most active in early manhood until growing maturity should bring the philosophic mind. If Hartley's system suggests a strident mechanical barrel organ, to the early Romantic poets it suggested a very different kind of instrument—the wind harp. The wind or aeolian harp was a German invention of the seventeenth century and is a stringed instrument with a sound box which resonates as the wind blows through the strings. The Coleridges possessed one which they hung in a window of the Clevedon cottage and it appears as a powerful symbol in several of his major poems, not only in *The Æolian Harp* of 1795 (see Part Two, p. 103). Very soon however, Coleridge abandoned his enthusiasm for Hartley and associationism as the idea of the faculty of the imagination came to occupy the central place in his philosophy of the human mind.

The talk of these months, however, was not limited to the philosophy of mind and shared poetic enthusiasms. Wordsworth and Coleridge were making plans and outlining projects continuously throughout the autumn. What they were doing out on the hills, up and down the coombes, was planning a long Coleridgean poem, *The Brook*, which came to nothing, and a collaboration on the theme of the *Wanderings of Cain*. The plan to write a long epic poem, of which *The Brook* was presumably an announcement, eventually became Wordsworth's long philosophical poem containing 'views of man, nature and society'. That both poets were casting back, in Hartleian fashion, to discover in the recollections of childhood the original impulses that formed them is attested not only by the serious interest in Hartley and the eventual appearance of Wordsworth's *Prelude* (it was left unpublished until after his death in 1850), but also by the series of five autobiographical letters that Coleridge wrote to Poole during these months. He had promised Poole some account of himself, but to have written it down may well indicate some more definite kind of literary intention. The subject could otherwise so easily have provided the occasion for several of the long evening conversations in Poole's sitting room in which the whole group so delighted during these months (see the example quoted from the letters on p. 14).

That autumn, Coleridge was immersed in 'the sense of sublimity' (see the letter to Thelwall on p. 33) and in the reading for his epic poem. What did come out of it all—the reading, the aesthetic preoccupations and the attempt at the subject of Cain's guilt for his brother's murder—was *Kubla Khan* and *The Ancient Mariner*. The idea for the ballad grew out of a four-day walking tour that Coleridge, William and Dorothy made along the foreshore to Porlock and Lynton.

Coleridge was still continuously in need of money and thought that he might get as much as £5 for a long ballad. The money would go towards easing the burden of debt which, despite the small fund subscribed to by Poole and his admirers, was still considerable. At the very end of this year, however, and in January 1798, two offers were made to him which confirmed him in his attempt to live by writing. In December he had an offer from Daniel Stuart to contribute verses or political essays regularly to the *Morning Post*, which he began to do. The arrangements were made through Stuart's brother-in-law James Mackintosh who had come across Coleridge earlier in London and knew something of his reputation. After his wife died Mackintosh married the daughter of Josiah Wedgwood who had made a fortune out of revolutionizing the making of pottery at his great works in Burslem, the centre of the industry. It was probably Mackintosh, therefore, who drew the attention of Wedgwood's sons, Josiah and Thomas, to Coleridge's existence. A few days before Christmas the younger Josiah Wedgwood sent Coleridge a draft for £100 which the poet returned, with a long letter to explain his refusal. Coleridge wrote that he was considering the offer of a Unitarian ministry at Shrewsbury. It was at Shrewsbury that Coleridge received the Wedgwoods' next letter offering him an annuity of £150, 'no condition whatever being annexed to it. Thus your liberty will remain entire, you will be under the influence of no professional bias, & will be in possession of a "permanent income not inconsistent with your religious & political creeds" so necessary to your health & activity.' It was in these terms, the need to be independent in opinion in order to write, that Coleridge had rejected the original offer. During his visit to Shrewsbury Coleridge stayed with a local dissenting minister, the father of William Hazlitt. Hazlitt's account of the occasion and the choice between the independence to write a great work of philosophy and a position as a minister appears in 'Sketches from Life' (p. 16).

'*Lyrical Ballads*'

Coleridge returned to Stowey, to poetry and the Wordsworths, to philosophy and a timely degree of financial independence. On 23 March, as Dorothy noted in her journal, Coleridge walked over to Alfoxden for dinner, bringing with him the completed ballad. There was now no great need to publish it immediately. Meanwhile he had written *Frost at Midnight*, and *Christabel* was begun in April by which time, as Coleridge states in Chapter 14 of the *Biographia Literaria*, the idea of *Lyrical Ballads* had emerged out of their long conversations on poetry and philosophy.

> During the first year that Mr Wordsworth and I were neighbours, our conversations turned frequently on the two cardinal points of

poetry, the power of exciting the sympathy of the reader by a faithful adherence to the truth of nature, and the power of giving the interest of novelty by the modifying colours of imagination. The sudden charm, which accidents of light and shade, which moon-light or sun-set diffused over a known and familiar landscape, appeared to combine the practicability of combining both. These are the poetry of nature. The thought suggested itself (to which of us I do not recollect) that a series of poems might be composed of two sorts. In the one, the incidents and agents were to be, in part at least, supernatural; and the excellence aimed at was to consist in the interesting of the affections by the dramatic truth of such emotions, as would naturally accompany such situations, supposing

William Wordsworth in 1798 by William Shuter

them real. And real in this sense they have been to every human being who, from whatever source of delusion, has at any time believed himself under supernatural agency. For the second class, subjects were to be chosen from ordinary life; the characters and incidents were to be such, as will be found in every village and its vicinity, where there is a meditative and feeling mind to seek after them, or to notice them, when they present themselves.

In this idea originated the plan of the 'Lyrical Ballads'; in which it was agreed, that my endeavours should be directed to persons and characters supernatural, or at least romantic; yet so as to transfer from our inward nature a human interest and a semblance of truth sufficient to procure for these shadows of imagination that willing suspension of disbelief for the moment, which constitutes poetic faith. Mr Wordsworth, on the other hand, was to propose to himself as his object, to give the charm of novelty to things of every day, and to excite a feeling analogous to the supernatural, by awakening the mind's attention from the lethargy of custom, and directing it to the loveliness and the wonders of the world before us; an inexhaustible treasure, but for which, in consequence of the film of familiarity and selfish solicitude we have eyes, yet see not, ears that hear not, and hearts that neither feel nor understand.

I cannot imagine that the 'plan' was so abstractly conceived, allocated and faithfully pursued. Writing the *Biographia* after a long interval, Coleridge had had time to allow the event to clear in his mind and, so to speak, to be distilled into the essential truth of the relationship. The passage is very interesting as a reconstruction of an important historical moment, but more important, it captures what is fundamentally characteristic of each author: Wordsworth's intense eye for the literal evidence and Coleridge's aspiration to reach a great and undivided world beyond the range of the senses.

Negotiations with Cottle to publish a volume of poems anonymously went forward rapidly and the scheme seems to have been settled by a visit from Cottle in May during which they all walked to Lynmouth and back. The prime aim again seems to have been to make money, this time for a tour to Germany, a plan which originated with Coleridge. Cottle was prepared to offer thirty guineas for the copyright. Both poets were composing rapidly at this time, and *Lyrical Ballads* was, as Wordsworth described it in the Advertisement to the original 1798 edition, an experiment. In no sense did it represent the whole of their output at the time. Wordsworth's long blank verse poem, now entitled *The Recluse*, was growing continuously; Coleridge wrote *The Nightingale*; *Fears in Solitude* and, in his Miltonic political vein, *France: An Ode*. The Ode expresses Coleridge's final disillusionment with the turn of events in France since 1789. The breaking point came with the invasion of Switzerland by Napoleon

Bonaparte's armies. When it first appeared in the *Morning Post* it was called a *Recantation*, and, in a letter to his brother George, Coleridge had again written of having snapped his 'baby squeaking trumpet of sedition', the expression he had already used two years earlier.

But if his relations with the Wordsworths was the closest possible at this time, an event occurred which he afterwards insisted caused him so much distress as to prevent his finishing *Christabel*, and to break for a time with his closest admirer Charles Lamb. In this month, Charles Lloyd published a novel, *Edmund Oliver*, that was a barely veiled portrait of Coleridge. In it Lloyd depicted a hero whose experiences, including a broken love-affair, an episode in the dragoons and opium-taking, which seemed to Coleridge to be breaking a number of confidences. Some of them must have come to Lloyd from Southey, who had contemplated writing a novel with the same title. The forcefulness of Coleridge's reactions and his subsequent two-year break with Lamb suggests that part of the pain he was suffering derived from an acutely uncomfortable recognition of some truth, however unflattering, in the revelation of a streak of selfishness and manipulation in Coleridge's relations with his friends. Even Wordsworth had expressed caution about the qualities of Coleridge's character. On hearing the news of Coleridge's annuity from the Wedgwoods he expressed the somewhat frosty hope that 'the fruit will be as good as the seed is noble'.

Cottle tried to patch up the quarrel, which was further complicated by the appearance in the *Morning Post* of a series of sonnets written by Coleridge under a pseudonym parodying his friends' poetic styles. Cottle was not successful. Coleridge seems never to have forgiven Lloyd and it was two years later before Lamb and he resumed correspondence on anything like friendly terms. Coleridge never had a very high opinion of novels but it is an interesting reflection on his character and stature when he was still only twenty five that two of his friends considered putting him at the centre of a novel.

In May 1798 Tom Poole's brother died just after his wife had given birth. In a letter of sympathy written on the 14th to Poole, Coleridge states: 'I have had lately some sorrows that have cut more deeply into my heart than they ought to have done—& I have found Religion & *commonplace Religion* too, my restorer & my comfort—giving me gentleness & calmness & dignity!' In the same letter he announces the birth of his second son, Berkeley. The choice of another eighteenth-century philosopher as a name for his second son is an interesting indication of the direction of Coleridge's enquiries at this stage in his philosophical development, because Berkeley's work must be sharply distinguished from the tradition of Locke and Hartley already outlined. Central to Berkeley's system was an attempt to deny that experience, or sensation was the basis of mind. He considered that psychological empiricism could only lead to materialism and atheism.

He was led to deny the existence of matter and to assert instead that all perceptions were perceptions of mental qualities, not of objects, the existence of which was not a matter for proof from experience, but depended exclusively on the existence of God.

Although Coleridge's study of Berkeley at this time is scarcely documented in his letters or notebooks, I am assuming that the naming of a second son was, for him, an act not less important than the naming of the first, and that the commemoration of Berkeley shows us that Coleridge was becoming interested in arguments against the popular current of empirical and materialist philosophy. It is also as well to remind ourselves that Coleridge was very well read from an early age in the tradition of idealist philosophy from Plato onwards. In 1796 he had written to Thelwall

> —I am, & ever have been, a great reader—& have read almost everything—a library cormorant—I am deep in all out of the way books, whatever of the monkish times, or of the puritanical era—I have read and digested most of the Historical Writers—; but I do not *like* History. Metaphysics, & Poetry, & Facts of mind—(i.e. Accounts of all the strange phantasms that ever possessed your philosophy-dreamers from Thoth, the Egyptian to Taylor, the English Pagan,) are my darling Studies. In short, I seldom read except to amuse myself—& I am almost always reading.

Thelwall, man of the radical left in politics, atheist and believer in natural rights, was perhaps not the most appropriate intellectual correspondent to sympathise with this side of Coleridge's philosophical pursuits, which may account for the jocular tone used to describe it. Nevertheless, Coleridge is telling him, just as Hamlet told Horatio, that there are more things in heaven and earth than Thelwall might dream of. It seems clear that Coleridge's early preoccupations with the vast and the sublime, dreams and the 'gorgeous nonsense of Plato' indicates a disposition of mind that had long become habitual and was already being used to correct his enthusiastic embrace of empirical philosophy even before his first visit to Germany and his encounter with the new idealist philosophies of Schelling and Kant.

Meanwhile, following a walk of a few days with the Wordsworths to the Cheddar Gorge on the river Avon near Bristol, Coleridge settled the printing of *Lyrical Ballads* in a letter to Cottle at the end of May. By the end of June he was visiting the Wedgwoods' home near Cobham in Surrey. They agreed to contribute to Coleridge's expenses in Germany. There could be little time to write more poems for Cottle's volume.

Although Coleridge's contribution consisted of only four poems, only one of which, *The Ancient Mariner*, was properly a ballad, these poems together make up a third of the total number of pages. The most important poem by Wordsworth, *Lines composed above Tintern Abbey during a Tour of the Wye,* was an afterthought, added when the rest of the volume was already set up in print. Seen in these terms, the contribution by Coleridge to *Lyrical Ballads* does not seem so negligible. Another factor must also be weighed against what has traditionally been called his indolence as a way of accounting for the disproportion. Coleridge was committed to regular publication for Stuart's *Morning Chronicle* from which none of the pieces could be reprinted if the poets wished to preserve the experimental and anonymous character of the work. Wordsworth disliked occasional publication and had been in full poetic flight since the early months of the year. *Tintern Abbey* is perhaps the best example of his power and fluency at this time. After staying a few days with Cottle in Bristol, he and Dorothy made a short walking tour to Tintern on the Wye. Four days later they were back and Wordsworth had completed what has always been considered one of his greatest poems.

While it is certainly false that Coleridge left England for Germany a poet and returned a philosopher, as has often been asserted, the completion of *Lyrical Ballads* and the departure for Germany of its two authors in September together make up a moment of curious finality in Coleridge's life. That after Germany they did not return to Somerset and the Quantock Hills was due primarily to the refusal of the owner of Alfoxden to renew Wordsworth's lease of the house on the advice of her local agent whose reaction to the interlopers was that shared by the majority of the neighbours. If I do not pursue in detail the relations between the two poets after Germany, it is for two reasons. This book is not intended to repeat biographical material that is readily available elsewhere, and secondly, because it has always seemed to me that in their later careers especially in the next years in the Lake District, Wordsworth came to be the major partner (if that is the right word for a relationship broken and never quite mended in which Coleridge became a kind of pensioner of Wordsworth's during many difficult years). In Somerset, however, their friendship developed quickly in a series of rich and intimate exchanges and without all the later qualifications. It was Coleridge, the better established in reputation and praise, who provided the setting and the major share of the intellectual context which culminated in the publication of *Lyrical Ballads*, an event of unequalled importance in the history of English poetry. At least as significant for any study of Coleridge, however, is that in this brief period of settlement and confidence, he produced most of the poems by which he is remembered.

Many of the details of the later dealings of Coleridge with Wordsworth appear in connection with some of the poems in Part Two and, again, in Part Three where Coleridge's travels, tours and sojourns are recorded.

5 Coleridge as Romantic Critic

In all violent states of *Passion* the mind *acts and plays a part*, itself the actor & the spectator at once!

Letter to Tom Poole, 6 May 1799 from Germany

We cannot see in what the state of literature would have been different had he been cut off in childhood, or had he never been born; for except a few wild and fanciful ballads, he has produced nothing worth remembrance.

Some Observations on the Biographia Literaria,
Anonymous, in *Blackwood's Magazine*, October 1817

Quality of mind

As we enter the field of Coleridge's work as literary critic, the discussion of his achievement and its background is complicated from the outset by a number of difficulties. It is not simply that at the end of the century he held a number of views which he and Wordsworth shared, and then changed his mind as a result of his philosophical studies at Göttingen in Germany between 1798 and 1799. This would be a very mechanical, and therefore false way of attempting to explain the development of Coleridge's critical thinking. From the beginning his enquiries are characterized by a certain quality of mind; the search, for example, for the unity that underlies multiplicity. Then, that mind is also coloured by an ineradicable faith in the existence of a personal God. Thirdly, Coleridge uses a number of key terms and expressions throughout his career (often taken from other writers), such as imagination, reason, understanding, with changing emphasis or even with different meanings. At crucial moments his language is often pictorial or metaphorical, with the result that, although the impression made on the reader at the time of reading is lively and forceful, it is not easy to be quite certain afterwards that one has grasped a meaning for the words. Again, up until the time of writing his literary memoirs, the *Biographia Literaria* and beyond, he was constantly reformulating his notions of poetry and its relation to the more general problems of a theory of knowledge, without ever making a definitive statement of his position. That he did not do so leaves us with a series of perceptions, suggestions and insights of an intensity which is sometimes blinding, but which oblige us to construct for ourselves the framework which, even in the *Biographia*, he cannot be said to have constructed for us. Furthermore, as I have already suggested, Coleridge's criticism is part of, and is illuminated by, his more general philosophical speculations and it will be necessary to touch on these when we come to consider Coleridge's view of poetry as a special kind of knowledge.

Finally, the commentator runs into two kinds of difficulty in attempting to write about Coleridge's thought on the nature of literature. In trying to make it clearer than Coleridge left it, he can all too easily make it appear simpler than it really is. Or, he can run the opposite risk of adopting Coleridge's terminology and procedures thereby making nothing clearer. What I intend to do, at the risk of simplification, is to try and show something of the development of Coleridge's thought, not by treating it chronologically as theoretical statements rise to the surface of his various critical writings over the years, but by comparing his early stance and the most readily available of the late formulations, that is the famous definition of imagination in Chapter 13 of *Biographia Literaria*. In doing so I have to bear in mind that Coleridge's thought is a continuous development, and that the attempt to explain these very processes of change and growth represented a most fundamental aspect of his philosophical enquiries. But Coleridge's *theory* of poetry and of creativity is only a part of his critical thinking. He was at the same time, and throughout his life, an extremely lively and acutely discerning reader of literature of all kinds. His talk and writings, his letters and rough notebook jottings are full of observations on other writers that mirror his own poetic feeling for language. As we shall see, it was he who established the kind of poet that we take Wordsworth to be, and whose response to the texture of Shakespeare's verse had seldom been equalled. At the time of the writing of the Preface, however, what motivated Wordsworth and Coleridge was primarily still the original political impulse that lay behind the first edition of *Lyrical Ballads*, of which the philosophical underpinning would remain undisclosed. What the two poets were proposing at this time was, basically, an art of and for the people. Justificatory theory was less important to them than the making of a certain kind of effect on their readers.

The Preface to 'Lyrical Ballads', 1800

By the end of 1799 the Wordsworths had settled at Dove Cottage just outside Grasmere, where Coleridge joined them the following April. Wordsworth was contemplating issuing a revised second edition of *Lyrical Ballads*. Coleridge offered him every encouragement, and threw himself energetically into preparing the new edition for printing. It was also Coleridge who urged on Wordsworth the task of writing an extended preface which would explain and justify their new kind of poetry. As Wordsworth reported many years later, it 'was written at the request of Mr Coleridge out of sheer good nature'. But he took the task seriously. The poets discussed the subject a good deal and the work was finished by the end of September. It has often been asked why, since the subject was more fitting to his temperament, Coleridge did not write it himself. The usual answer is that had he undertaken it, the Preface would never have appeared. Evidence appears continuously to support the theory of Coleridge's incorrigible indolence but, in fact, he was extremely busy at this time completing his excellent translation of Schiller's tragedy, *Wallenstein*. He had also committed himself to the publisher, Longman, to write an account of his tour in Germany. Admittedly this last, like so much else, never appeared. 'You spawn plans like a herring', wrote Southey a little later. But the fact is that Coleridge was writing at this time expressly, as on so many other occasions, for the money.

Furthermore, in July of this year Coleridge moved his family to the Lake District, to Greta Hall on the river Derwent near Keswick, in order to be permanently near Wordsworth. Thomas Poole disapproved of the arrangement, charging Coleridge with 'prostration' before Wordsworth. Coleridge's third son, Derwent, was born on 17

September in the new house and his health caused both parents considerable anxiety. 'He creaks like a barn door when he breathes', wrote Coleridge. Amidst all these events he also found time to revise *The Ancient Mariner* and complete Part 2, but not all, of *Christabel* for the new edition. Perhaps the most important factor in his urging on of Wordsworth was his desire to make for Wordsworth a place as a poet worthy of his own high esteem of him. To lean too heavily on the view of Coleridge as indolent and distracted can prevent our seeing just how much varied work he did at this time and throughout his life. Finally, it should be recalled that the Cumberland climate did not suit Coleridge; he suffered almost continuously throughout these years from colds and persistent stomach trouble, against which he had increasing recourse to opiates.

Given the weight that Coleridge lent to Wordsworth during these months, I think we can safely assume that Coleridge assented to the views expressed in the Preface. The occasion may have felt to him to be only a continuation of the relationship that had, two years earlier, resulted in the appearance of the first edition of *Lyrical Ballads*. The effects of the year in Germany and his intensive study of New German philosophy at Göttingen were not yet apparent.

Wordsworth's view of Poetry in the Preface

The 1800 prose essay is polemical in character in that it attempts at once to justify and persuade readers to appreciate a radically new view of what poetry is. It proceeds partly by attacking the practice of earlier eighteenth-century poets and partly by advocating a new way of thinking about poetry.

Even in the earlier part of the century the neoclassical idea of poetry was seldom advocated or practised in anything like a pure state. Nor, until Dr Johnson formulated it, was the theory ever very clearly perceived. Poetry, for Johnson, is 'just representation of general nature'. Art, that is, is justified in two ways. First, it is an imitation of nature, but, second, what it is that art imitates is not the accidental and occasional features of nature as we perceive them through the senses, but a selection of experience that emphasizes its generalized and characteristic, or representative character. Already we can see how such a view would clash with the assertions of eighteenth-century philosophers who insist that all knowledge begins in particulars and that its particularity is the essential characteristic of all knowledge. And it is with this new philosophical tradition, as we have seen in the previous section, that Wordsworth takes his stand in the Preface.

If I do not give a complete analysis of the view of poetry expressed in the Preface it is because my main emphasis must be placed on Coleridge's later work and on those points over which he came to disagree with what was written there. Two cardinal features must be looked at to establish the area: Wordsworth on the language of poetry, and his answer to the question what is a poet. From the position he adopts in these two cases the answer to his own third question, 'What is poetry', can be deduced.

To deal with language first. Wordsworth claims that the poems are written in a selection of the real language of men and, later, that there is no essential difference between the language of poetry and the language of prose. It follows, therefore, that whatever it is that characterizes the essence of poetry, that essence is not to be found in language, but elsewhere. The elsewhere is the poet himself, above all in those innermost feelings that he draws from the deepest and most permanent source of life; that is, from nature. The feelings of those human beings most closely and continuously in touch with nature are the profoundest and most educative, and it is with such people that Wordsworth identifies himself. The poet, therefore, is not a special kind of person but one more aware, more sensitive and more reflective than is common. He is a kind of translator and the only restriction under which he works is to achieve a balance between pleasure and stimulation in his reader. Perhaps in the notion of balancing and reconciling we can detect something of Coleridge's presence, but for the rest, the notion is empirical and, in the sense that the poet ranges himself with common humanity, democratic.

So for Wordsworth poetry is not in the language of the poem but is anterior to the poem. Poetry lies in the passions and enjoyments of men which the poet then expresses as best he can. What he knows best is his own emotional life and to it he pays particular attention. His imagination allows him to pretend to enter other situations and other lives on the reassurance that, since he seeks out the most permanent of human emotions, these will not be altogether different from his own in kind. Wordsworth's theory is an important one, which is still very much alive, in that he conceives of the content of poetry as being sincere self-expression and of the poem as the container. Although they imply other associated meanings, his two definitions of poetry in the Preface as 'emotion recollected in tranquillity' and 'the spontaneous overflow of powerful feelings' both assert the separateness of content and container.

At one stroke, Wordsworth achieved a radical re-ordering of the relationship between poetry and the world of experience. Poetry no longer imitated life so much as recorded the poet's own life. The artist's faithfulness as an imitator gave way to his sincerity as a recorder when it came to the judgment of his performance.

Coleridge on Wordsworth's view

Coleridge addressed himself to the Preface in a long letter to Southey written from Keswick in July 1802. Among the outlines of several schemes he is contemplating, he sketches an anthology of contemporary poetry.

> The object is not to examine what is good in each writer, but what has ipso facto pleased, & to what faculties or passions or habits of the mind they may be supposed to have given pleasure. Of course, Darwin & Wordsworth having given each a defence of *their* mode of Poetry, & a disquisition on the nature & essence of Poetry in general, I shall necessarily be led rather deeper—and these I shall treat of either first or last. But I will apprize you of one thing, that altho' Wordsworth's Preface is half a child of my own Brain & so arose out of Conversations, so frequent, that with few exceptions we could scarcely either of us perhaps positively say, which first started any particular Thought—I am speaking of the Preface as it stood in the second Volume [edition?]—yet I am far from going all lengths with Wordsworth. He has written lately a number of Poems (32 in all) some of them of considerable Length (the longest 160 Lines) the greater number of these to my feelings very excellent Compositions, but here & there a daring Humbleness of Language & Versification, and a strict adherence to matter of fact, even to prolixity, that startled me. His alterations likewise in *Ruth* perplexed me, and I have thought & thought again, & have not had my doubts solved by Wordsworth. On the contrary, I rather suspect that some where or other there is a radical Difference in our theoretical opinions respecting Poetry—this I shall endeavour to go to the Bottom of—and acting the arbitrator between the old School & the New School hope to lay down some plain, & perspicuous, tho' not superficial, Canons of Criticism respecting Poetry. —What an admirable Definition Milton gives quite in an obiter way—when he says of Poetry—that it is 'simple, sensuous, passionate.'!—It truly comprizes the whole, that can be said on the subject. In the new Edition of the L. Ballads there is a valuable appendix, which I am sure you must like, & in the Preface itself considerable additions, one on the Dignity & nature of the office & character of a Poet, that is very grand, & of a sort of Verulamian Power & Majesty—but it is, in parts, (and this is the fault, *me judice*, of all the latter half of that Preface) obscure beyond any necessity—& the extreme elaboration & almost constrainedness of the Diction contrasted (to my feelings) somewhat harshly with the general style of the Poems, to which the Preface is an Introduction. . . .

He closes the topic with the assurance:

> However, I need not say, that any diversity of opinion on the subject between you & myself, or Wordsworth and myself, can only be small, taken in a *practical* point of view.

'Getting to the bottom of it' became a preoccupation for the next fifteen years of Coleridge's life, broken and disordered years as they were. But he strikes an interesting note when he writes of 'acting the arbitrator between the old School and the new School'. Coleridge could scarcely ever have been free from the pressures of his knowledge of history and here it produces a characteristic response: the reconciling stance between opposites.

In the same long letter to Southey, Coleridge laments the passing of his gift for poetry.

> As to myself, all my poetic Genius, if ever I really possessed any *Genius*, & it was not rather a mere general *aptitude* of Talent, & quickness in Imitation is gone—and I have been fool enough to suffer deeply in my mind, regretting the loss—which I attribute to my long & exceedingly severe Metaphysical Investigations—& these partly to Ill-health, and partly to private afflictions which rendered any subject, immediately connected with Feeling, a source of pain & disquiet to me.

He then quotes some lines from *Dejection*, and goes on to say that his relations with his wife are better since he had raised the possibility of separating from her. I shall leave to the discussion of the whole poem *Dejection: An Ode* (see p. 136) any account of Coleridge's mood and health during these months. What I am concerned with at this point is the fact that he had already begun to explain the difference between Wordsworth's view of poetry and his own. Within the next two years, before the breakdown that forced him to leave his wife and seek better health in a warmer climate, he had achieved the distinction between Fancy and Imagination which comes so abruptly at the centre of the *Biographia Literaria* and which is the pivot on which his whole aesthetic theory turns. In January 1804 he was writing in a letter on the virtues of Wordsworth as a poet.

> Wordsworth is a Poet, a most original Poet—he no more resembles Milton than Milton resembles Shakespeare—no more resembles Shakespeare than Shakespeare resembles Milton—he is himself: and I dare affirm that he will hereafter be admitted as the first & greatest philosophical Poet—the only man who has effected a complete and constant synthesis of Thought and Feeling and combined them with Poetic Forms, with the music of pleasurable passion and with Imagination or the *modifying* Power in that highest sense of the word in which I have ventured to oppose it to Fancy, or the *aggregating* power—in that sense in which it is a dim Analogue of Creation, not all that we can *believe* but all that we can *conceive* of creation. Wordsworth is a Poet, and I feel myself a better Poet, in knowing how to honour *him*, than in all my own poetic Compositions, all I have done or hope to do—.

It is remarkable just how many of his major concerns Coleridge manages to hint at in this very compact early formulation. The conciseness and assurance suggest forcibly that he had already consciously worked out many of his most important themes. The thought also proceeds in characteristic fashion, by distinction (what he later called *desynonymizing*) and by qualification, so that its flow is not always immediately clear. First, Coleridge names his three major English poets: the highest standards by which all else would be judged. Then, keen to make propaganda on behalf of a Wordsworth still incomprehensible to the educated reading public, he asserts Wordsworth's kind of originality: the complete synthesis of thought and feeling. Thirdly, this synthesis combined with forms is a product of the poetic imagination. Coleridge then defines imagination as a power similar to God's power of creation, even if the similarity is only a 'dim' one, or not very close. Be that as it may, the human imagination has more in common with divine creativity than it has with the power of fancy which operates by aggregating or collecting rather than by modifying. The difference appears to be this: that the imagination works on the materials that come to it and changes them in some way which is creative in the sense that God made and makes all creation. In the operation of fancy the materials collected remain as they are, a bundle of things unchanged from what they were before they were brought together.

At a first approach to Coleridge's distinction, one is reminded of Burke's similar procedure; there the Sublime is distinguished from the Beautiful, here the Imagination from the Fancy. But in Coleridge's desynonymizing act much more is implied than in Burke's. Burke relies on formulating how we might feel in certain circumstances to promote a general theory of perception, Coleridge is opposing to each other two theories of perception. To make this implication clearer I must go back to Coleridge's correspondence of 1801. In February of that year he wrote three philosophical letters to Josiah Wedgwood as an earnest, perhaps, of the serious philosophical work that the Wedgwood annuity was intended to make possible. In these letters Coleridge undertakes the demonstration of Locke's dependence on Descartes, the seventeenth-century French philosopher, for his theory of mind. Coleridge also tries to show that, in assuming that Descartes believed that human beings are born already holding certain ideas, Locke misconceived what Descartes's work was about. This demonstration allows Coleridge to go on to express an acute dissatisfaction with Locke's empirical theory of knowledge and to explain Locke's great reputation in political and social terms.

The refutation of Locke's theory is part of a grander scheme of study that Coleridge had in hand. A month later he wrote to Tom Poole that he was engaged in 'the most intense Study', in which he had succeeded in overthrowing 'the doctrine of Association, as taught by Hartley, and with it all the irreligious metaphysics of modern

Infidels—especially, the doctrine of Necessity'. The exercise had meant abandoning the book on his German travels, but he hopes to persuade Longman to accept instead 'a work on the originality & merits of Locke, Hobbes, & Hume which Work I mean as a *Pioneer* to my greater work, and as exhibiting a proof that I have not formed opinions without an attentive Perusal of the works of my Predecessors from Aristotle to Kant'. In a second letter to Poole on this vast subject Coleridge prefaces his continued attack on the modern English empirical tradition by asserting: 'My opinion is this—that deep Thinking is attainable only by a man of deep Feeling, and that all Truth is a species of Revelation.' His enquiries into the tradition take him back from Locke to Newton, whose demonstration of the laws of the physical universe had prompted Locke into a similar kind of search for the laws of the human universe.

Newton was a mere materialist. *Mind* in his system, is always *passive*,—a lazy *Looker-on* on an external world. If the mind be not passive, if it be indeed made in God's Image, and that, too, in the sublimest sense, the *Image of the Creator*, there is ground for suspicion that any system built on the passiveness of the mind must be false, as a system.

In a letter of September 1802 Coleridge's continuous pursuit of this theme again rises to the surface in a discussion of, among other literary matters, a recent volume of Bowles's later poems.

There reigns thro' all the blank verse poems such a perpetual trick of *moralising* every thing—which is very well, occasionally—but never to see or describe any interesting appearance in nature, without connecting it by dim analogies with the moral world, proves faintness of Impression. Nature has her proper interest; & he will know what it is, who believes & feels, that every Thing has a Life of its own, & that we are all *one Life*. A Poet's *Heart & Intellect* should be *combined*, *intimately* combined & *unified*, with the great appearances in Nature—& not merely held in solution & loose mixture with them, in the shape of formal Similies. I do not mean to *exclude* these formal Similies—there are moods of mind, in which they are natural—pleasing moods of mind, & such as a Poet will often have, & sometimes express; but they are not his highest, & most appropriate moods. They are 'Sermoni propriora' which I once translated—'Properer for a Sermon.' The truth is—Bowles has indeed the *sensibility* of a poet; but he has not the *Passion* of a great Poet. His latter writings all want *native* Passion—Milton here & there supplies him with an appearance of it—but he has no native Passion because he is not a Thinker—

The letter continues touching fleetingly on a number of personal and general literary topics and comes to rest for a moment on a comparison between Greek and Hebrew poetry. Of Greek poetry, and its fondness for 'godkins' and 'goddesslings', Coleridge says: 'At best, it is but Fancy, or the aggregating Faculty of the mind—not *Imagination*, or the *modifying*, and *co-adunating* Faculty.' 'Co-adunating' is one of a number of adjectives that Coleridge borrowed or invented in his efforts to describe exactly the activity of the imagination. Here the word, borrowed from the jargon of botany and physiology, means joining together.

So, what Coleridge has done is to distinguish two 'faculties' or activities of the mind, making one creative, remaking the objects of experience so as to give life to them, the other merely reproductive in a mechanical sense of the objects of experience.

He did not invent the notion of the imagination. Its nature and existence had been a preoccupation of philosophers interested in the workings of the human mind throughout the eighteenth century. And, as we have seen, not all of them, Berkeley is one example, and there were others whom Coleridge had certainly read seriously, assumed that the mind always behaved like an adding machine. But, although recent writers had speculated on the activity of the imagination, few had emphasized its inherent quality, its function as part of the constitution of the mind, or grasped the importance of the mind so constituted acting on experience, rather than being acted upon by experience.

Idealism and Romanticism

The notion that, in experiencing, the self plays an active and constitutive rôle is one of the utmost importance in any view we might take of the meaning, or meanings, of the word Romanticism. Its assertion is usually associated with the tradition of late eighteenth- and early nineteenth-century philosophy in Germany known as idealism. Extreme Romantic Idealism arrived at a point at which it was asserted that the mind could know only itself, that all things were the product of thought. But the philosophical movement against mechanical or rational views of the mind began with the work of Immanuel Kant, whose *Critique of Pure Reason* first appeared in 1781.

Coleridge and Kant

Although Coleridge most certainly became acquainted with the work of Kant while he was studying in Germany, he does not seem to have given serious attention to it until 1803. By this time, as we have just read, he was beginning to work out his own dissatisfaction with empiricism into a new system. When he came to write the *Biographia* he said disappointingly little about his relationship to Kant's critical attack on Reason as a sufficient instrument by which to know and explain reality. Kant's dissatisfaction with the explanatory power of unaided reason parallels Coleridge's with empiricism and association-ism. Kant's 'Copernican revolution' consisted of asserting that far from the mind conforming to objects outside the mind, it is objects that conform to the mind. Coleridge came to Kant in the hope of reinforcing his intuition that, in the act of perception, the mind is active and not merely a passive onlooker. But if Kant's outlook is primarily logical, Coleridge's impulse is essentially psychological. That is, he sought an account of the mind that would accommodate the notion that thought was rooted in feeling and must report truth-fully on actual experiences. We recall his early habituation of the idea of the *vast*, his assurance that the world of belief reached far beyond the horizon of sense perception.

Kant's solution, in so far as it is relevant to Coleridge's similar search, is to propose two worlds of knowledge, that of the senses which comes at us through experience but which is organised by the mind, and that of the intellect. The world of the intellect is dictated by the constitution of the mind, and, logically, must precede the world of experience. What is known through experience takes the shape of the mind. Therefore there is much that must remain unknowable. In this context a remark of Coleridge's in a letter of 1806 is illuminating. He is attempting to distinguish thoughts from things. 'No *thought*, which I have of any *thing* comprizes the whole of that Thing. I have a distinct Thought of a Rose-Tree; but what countless properties and goings-on of that plant are there, not included in my *Thought* of it?' Coleridge is here expressing a very Kantian notion, yet there is an important distinction we must make between their philosophies in order to make clearer Coleridge's own philosophical scheme. Neither is a pure romantic idealist; that is, neither held that all we can know is our own thoughts in that they both held that the material of thought is given and is then worked upon by the mind. For Kant, however, the structure of the human sensibility and the mind is constant, whereas for Coleridge on the other hand this inner structure is continuously growing and developing, acting upon and acted upon by the world of experience in continuous interchange and interpenetration. Coleridge's position in this respect has impressed a number of com-mentators as a rich psychological theory of human development, but it has often been considered too elusive to grasp as a theory of the mind. What one has to be able to picture is a reciprocal action between a developing mind and a ceaselessly flowing world of experience. Coleridge captures the notion often for himself by means of a poetic image.

> The *white rose* of Eddy-foam, where the stream ran into a scooped or scalloped hollow of the Rock in its channel—this Shape, an exact white rose, was for ever overpowered by the Stream rushing down in upon it, and still obstinate in resurrection it spread up into the

scallop, by fits & starts, *blossoming* in a moment into a full Flower.—
Hung over the Bridge, & musing considering how much of this
Scene of endless variety in Identifying was Nature's—how much
the living organ's!—What would it be if I had the eyes of a fly!—
What if the blunt eye of a Brobdingnag!—

In this notebook entry for 1803 Coleridge has supplied us with the
perfect emblem for his philosophical endeavours. The image of the
rose is constantly unmade and remade by the rush of the waterfall,
and the sentence conveys most musically the wonder and beauty of
its continuous rebirth. But having come to rest for the moment on the
image itself, Coleridge's speculative imagination darts off characteristically to wonder how the scene would impress itself on a radically
different mode of perception and asks what it might be like to
experience the world as fly or giant.

During these years Coleridge leaned heavily on Kant and the later
developments from Kant towards idealism, but it is not to my purpose
to establish his indebtedness in any detail. He asserted in the *Biographia*
that his reading of German philosophy merely confirmed for him the
insights he had already achieved from reflection on the earlier English,
Scottish and European traditions. Coleridge certainly used Kantian
terminology and method as he required them, but only to his own
purposes. These were to construct a dynamic philosophy of the human
mind that took account of man's creativity and moral freedom, his
experience and his existence as the creation of a personal God. And
these elements of his developed thought are to be discovered in the
occasional glimpses we catch in notebooks and letters of Coleridge's
struggle towards philosophical articulateness.

The struggle was not purely theoretical or metaphysical. Nor does
it seem to be the case that the poet was killed off by the philosopher.
There is no reason not to accept much of Coleridge's own account of
his case: that philosophizing in these years acted as an anodyne to his
rapidly worsening health and the rupture between himself and his
wife. Laudanum and philosophy kept him going at a time when the
effort to write poetry would have demanded too much of himself and
his feelings, as he wrote to Southey.

The dark years

The break came in 1804. After a year or more of tentatively exploring
the idea of going to live in a warmer climate for the sake of his health,
it was arranged that he should travel to Malta. He left Keswick in
January for London, became very ill and stayed for a short time in
Essex with Sir George and Lady Beaumont to recover, finally leaving
from Portsmouth early in April for a voyage of eight or nine weeks. He
never lived with his family again; and Robert Southey was left at

Greta Hall to become the father to two families. Coleridge's two years in the Mediterranean did little for his health or for his philosophical and literary advancement. His own story was that his papers were sunk by a French privateer while on their way to England by sea.

The only substantial remains of his restless activities as writer and thinker until the year of publication of *Biographia Literaria* are the various series of lectures on poetry, and on Shakespeare in particular, which he gave in London and Bristol at different times, and the editing of *The Friend* from Kendal in 1809, where he was helped by Sara Hutchinson. *The Friend* a 'literary, moral and political weekly paper', failed after ten numbers had appeared, and, of the lectures, many exist only in imperfectly reported accounts by listeners. Sometimes Coleridge digressed from his announced theme and on some occasions he was unable to appear at all. In 1811 Josiah Wedgwood, the surviving brother, saw fit to withdraw his half of the legacy that had been settled on Coleridge. That he was kept going at all during the years to 1816 was due almost entirely to the loyal support of friends. It was at the insistence of Joseph Henry Green, a lecturer in medicine who had heard Coleridge at the Royal Institution, that he was finally persuaded to attempt a cure for his addiction if not for his continuous illnesses. He became a patient in the house of Dr James Gillman of Highgate in April 1816.

The occasion of 'Biographia Literaria'

The idea of writing a literary autobiography grew out of the need to find money to help his eldest son Hartley who was about to go up to Merton College, Oxford. At the same time Coleridge would prepare a new edition of his verse. Both tasks were begun in 1815 and *Biographia Literaria* and *Sybilline Leaves* appeared in 1817.

So the *Biographia* is something of an accompaniment, an occasional piece and not the great work so often announced. It is not Coleridge's philosophical system, his *Organon* or *Logosophia*, but a miscellany, a disparate collection of writings held together, in intention at least, by the thread of the writer's own life as a man of letters and the history of his literary opinions. But these last, as I have attempted to show in this section, are, as he himself insisted, inseparable from the development of his philosophical views. Philosophical enquiry, therefore, occupies a large and, for modern readers interested in Coleridge primarily as poet and critic, somewhat indigestible part of the early chapters.

The refutation of the contemporary tradition of mechanistic explanation in philosophy was a necessary preliminary to the exposition of the new dynamic philosophy and the central role in it of the creative imagination which was to supplant the former. No sooner, however, has he launched, in Chapter 12, into the exposition of the new philosophy (much of which is a transcription of the work of the German follower of Kant, F. W. J. von Schelling) than in the next chapter he cuts himself short in mid-flight, realizing that such an exposition, from which he was to derive the poetic imagination, would be out of place in what was, after all, intended as a personal literary miscellany. Having interrupted himself so abruptly, he closes chapter 13 with the gnomic distinction between fancy and imagination.

Imagination, or the Esemplastic Power

The IMAGINATION then, I consider either as primary, or secondary. The primary IMAGINATION I hold to be the living Power and prime Agent of all human Perception, and as a repetition in the finite mind of the eternal act of creation in the infinite I AM. The secondary Imagination I consider as an echo of the former, co-existing with the conscious will, yet still as identical with the primary in the *kind* of its agency, and differing only in *degree*, and in the *mode* of its operation. It dissolves, diffuses, dissipates, in order to recreate; or where this process is rendered impossible, yet still at all events it struggles to idealize and to unify. It is essentially *vital*, even as all objects (*as* objects) are essentially fixed and dead.

FANCY, on the contrary, has no other counters to play with, but fixities and definites. The Fancy is indeed no other than a mode of Memory emancipated from the order of time and space; while it is blended with, and modified by that empirical phenomenon of the will, which we express by the word CHOICE. But equally with the ordinary memory the Fancy must receive all its materials ready made from the law of association.

This definition is the focal point from which the rest of the writing radiates. I hope enough has been said in the earlier parts of the section to enable the reader to see directly the connection between a theory of poetry and the mode of its creation, and a philosophy of knowing which is essentially dynamic and creative. In making the distinction Coleridge is reflecting Kant's two worlds of intelligence and the senses. Imagination is part of our way of knowing. Fancy, on the other hand, belongs to the world of experience. Not that to say so denies all or any importance to the world of experience and the associations that are gathered from it by the Fancy. Far from it; Coleridge does not follow Schelling, from whose *Transcendental Idealism* of 1800 he took so much of his emphasis on the primacy of the imagination in the act of knowing, so far as to assert that the reality inhabited by consciousness is a reality of its own exclusive creation. This is the full significance of Romantic Idealism, and Coleridge rejects it. Tempted as he must have been to it as a belief, he could not reconcile complete subjectivism and his belief in a personal and creating God—the infinite I AM of the definition. If the mind knew only that reality which it created for itself, then God had no place beyond human consciousness, and then, Coleridge asserted, the only possible belief could be what he called 'pantheism'. There could be nothing known that was *not* God. On the contrary, one cannot read Coleridge for very long without being struck again and again by the way in which the writing carries the pressures and flux of his own experience. It is as though his philosophical development during the period we have been considering is a ceaseless attempt to bring his experience into consciousness and find a satisfactory explanation for its mysterious and paradoxical effects on him.

His profoundest intuition was a religious one, which reappears in various guises throughout his work as the conviction of the unity of all life. This intuition could only come from within, as he felt, and not from experience. It followed for him that the agent of this intuition was the imagination which *created* a reality out of the flux of impressions under the guidance of this intuition. Despite sharp disagreement among interpreters as to what Coleridge intended by the 'primary imagination', it seems best to read the words as descriptive of that spontaneous consciousness with which we deal creatively with experiences as we meet them. In Chapter 12 he states as an axiom that 'To know is in its very essence a verb active'. Later, in Chapter 18, he asserts that 'The *rules* of the IMAGINATION are themselves the very powers of growth and production.'

To the 'secondary imagination' is reserved the meaning of a special *self*-consciousness which works deliberately to recombine the disparates of experience, reconciling opposite and discordant qualities in order to create new forms out of them. It follows that great poetry is the product of the secondary imagination, and Coleridge comes at his definition of poetry in Chapter 14 by way of opposing the view that Wordsworth expressed in his 1800 Preface, that there is no essential difference between poetry and prose. For Coleridge if the elements of a poem and a prose composition are the same, the distinction lies in the different combinations and ends which the elements serve:

> A poem is that species of composition, which is opposed to works of science, by proposing for its *immediate* object pleasure, not truth; and from all other species (having *this* object in common with it) it is discriminated by proposing to itself such delight from the *whole*, as is compatible with a distinct gratification from each component *part*.

How we recognize a poem is to read it as a particular kind of structure not as an illustration of general truths. What is communicated by this structure is *pleasure* and not information of any extractable kind. Frequently reformulated, this view of poetry has provided the *motif* for the discussion of the nature of poetry ever since Coleridge. At its weakest, it has appeared in the slogans, 'art for art's sake' or 'art is useless', but has remained a powerful instrument with which to oppose all those alternative views of literature which read imaginative works as biographical evidence or as expressions of a commitment to particular religious or ideological beliefs.

But if a poem is primarily a structure which is so designed as to give pleasure, two questions immediately arise. What is its relation to truth, and, how do we tell a good poem from a less good poem when poems are no longer expressions of beliefs? These are, of course, Wordsworth's questions in the Preface, and the remaining major chapters of *Biographia Literaria*, on Shakespeare and Wordsworth, provide Coleridge's answers to them.

In Chapter 14 he proceeds to distinguish between a poem and poetry. Poetry is not a matter of writing in verse or prose. For Coleridge the question, 'What is poetry?' is nearly the same as 'What is a poet?', and he wants to distinguish his own answer from the one proposed by Wordsworth in 1800 in which Wordsworth claims that a poet is a man like other men, but who 'from practice . . . has acquired a greater readiness and power in expressing what he thinks and feels'. Coleridge's definition shifts the emphasis away from the *content* of the poet's mind to the activity or *process* going on in that mind. From our reading of his philosophical development earlier, this is much as we should expect. He then continues by explaining the nature of that activity:

> The poet, described in *ideal* perfection, brings the whole soul of man into activity, with the subordination of its faculties to each other, according to their relative worth and dignity. He diffuses a tone and spirit of Unity, that blends, and (as it were) fuses, each into each, by that synthetic and magical power, to which we have exclusively appropriated the name of Imagination. This power . . . reveals itself in the balance of opposite or discordant qualities: of sameness, with difference; of the general with the concrete; the idea, with the image; the individual with the representative; the sense of novelty and freshness, with old and familiar objects; a more than usual state of emotion, with a more than usual order; judgment ever awake and steady self-possession, with enthusiasm and feeling profound or vehement; and while it blends and harmonises the natural and the artificial, still subordinates art to nature; the manner to the matter; and our admiration of the poet to our sympathy with the poetry.

The foregoing is Coleridge's answer to the question 'What is the relation between poetry and truth?' Poetry is its own truth in that it is a product of the imaginative activity of the poet. At the same time Coleridge has given one kind of answer, an *ideal* answer that is, to the question, 'How do we recognize good poetry?'

But there is also another kind of answer provided in the remainder of *Biographia Literaria*. Coleridge proceeds to give *examples* of good poetry, with Shakespeare and Wordsworth as the centre of his demonstration.

Coleridge and Shakespeare

Shakespeare is Coleridge's 'poet described in ideal perfection'. As he turns to what he calls 'practical criticism' in order to justify his view, so in Chapter 15, his first task is to locate the specific symptoms of poetic power in the early work of Shakespeare. He describes four such qualities: the sense of musical delight, the choice of subjects remote from the private interests and circumstances of the poet, the use of imagery modified always by a predominant passion and, finally, depth and energy of thought. It is in respect of the depth and intensity of thought that Shakespeare's greatness shows. 'No man', he writes in the next sentence, 'was ever yet a great poet, without being at the same time a profound philosopher. For poetry is the blossom and the fragrancy of all human knowledge, human thoughts, human passions, emotions, language.' The metaphor of blossoming here is far from accidental. For, just as Nature unfolds herself through the activities of the vegetable world, so poetry is the unfolding of the whole of human consciousness.

Coleridge's interest in Shakespeare is not unique in his time. We only have to think of Blake's illustrations to some of the plays, or of the whole tradition of scholarly criticism of Shakespeare throughout the eighteenth century, to correct any false impression of that kind. Sir George Beaumont and other members of the Sketching Society habitually practised their art on Shakespearian themes, but never before had it been suggested that Shakespeare was a *philosopher*. Coleridge stands against the opposing view of Shakespeare that Milton expresses in *L'Allegro*, of Shakespeare 'warbling his native wood-notes wild' as genius by nature and almost by accident. Coleridge does not develop his position in *Biographia Literaria*, but it is to be found amply extended and repeated in his long series of lectures on Shakespeare and poetry, of which the most useful collection is that of Professor T. M. Raysor which first appeared in 1930. I have included as Appendix D (p. 206) Coleridge's most concise statement on Shakespeare's art, and examples of his practical analysis of *Hamlet* appear in Part Two (p. 143).

Shakespeare and Wordsworth

The view of Wordsworth's poetry that Coleridge has expanded in Chapters 17 to 22 has remained definitive. In Chapter 22 he lists its characteristic excellences: An austere purity of language, the weight and sanity of his thought, the sinewy strength of single lines and paragraphs, the perfect truth of nature in his images, a meditative pathos, a union of deep and subtle thought with sensibility and, lastly and pre-eminently, 'the gift of IMAGINATION in the highest and strictest sense of the word'. In imaginative power, Coleridge summarizes, Wordsworth stands nearest of all modern writers to Shakespeare and Milton. These figures represent between them in their entirely different ways the three peaks of English poetry by which the rest is to be judged. Coleridge does not discuss Milton in the *Biographia* as he has no reason to qualify Milton's traditional reputation. His assessment of Shakespeare, on the other hand, constitutes a radical revaluation, one which has provided the framework for all later approaches to him. The feature that, for Coleridge, unites Shakespeare and Wordsworth is the organic principle to be discovered in their works deriving from their individual creative imagination. Because this principle is organic and not mechanical or external, its existence is not immediately apparent. Neither Shakespeare nor Wordsworth *appears* to be a philosophical poet. Hence the traditional judgment that Shakespeare was a natural, untutored genius. Hence also the contemporary dismissal of Wordsworth as banal, or silly. On the contrary, asserts Coleridge, it is the *appearance* of naturalness that, in their case, is the guarantee of their profundity as poets of the imagination. In their works are balanced and reconciled the appearance of naturalness and the reality of the voluntary effort that is necessary to make poems. If Shakespeare is the ideal poet by whose standard all others are to be judged, then Wordsworth is, from among all his contemporaries, the greatest modern English poet. The poems of both celebrate the creative imagination.

Finally, it is for his formulation of the creative imagination that we must place Coleridge in the centre of what is usually called the Romantic Revival in literature and thought. He, as much as any other poet or thinker in England, made articulate the Romantic belief that the self acts in its own experience and is not merely acted upon. We can see the dawning of this intuition very early in Coleridge in the quotation from the letter to Tom Poole placed as an epigraph to this section. What followed for the Romantics, and for all subsequent imaginative writers up until our own time, was that the exploration of the self could be a legitimate subject for art, and that the roots of human self-awareness and action are neither rational nor rationally predictable. There are, however, few necessary victories in history; this view of the self and its creative potential has not prevailed, and the reputation of the English Romantic poets has never been a secure one.

To end this section I want to draw attention to another complex figure of English Romanticism, much more isolated than ever Coleridge was in his own time. William Blake developed as an artist, poet and illustrator, in a tradition very different from that of Wordsworth and Coleridge. Yet many times in writing about Coleridge, I have been reminded of the occasional and striking similarity in their beliefs. The following quotation from Blake for example, corresponds very closely to Coleridge's distinction between Fancy and Imagination, and, for all its very different mode of expression, to Coleridge's formulation of what he means by a symbol in *The Statesman's Manual* (see p. 99). 'Fable or Allegory are a totally distinct & inferior kind of Poetry. Vision or Imagination is a Representation of what Eternally Exists, Really & Unchangeably. Fable or Allegory is Form'd by the daughters of Memory. Imagination is surrounded by the daughters of Inspiration.'

At this level Blake is less isolated a figure than he certainly appears to be, and Coleridge's intuition receives an important kind of confirmation. Both poets, in their very different ways which sometimes meet, identified and protested against the reduction of human life to the forces of mechanical explanation or abstraction at their first appearance in eighteenth century rationalist and empirical philosophy. Given the ever-increasing pressure of the same forces in our own day, it should be clear why I suggest that history has no necessary victories.

6   Epilogue

The final phase

One reason why *Biographia Literaria* is imperfect and unsatisfactory to read as a single work is that, like so much of Coleridge's output, it is an occasional piece. There is also another, internal reason, the nature of which I have indicated in the foregoing section. Coleridge's explanation of the concept of the creative imagination had to remain tentative because it put him in an impasse. It was impossible for him to reconcile his belief in a world ordained by God and designed to serve God's inscrutable purposes, and a theory of man's freedom to create his own universe of awareness with the faculty of imagination as its instrument. A further reason for the difficulty one encounters in attempting to deal with these problems in Coleridge's terms is the difficulty of certain ideas. 'An idea', he wrote in the *Biographia*, 'in the highest sense of that word, cannot be conveyed but by a symbol'. As we shall see from the extract from the Notebooks quoted on p. 145, Coleridge valued dim or obscure ideas above clear notions which he suspected because they were clear. One may immediately leap to the conclusion that this preference is nothing but another manifestation of an irrational predilection for the sublime, but Coleridge was not afraid to do the work involved in making good this and other claims.

It is beyond the scope of this book to follow Coleridge's thought in any detail through the last phase of his life when he abandoned literature for religious philosophy. But his last works do not represent a break in the continuity of his thought. *The Statesman's Manual* of 1816, the two *Lay Sermons* of the following year, *Aids to Reflection* of 1825 and *On the Constitution of Church and State* of 1830 are all concerned with the attempt to fix and reconcile principles in politics, morals and religion. The method and the attempt at a universal reconciliation are very similar to his earlier enquiries; only now, the centre of his considerations has changed from man to God. For Coleridge, the Bible, as he emphasizes in *The Statesman's Manual*, is the 'best guide to political skill and foresight'. Relations between men cannot be regulated by external or mechanical means; hence political revolution or the extension of the franchise, of themselves, cannot guarantee social improvement. It is from such positions that Coleridge has been called, like Edmund Burke before him, a conservative or reactionary political thinker. But, in so many respects it is meaningless to attach party labels to Coleridge's political views. What he attacks is:

> this accursed practice of ever considering *only* what seems *expedient* for the occasion, disjoined from all principle or enlarged systems of action, of never listening to the true and unerring impulses of our better nature—, which has led the colder-hearted men to the study of political economy, which has turned our Parliament into a real committee of public safety.

In his pursuit of principle and enlarged systems, Coleridge did propose institutional changes in the structure of society which would, as he writes in Chapter 5 of *On the Constitution of Church and State*, ensure the 'harmonious development of those qualities and faculties that characterise our humanity'. Coleridge felt that the real alternative to the external and mechanical regulation of social relations or to more political expediency, was to propose arrangements for the education of the population. To this end he proposed that the resources of all the Churches should be assembled into a 'nationalty', or national church, and that these accumulated resources should be devoted to the establishment of a 'clerisy' or body of educators, consisting of clergymen of all denominations, and of school-teachers.

If we think for a moment of the enormous difficulties that universal education has imposed on modern societies, then we are led to contemplate the neat and final paradox of the late Coleridge. Bringing to bear on these proposals all our knowledge of all that Coleridge had done and experienced; in other words, his continuous and developing education as man, poet and thinker; we cannot help feeling that he escapes altogether from the embrace of any system, his own or any other.

These late works are not without interest to us as readers of literature. For example a distinction that he makes in the course of an illustration of the relation between 'idea' and 'symbol' in *The Statesman's Manual*, is important to our understanding of his methods and procedures as a literary theorist.

> In the Scriptures [*histories*] are the living educts of the imagination; of that reconciling and mediatory power, which, incorporating the reason in images of the sense, and organising (as it were) the flux of the senses by the permanence and self-circling energies of the reason, gives birth to a system of symbols, harmonious in themselves, and consubstantial with the truths of which they are the conductors . . . An allegory is but a translation of abstract notions into picture language.

The expression here is characteristically dense and compact, and I must lay aside any discussion of what Coleridge means here by 'reason' which he is using in a Kantian sense and relates to the apprehension of ultimate realities unaffected by the world of experience. But what is important to grasp is the importance he attaches to the word 'symbol'. Not only does it represent and reconcile opposite or discordant qualities, but at the same time it mediates in language, as does the imagination in perception, between the word for the thing concretely experienced and the ideal, changeless character of the universe. There is nothing prior in experience to this symbolizing process, so that, as we have already seen from our study of the poetic imagination in the previous section, there is nothing prior to a symbolising language. Poetry is not written about something which is not poetry. Such a view takes us back to the distinction I tried to draw between Wordsworth's and Coleridge's view of what poetry is. A twentieth-century American poet, Archibald MacLeish, has expressed the same idea in the following words: 'A poem must not mean, but be.' And this discussion of an ideal Platonic world inhabited by art reminds me of a poem by W. B. Yeats. *Among School Children* seems to me to be a poem about this notion of 'symbol', or 'image' as Yeats himself calls it. I do not assume in pointing to Yeats that there is any immediate influence passed on from Coleridge. What I mean by it is rather a way of stressing Coleridge's profound and ultimate importance to what, in the modern age, many poets and critics have taken imaginative literature to be.

Part Two

Critical Survey

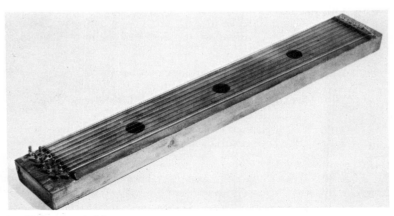

An Æolian or wind harp

Coleridge's Verse

Love to all the Passions & Faculties, as Music to all the varieties of
sound.

s. t. coleridge, Notebook entry

An epicure of sound.

w. wordsworth on Coleridge

Although he made verse throughout his life, most of the poems by
which Coleridge is remembered were written before his departure for
Malta in 1804. While it is true that he did write some notable and
poignant verse in his later years, his greatest achievements fall readily
within the period of his close friendship with Wordsworth. Even
during these years, however, poetry was only a small part of Coleridge's
general literary production. He was at the same time reviewer,
political commentator and translator to the extent that most of his
poems are marked by the presence within the poem of the occasions
out of which they grew. In this respect they are quite unlike most of
Wordsworth's major poems. By making this distinction I do not wish
to imply that a poem marked by the occasion is necessarily more
limited than one which is not. Many great poems in the English
language are 'occasional' poems in this sense. In Coleridge's case the
occasions are immediate and explicit, public or private. Most often
they are concerned with intimate details of his private life which
become, in the poems, materials to be explored and searched through
and which unfold a more general speculation on life. The results of
the speculating climax are then returned to the materials, the occasion,
to enrich them and to leave us with them, wife or friends, baby or
honeymoon cottage, bathed in the reflected light of Coleridge's
philosophizing vision.

> And last, a matron now, of sober mien,
> Yet radiant still and with no earthly sheen,
> Whom as a faery child my childhood woo'd
> Even in my dawn of thought—Philosophy;
> Though then unconscious of herself, pardie,
> She bore no other name than Poesy.
>
> *The Garden of Boccaccio*, published 1829

It may be objected that his two best known poems *The Ancient
Mariner* and *Kubla Khan* give no hint of their occasions, and that they
have none is one aspect of the difficulty these two poems create for
the critic (if not for the reader). But even in these two cases, Coleridge

seems to have manufactured an occasion for them: a prose commentary for *The Ancient Mariner*, an apologetic preface for *Kubla Khan*.

What I am driving at is the ground of Coleridge's acknowledgement of the difference between his own and Wordsworth's practice as poets; the nature of his dissatisfaction with his own poetry when compared with that of his admired friend. His own work seemed to him to require an occasion to justify its existence on the page. He seemed to sense that he himself was not a poet in the way that Shakespeare, Milton and Wordsworth were.

But Wordsworth can help us here. If Coleridge insisted that 'the sense of musical delight' is the essential characteristic of good poetry, then, in describing him as 'an epicure of sound', Wordsworth points to a particular and distinguishing characteristic of Coleridge's own verse, its musicality. Music of all kinds, heavenly, natural or composed, permeates all the varying textures of Coleridge's verse, whether as arrangements of sounds in the language used, or as an image of some grander vision of a philosophical harmony. Its importance can be felt and appreciated immediately in *The Eolian Harp* whether we are discussing the subject matter, the mood or the language of this poem of 1795.

The Eolian Harp

My pensive Sara! thy soft cheek reclined
Thus on mine arm, most soothing sweet it is
To sit beside our Cot, our Cot o'ergrown
With white-flower'd Jasmin, and the broad-leav'd Myrtle,
5   (Meet emblems they of Innocence and Love!)
And watch the clouds, that late were rich with light,
Slow saddening round, and mark the star of eve
Serenely brilliant (such should Wisdom be)
Shine opposite! How exquisite the scents
10   Snatch'd from yon bean-field! and the world *so* hush'd!
The stilly murmur of the distant Sea
Tells us of silence.

              And that simplest Lute,
Placed length-ways in the clasping casement, hark!
How by the desultory breeze caress'd,
15   Like some coy maid half yielding to her lover,
It pours such sweet upbraiding, as must needs
Tempt to repeat the wrong! And now, its strings
Boldlier swept, the long sequacious notes
Over delicious surges sink and rise,
20   Such a soft floating witchery of sound
As twilight Elfins make, when they at eve
Voyage on gentle gales from Fairy-Land,

Where Melodies round honey-dropping flowers,
Footless and wild, like birds of Paradise,
25 Nor pause, nor perch, hovering on untam'd wing!
O! the one Life within us and abroad,
Which meets all motion and becomes its soul,
A light in sound, a sound-like power in light,
Rhythm in all thought, and joyance every where—
30 Methinks, it should have been impossible
Not to love all things in a world so fill'd;
Where the breeze warbles, and the mute still air
Is Music slumbering on her instrument.

And thus, my Love! as on the midway slope
35 Of yonder hill I stretch my limbs at noon,
Whilst through my half-clos'd eye-lids I behold
The sunbeams dance, like diamonds, on the main,
And tranquil muse upon tranquillity;
Full many a thought uncall'd and undetain'd,
40 And many idle flitting phantasies,
Traverse my indolent and passive brain,
As wild and various as the random gales
That swell and flutter on this subject Lute!
And what if all of animated nature
45 Be but organic Harps diversely fram'd,
That tremble into thought, as o'er them sweeps
Plastic and vast, one intellectual breeze,
At once the Soul of each, and God of all?
But thy more serious eye a mild reproof
50 Darts, O belovéd Woman! nor such thoughts
Dim and unhallow'd dost thou not reject,
And biddest me walk humbly with my God.
Meek Daughter in the family of Christ!
Well hast thou said and holily disprais'd
55 These shapings of the unregenerate mind;
Bubbles that glitter as they rise and break
On vain Philosophy's aye-babbling spring.
For never guiltless may I speak of him,
The Incomprehensible! save when with awe
60 I praise him, and with Faith that inly *feels*;
Who with his saving mercies healéd me,
A sinful and most miserable man,
Wilder'd and dark, and gave me to possess
Peace, and this Cot, and thee, heart-honour'd Maid!

OCCASION. The poem was written at Clevedon, Somerset, a few
weeks before his marriage to Sara Fricker. The original note dates
it as 20 August 1795, and it is, therefore, a kind of prothalamium. The

setting, the cottage 'o'ergrown with white flower'd Jasmin', is the same as that described in *Reflections on having left a place of retirement* (see p. 57).

THEME. The poem begins by evoking a mood of silence and domestic contentment at twilight. The love between the couple is new and innocent. The breeze which rises outside the window does not disturb the tranquillity but rather enhances it because it evokes a harmonious music from the wind-harp lying by the open window. Just as the breeze causes the music so it stirs the poet into thought. At first his thought is merely fanciful, but the wind caressing the harp becomes a metaphor for the poet's sense of the unity of all life.

> O! the one Life within us and abroad
> Which meets all motion and becomes its soul.

These and the next six lines to the end of the paragraph are of a later date than the rest of the poem. They first appeared in the text of 1828, but they no longer read like an interpolation and they carry the mood to a rising speculation and pause before the thought moves on. The lines are also full of Coleridge's verbal music, a subtle alliteration and assonance, with an anticipation of important vowel sounds which create the pace at which the poem must be read. Notice, for example, that the line 'Which meets all motion and becomes its soul' is balanced between the long diphthong of 'motion' and the same sound of 'soul', keeping the voice up at the end of the line. 'Soul' gives us the echo of 'all' in the same line and elsewhere, and takes up the accompaniment of the sibillant whispering of the s- and sh- sounds. In line 33 the key word 'music' is anticipated by 'mute' in the preceding line, 'instrument' by 'still'.

Harp and thought accompany each other through the next section of the poem in which the harp not merely suggests the harmony of all life but becomes a strict analogy for the influence of the

> intellectual breeze,
> At once the Soul of each, and God of all,

This imaginative sweep pauses on the question mark and, in the pause, Coleridge remembers the presence of his wife, whom he has by now completely forgotten. He feels guilty, his mind is 'unregenerate', philosophy a 'bubble' or 'aye-babbling spring'. And the poem is completed by a return to the mood and setting of the opening lines. The poet will try to copy the humble faith of his wife-to-be.

But the paradox of philosophy springing boldly up from humble faith is not resolved. Coleridge did not tear up the poem; the tension persisted and he remained a man in many respects 'wilder'd and dark' throughout his life.

Coleridge thought of *The Eolian Harp* as his favourite among his own poems and made slight revisions and restorations to it when it appeared in subsequent collections of his poems. Yet its effect is not entirely satisfactory. It is not only that the poet breaks off his train of speculation under the rebuke implied in his wife's look, the slackening of tension is also to be found in the language of the final paragraph. One notices the awkwardness of the double negative in lines 50–51 and the succession of coupled adjectives and verbs which of themselves suggest something of the poet's hesitations. In intention the poem is an illustration of Hartleian associationism, but the doctrine appears to clash with the 'Faith that inly *feels*'. It is as though there is another, inner ground of consciousness which is barely hinted at in the poem. One might be tempted to seize on the word 'organic' to support such a view, as Coleridge uses the word in his later writings to oppose it to the idea of the mechanical. But here, I feel, it is only a near synonym for 'animate' in the previous line (line 44) and belongs to that sub-Miltonic rhetoric on which Coleridge sometimes falls back even in other, more satisfying poems.

NOTE. The aeolian or wind-harp was a German invention of the early seventeenth century consisting of a sounding board designed to amplify, as in any stringed instrument, the vibrations of the strings stretched over it. Lying near an open window it would produce a thin 'etherial' sound in response to the wind blowing over it, producing a 'natural' music. Its appropriateness as a metaphor for Romantic poetry is obvious. Compare its appearance in *Dejection: an ode* on p. 136. Wordsworth used it in his verse:

> It was a splendid evening; and my Soul
> Did once again make trial of the strength
> Restored to her afresh; nor did she want
> Æolian visitations; but the harp was soon
> > defrauded.
> > > (*Prelude*, 1805, Book 1)

Shelley and Hazlitt both referred to it explicitly when attempting to define the nature of poetry. Robert Bloomfield, the farmer-poet, whose long poem *The Farmer's Boy* published in 1800 was a best-seller of the period, collected an anthology of wind harp literature in 1808. An eighteenth-century example of an address to an aeolian lyre is Gray's *The Progress of Poesy*, where it serves as a poetical device with which to open a poem on the subject of poetry.

The grandest paradox of existence and imaginative speculation appears in the title of *This Lime Tree Bower my Prison* which, for me, is an almost perfect example of Coleridge's conversation poems.

Charles Lamb, after H. Meyer

This Lime Tree Bower my Prison
(Addressed to Charles Lamb, of the India House, London)

In the June of 1797 some long-expected friends paid a visit to the author's cottage; and on the morning of their arrival, he met with an accident, which disabled him from walking during the whole of their stay. One evening, when they had left him for a few hours, he composed the following lines in the garden-bower.

> Well, they are gone, and here must I remain,
> This lime-tree bower my prison! I have lost
> Beauties and feelings, such as would have been
> Most sweet to my remembrance even when age
> 5   Had dimm'd mine eyes to blindness! They, meanwhile,
> Friends, whom I never more may meet again,
> On springy heath, along the hill-top edge,
> Wander in gladness, and wind down, perchance,
> To that still roaring dell, of which I told;
> 10 The roaring dell, o'erwooded, narrow, deep,

And only speckled by the mid-day sun;
Where its slim trunk the ash from rock to rock
Flings arching like a bridge;—that branchless ash,
Unsunn'd and damp, whose few poor yellow leaves
15 Ne'er tremble in the gale, yet tremble still,
Fann'd by the water-fall! and there my friends
Behold the dark green file of long lank weeds,
That all at once (a most fantastic sight!)
Still nod and drip beneath the dripping edge
20 Of the blue clay-stone.

       Now, my friends emerge
Beneath the wide wide Heaven—and view again
The many-steepled tract magnificent
Of hilly fields and meadows, and the sea,
With some fair bark, perhaps, whose sails light up
25 The slip of smooth clear blue betwixt two Isles
Of purple shadow! Yes! they wander on
In gladness all; but thou, methinks, most glad,
My gentle-hearted Charles! for thou has pined
And hunger'd after Nature, many a year,
30 In the great City pent, winning thy way
With sad yet patient soul, through evil and pain
And strange calamity! Ah! slowly sink
Behind the western ridge, thou glorious Sun!
Shine in the slant beams of the sinking orb,
35 Ye purple heath-flowers! richlier burn, ye clouds!
Live in the yellow light, ye distant groves!
And kindle, thou blue Ocean! So my friend
Struck with deep joy may stand, as I have stood,
Silent with swimming sense; yea, gazing round
40 On the wide landscape, gaze till all doth seem
Less gross than bodily; and of such hues
As veil the Almighty Spirit, when yet he makes
Spirits perceive his presence.

        A delight
Comes sudden on my heart, and I am glad
45 As I myself were there! Nor in this bower,
This little lime-tree bower, have I not mark'd
Much that has sooth'd me. Pale beneath the blaze
Hung the transparent foliage; and I watch'd
Some broad and sunny leaf, and lov'd to see
50 The shadow of the leaf and stem above
Dappling its sunshine! And that walnut-tree
Was richly ting'd, and a deep radiance lay
Full on the ancient ivy, which usurps

Those fronting elms, and now, with blackest mass
55 Makes their dark branches gleam a lighter hue
Through the late twilight: and though now the bat
Wheels silent by, and not a swallow twitters,
Yet still the solitary humble-bee
Sings in the bean-flower! Henceforth I shall know
60 That Nature ne'er deserts the wise and pure;
No plot so narrow, be but Nature there,
No waste so vacant, but may well employ
Each faculty of sense, and keep the heart
Awake to Love and Beauty! and sometimes
65 'Tis well to be bereft of promis'd good,
That we may lift the soul, and contemplate
With lively joy the joys we cannot share.
My gentle-hearted Charles! when the last rook
Beat its straight path along the dusky air
70 Homewards, I blest it! deeming its black wing
(Now a dim speck, now vanishing in light)
Had cross'd the mighty Orb's dilated glory,
While thou stood'st gazing; or, when all was still,
Flew creeking o'er thy head, and had a charm
75 For thee, my gentle-hearted Charles, to whom
No sound is dissonant which tells of Life.

OCCASION. Again the poem grows naturally out of its occasion and
recalls what was perhaps an all too typical moment in Coleridge's
domestic life. He wrote to Southey on 17 July 1797:

> Charles Lamb has been with me for a week—he left me Friday
> morning. The second day after Wordsworth came to me, dear Sara
> accidentally emptied a skillet of boiling milk on my foot, which
> confined me during the whole time of C. Lamb's stay & still
> prevents me from all *walks* longer than a furlong.—While Words-
> worth, his Sister, & C. Lamb were out one evening; sitting in the
> arbour of T. Poole's garden, which communicates with mine, I
> wrote these lines, with which I am pleased—

It is not very difficult to picture to oneself the overcrowded little
kitchen of the Nether Stowey cottage and the mood in which Mrs
Coleridge set about cooking for these perhaps not altogether welcome
extra bodies. She had much to put up with.

THEME. The poem tells us why it addresses itself especially to Charles
Lamb. Lamb, like Coleridge at the moment in his bower, spends most
of his time in prison—'many a year, In the great City pent' and will
enjoy the wandering walk with a particular intensity. Just as prison
and freedom to wander are contrasted, so presence and absence are
played off against each other throughout the poem. Deprived of

'beauties and feelings' the poet takes his friends' walk *in imagination* and so, through the imagination, creates for himself the experience he has 'lost'. Furthermore, the kinds of experience the friends enjoy are contrasted as they move from 'hill-top edge' to the 'roaring dell, o'erwooded, narrow, deep' and out again to the 'many-steepled tract magnificent' open to the sky and the purple shadows of the Holms, the islands in the Bristol Channel.

The atmosphere of this poem matches very well that of Dorothy Wordsworth's Alfoxden diary of the following year. Two entries are of particular interest in relation to *This Lime Tree Bower*. The first is for 26 February, part of which reads: 'A very clear afternoon. We lay side-long upon the turf, and gazed on the landscape till it melted into more than natural loveliness. The sea very uniform, of a pale greyish blue, only one distant bay, bright and blue as a sky; had there been a vessel sailing up it, a perfect image of delight.' It is surely the same delight that suffuses the poem like the clear wintry light on the sea in the prose extract.

The entry for 10 February is as follows: 'Walked to Woodlands [*a house in the neighbourhood*] and to the waterfall. The adder's-tongue and the ferns green in the low damp dell. These plants now in perpetual motion from the current of the air; in summer only moved by the drippings of the rocks. A cloudy day.'

Some further significance attaches to the correspondence of the two journal entries and the descriptions in the poem than that of the closeness of the experiences these friends shared during this period at Nether Stowey. The progression in the walk from dell to hill-top possesses a further suggestiveness. The significance of hill-top expressing delight and achievement is clear. It is also traditional. But the secluded dell also has its tradition, particularly in Dutch seventeenth-century landscape painting which had become a fashionable taste by the time Coleridge was writing. William Gilpin exercised a considerable influence on its diffusion in England. The dark dell in such paintings (see the reproduction opposite of Thomas Gainsborough's *Cornard Wood* of 1748) symbolized philosophical reflection. The dell in the poem provides a 'fantastic sight'. The leaves and weeds are animated, not by sun and wind, but by the spray from the waterfall and the drips from the rocks in a *semblance* of life. Coleridge in writing his poem by imagining himself there with his friends, creates a semblance of his presence and of the experience.

That the episodes are chosen for their connection with the aesthetic of the Sublime is made clear in the following apostrophe to the features of the landscape, sun, clouds, distant groves. The Miltonic construction of 'many-steepled tract magnificent' might have prepared us for this attempt to heighten the tone. The lines 32–37 seem to me to be a falling-off from the rest of the poem, contrasting harshly with the completely natural and appropriate language and cadence of the rest.

Cornard Wood *by Thomas Gainsborough*

But the heightening which Coleridge felt to be necessary at this point is magnificently recovered in the following lines where Coleridge achieves, beyond the reach of the mode of the Sublime, his aching to behold and know something great. In the letter to Thelwall of 14 October 1797 (see p. 31) in which he describes this longing he quotes these next lines 38–43 with the comment 'It is but seldom that I raise & spiritualize my intellect to this height—'.

But having done so, having raised his intellect to this spiritual height by way of the Sublime through an imagined participation, he is able to turn this enhanced perception on to his own imprisonment. The bower is now transformed as Coleridge registers the unique details of the actual scene around him; sunshine and shadow on individual leaves, the black of the ivy on the black of the elms, the solitary bee singing in the bean-flower: its thin, droning music oscillating between the short 'i' and long 'e' sounds.

The awakening to love and beauty in Nature is not merely a consolation to the imprisoned poet, but rather the announcement of a new principle of being discoverable only in joy. The poem closes with the set of the sun, but is held in a slow suspension of any further movement by the single sharp detail of the imagined last rook disappearing. 'Creeking o'er thy head' is marvellously placed in the poem. 'No sound is dissonant' because that single rook, like the solitary bee, has resolved into a complete harmony those paradoxes of presence and absence, of imprisonment and freedom with which the poem began.

NOTE. Charles Lamb's 'strange calamity' had occurred a year earlier. In a fit of insanity his sister killed their mother and Charles dedicated himself to caring for her. At about the same time he had also suffered occasional and severe mental disturbance, so, for him in the poem, Nature fulfills a particular restorative function. The influence of Nature is the subject matter of *Frost at Midnight*.

Frost at Midnight

The Frost performs its secret ministry,
Unhelped by any wind. The owlet's cry
Came loud—and hark, again! loud as before.
The inmates of my cottage, all at rest,
5   Have left me to that solitude, which suits
Abstruser musings: save that at my side
My cradled infant slumbers peacefully.
'Tis calm indeed! so calm, that it disturbs
and vexes meditation with its strange
10   And extreme silentness. Sea, hill, and wood,
This populous Village! Sea, and hill, and wood,
With all the numberless goings-on of life,

Inaudible as dreams! the thin blue flame
Lies on my low-burnt fire, and quivers not;
15 Only that film, which fluttered on the grate,
Still flutters there, the sole unquiet thing.
Methinks, its motion in this hush of nature
Gives it dim sympathies with me who live,
Making it a companionable form,
20 Whose puny flaps and freaks the idling Spirit
By its own moods interprets, everywhere
Echo or mirror seeking of itself,
And makes a toy of Thought.

                              But O! how oft,
How oft, at school, with most believing mind,
25 Presageful, have I gazed upon the bars,
To watch that fluttering *stranger*! and as oft
With unclosed lids, already had I dreamt
Of my sweet birth-place, and the old church-tower,
Whose bells, the poor man's only music, rang
30 From morn to evening, all the hot Fair-day,
So sweetly, that they stirred and haunted me
With a wild pleasure, falling on mine ear
Most like articulate sounds of things to come!
So gazed I, till the soothing things, I dreamt,
35 Lulled me to sleep, and sleep prolonged my dreams!
And so I brooded all the following morn,
Awed by the stern preceptor's face, mine eye
Fixed with mock study on my swimming book:
Save if the door half opened, and I snatched
40 A hasty glance, and still my heart leaped up,
For still I hoped to see the *stranger's* face,
Townsman, or aunt, or sister more beloved,
My playmate when we both were clothed alike!

    Dear Babe, that sleepest cradled by my side,
45 Whose gentle breathings, heard in this deep calm,
Fill up the interspersèd vacancies
And momentary pauses of the thought!
My babe so beautiful! it thrills my heart
With tender gladness, thus to look at thee,
50 And think that thou shalt learn far other lore,
And in far other scenes! For I was reared
In the great city, pent 'mid cloisters dim,
And saw nought lovely but the sky and stars.
But *thou*, my babe! shalt wander like a breeze
55 By lakes and sandy shores, beneath the crags
Of ancient mountain, and beneath the clouds,

Which image in their bulk both lakes and shores
And mountain crags: so shalt thou see and hear
The lovely shapes and sounds intelligible
60   Of that eternal language, which thy God
Utters, who from eternity doth teach
Himself in all, and all things in himself.
Great universal Teacher! he shall mould
Thy spirit, and by giving make it ask.

65   Therefore all seasons shall be sweet to thee,
Whether the summer clothe the general earth
With greenness, or the redbreast sit and sing
Betwixt the tufts of snow on the bare branch
of mossy apple-tree, while the nigh thatch
70   Smokes in the sun-thaw; whether the eave-drops fall
Heard only in the trances of the blast,
Or if the secret ministry of frost
Shall hang them up in silent icicles,
Quietly shining to the quiet Moon.

OCCASION.   Hartley Coleridge appears as a special kind of child in
a number of Coleridge's poems. He is the 'dear babe' of *The Nightingale*,
written in April 1798 and first published in *Lyrical Ballads*. There is
an entry in the so-called Gutch (after a later owner) Notebook which
refers to his appearance in that poem. 'Hartley fell down & hurt
himself—I caught him up crying and screaming—& ran out of doors
with him.—The moon caught his eye—he ceased crying immediately
—& his eyes & the tears in them, how they glittered in the Moonlight!'
Hartley is also the 'limber elf' of the Conclusion of Part II of *Christabel*.
A little later in the Gutch Notebook, however, there is a number of
entries referring to childhood, and one which names Hartley specifically. One notes from among them the phrase, 'Nature how lovely a
school mistress'. The previous entry reads:

The reed-roof'd Village, still bepatch'd with snow
Smoked in the sun-thaw.

Coleridge's preoccupation with parenthood and infancy (his wife was
expecting their second child) provides the context out of which the
poem grows.

THEME.   Out of the preoccupation the poem traces the movement of
the mind over the subject of education, that of the poet contrasted
with that of the child. To put the subject so abstractly, however, is to
obliterate the very beautiful control that is exerted by the opening
sentence over the delicate movement of the rest of the poem. The frost
is part of the silence, sharpening it even in the play of 's-', 't-', and '-st'
sounds in the first line. Only when everything else is still, so still that

114

the silence impinges on those 'abstruser musings' in which one engages late at night, is the mind forced to attend to the quality of the stillness. All the numberless goings-on of life are inaudible as dreams. Yet it is only in this silence that one can feel the unobservable secret influences that are at work in life. Frost, whether it is making patterns on the window or icicles under the eaves, works below the threshold of perception. Other influences work in the same way; they are not observable and yet they influence us in important ways. They minister to us. In the silence only the movement of the poet's mind itself is palpable and can be registered. The only thing analogous to it is the film of smoke fluttering in the otherwise unquivering flame of the dying fire.

The film and its superstitious association with the arrival of a stranger reminds him forcefully of his own childhood at school. The metaphor of 'ministry' or education by secret influence and the memory of his own school time come together at this moment and flow together through the remainder of the poem. The achievement of the poem is that the process is not made articulate by description, but *experienced* in the attentive reading that the poem demands.

The poet contrasts his own schooldays with the education his son shall have. 'Pent' in a kind of prison, his mind was never on the present, but either *dreaming* of memories of his birthplace or superstitiously anticipating a visitor to relieve his pretended concentration on the 'swimming book'. His son's education, on the contrary, will be free and natural. He shall:

> Wander like a breeze
> By lakes and sandy shores, beneath the crags
> Of ancient mountain, and beneath the clouds
> Which image in their bulk both lakes and shores
> And mountain crags:

in such a way that, seeing the bulk of the landscape reflected in the clouds, all parts of the natural world fittings together in complete harmony, he shall learn to see and hear God in all things.

In the line: 'Himself in all, and all things in himself' Coleridge reaches the central insight of the poem, and, if we compare the language and the rhythm of this moment of revelation and the route of its achievement with that of the similar aspostrophe to the landscape in *This Lime Tree Bower*, we can appreciate the mastery of *Frost at Midnight*. Language and subject meet naturally and appropriately without any sense of strain or break in the overall mood of calm reflection that pervades the entire poem.

The lyricism of the opening of the final paragraph is completely in keeping with the heightening that has just been achieved, communicating the joy with which the father addresses the sleeping son. The poet is confident that the secret and beneficial influences of Nature will work on the infant even in sleep, just as:

> the nigh thatch
> Smokes in the sun-thaw; whether the eave-drops fall
> Heard only in the trances of the blast,
> Or if the secret ministry of frost
> Shall hang them up in silent icicles,
> Quietly shining to the quiet Moon.

The final placing of the moon bathes the whole of the foregoing in its clear, soft light. We scarcely need to be conscious that it is a *reflected* light to experience its rightness at the very end of the poem. It completes the mood of reflectiveness, and its resonance persists beyond the end.

NOTES. A comparison with the original passage from *The Task* on p. 41 illuminates the complexity of questions of a poet's indebtedness to his precursors. Cowper is bookish and Miltonic in tone, most successful when, in the opening lines, he seems to suggest that to read Milton by a warm fire at home is one of the desirable pleasures. The tone is elsewhere apologetic. Idle fancies dreamed up in the firelight are an indulgence that requires a mask of seriousness. That there has been a radical shift of sensibility from Cowper to Coleridge can be felt immediately in Coleridge's tone. He needs no such justification for recording those 'momentary pauses of the thought'. Nor does he feel obliged to apologize if idle fancies make a 'toy' of thought.

The comparison and the distinctions I have drawn from it lead us to a further point about the nature of Romantic poetry, namely, that the play of the mind is a subject for poetry. The processes of the poet's own mind, its mobility and alterations of mood become the subject matter and all manner of feelings are interesting and available to exploration; blankness and desolation as well as joy and imagined richness. Dreams or visions of impossible objects take on their own dramatic force as 'reality' is no longer perceived as a given condition of existence, so much as something to be continually re-experienced and re-created in poetry. *Frost at Midnight* is one such very successful rendering which, in its evocation of the interior drama of a mind recollecting, describing and predicting, was an important influence on Wordsworth's *Lines composed a few miles above Tintern Abbey* written a few months later.

At the moment of referring to one of Wordsworth's greatest poems one is reminded of the continuous influence of Milton on these two poets. His presence in *Frost at Midnight* is less substantial than it is in either *The Task* or *Tintern Abbey*, but it is there nevertheless, subtle and shadowy. Coleridge's 'eave-drops . . . heard only in the trances of the blast' are Milton's in *Il Penseroso*.

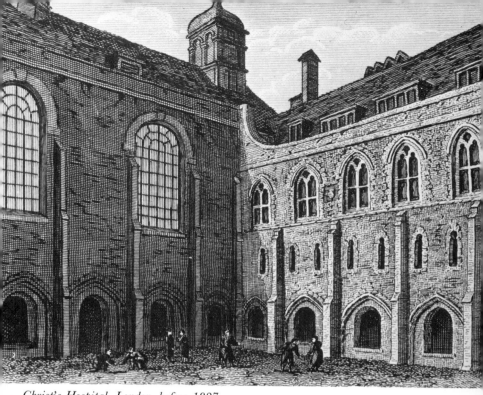

Christ's Hospital, London, before 1827

Cornfield by Moonlight *by Samuel Palmer*

While rocking winds are Piping hard,
Or usher'd with a shower still,
When the gust has blown his fill,
Ending on the russling leaves,
With minute drops from off the Eaves.

But Milton's eave-drops are heard in the morning, whereas Coleridge's scene is transformed by moonlight. The effect of the placing of the moon at the very end of the poem is to bring the poem back into one's remembrance bathed in its serene, mysterious light. The Romantic poets can be said to have discovered a new world of imagination and mystery when the daytime world is seen transmuted by moonlight. Poets had traditionally celebrated its beauty, its sympathy with the melancholy of unrequited lovers, but the moon's appearance in a Romantic poem is something altogether richer in suggestions of mystery and the irrational. Even Wordsworth, who, as Coleridge himself was quick to assert, was often very literal-minded about the world of appearances, succumbs to its fascination and inexplicability in one of the Lucy poems of 1800, *Strange fits of passion have I known*, where the sudden dropping of the moon behind his beloved's cottage plunges him into an irrational fear that she may be dead. In painting too, moonlight transforms the common world. Washington Allston painted moonlit landscapes, and perhaps the best known example of the time is Samuel Palmer's *Cornfield by Moonlight*. Readers can judge for themselves the significance of the appearances of the moon in *The Ancient Mariner* and its relation to the Mariner's restoration to the world of men.

The Rime of the Ancient Mariner

The extreme length of this poem precludes our reprinting it here. The reader is accordingly invited to have a text beside him so that both poem and commentary may be viewed together.

OCCASION OF THE POEM. In the division of the tasks for *Lyrical Ballads*, Coleridge's contribution of ballads was intended to be much longer than the single poem *The Ancient Mariner*. The first part of *Christabel* was written at about the same time and the completion prevented, according to Coleridge's own account, by his discovery of the painful betrayal of confidence on the part of Charles Lloyd. There is also extant a fragment of another poem in the same genre, *The Ballad of the Dark Ladie*, dating from these early months of 1798, which bears echoes and hints of the other two attempts. The appearance side by side of at least three such poems in the volume to balance Wordsworth's contribution, would have made a great deal of difference to later approaches to *The Ancient Mariner* and to the enquiry into what Coleridge had in mind when he proposed to write a series of ballads on supernatural themes. (It is not my aim, however, to point to what might have been or to assert a special privilege for the poet's intention when we come to consider our response to so singular an achievement as *The Ancient Mariner*. On the other hand I have no wish to exclude that knowledge of a poem drawn from other sources than that of the black marks on the pages before us.)

In 1828 Coleridge published a prose fragment, the second canto on the subject of *The Wanderings of Cain* together with a prefatory note. In this he explains the genesis of the work. He and Wordsworth were to compose a prose piece in collaboration in order to raise some money for a walking tour. Wordsworth was to write the first canto, Coleridge the second, and whoever finished his part first was to go on and write the completion.

> Methinks I see his grand and noble countenance as at the moment when having despatched my own portion of the task at full finger-speed, I hastened to him with my manuscript—that look of humorous despondency fixed on his almost blank sheet of paper, and then its silent mock-piteous admission of failure struggling with the sense of the exceeding ridiculousness of the whole scheme—which broke up in a laugh: and the Ancient Mariner was written instead.

THEME. It has long been accepted that the connection between the story of Cain's years of guilty wandering after the murder of his brother Abel has a more than accidental relation to the theme of the journey through crime, punishment and expiation suffered by the Mariner. In the Cain story the grounding of Cain's suffering in religion, in his pursuit by a severe, if ultimately merciful God, is not in doubt. Reactions to *The Ancient Mariner* on the whole, have chosen rather to emphasize the psychological origins of the Mariner's guilt and suffering. It has been read most often as an epic of *secular* experience and many critics have attempted to resolve the apparent paradox of the poem's independence of any easily paraphrasable meaning, by concentrating on those elements within it which seem to refer us back to its author's life. The poem can then be read as an account of Coleridge's own experience of desolation following the loss of his early hopes for himself, or as a lament for the suffering he imposed on himself as a consequence of destroying his imaginative power to make poetry. There are several accounts of this kind, among which two are particularly persuasive: that of Robert Penn Warren of 1946 (reprinted in his *Selected Essays*, 1958), and that of George Whalley (most readily available in the volume on Coleridge in the series *Twentieth Century Views*, [1967]).

Critics who wrote about it on its first appearance in 1798 could not make much of it. Writing anonymously in the *Critical Review* for October 1798 Southey called it 'a Dutch attempt at German sublimity'. (Coleridge was in Germany at the time, and relations between

them had not yet been completely restored after their earlier disagreements of 1795.) *The Monthly Review* of May 1799 called it 'the
strangest story of a cock and bull that we ever saw on paper: yet,
though it seems a rhapsody of unintelligible wildness and incoherence
(of which we do not perceive the drift, unless the joke lies in depriving
the wedding guest of his share of the feast), there are in it poetical
touches of an exquisite kind'. A corrective to this kind of philistine
response, which is in any case a constant accompaniment to literary
production, is that of Charles Lamb who wrote immediately to
Southey to remonstrate with him.

> If you wrote that review in *Crit. Rev.*, I am sorry you are so sparing
> of praise to the *Ancient Mariner*—so far from calling it as you do,
> with some wit, but more severity, 'A Dutch Attempt', &c., I call it a
> right English attempt, and a successful one, to dethrone German
> sublimity. You have selected a passage fertile in unmeaning
> miracles, but have passed by fifty passages as miraculous as the
> miracles they celebrate. I never felt so deeply the pathetic as in
> that part,
>> A spring of love gush'd from my heart,
>> And I bless'd them unaware.
>
> It stung me into high pleasure through sufferings. Lloyd does not
> like it; his head is too metaphysical, and your taste too correct; at
> least I must allege something against you both, to excuse my own
> dotage.
>> So lonely 'twas, that God himself
>> Scarce seem'd there to be!—&c., &c.

Lamb wrote to Wordsworth two years later, in January 1801, of the
continued effect of the poem on him. 'For me, I was never so affected
with any human Tale. After first reading it, I was totally possessed
with it for many days—I dislike all the miraculous part of it, but the
feelings of the man under the operation of such scenery dragged me
along like Tom Piper's magic whistle.' Wordsworth, for his part, did
not like the poem and felt that its effect spoiled the rest of the volume,
but Lamb's response, which is a genuinely felt one, is the type of many
later responses which have taken the Mariner's experience to be the
centre of this extraordinary poem. It is a voyage of appalling discovery in a ship flung to the other side of the world through terrible
adventures, like those of the seventeenth century travel books that
Wordsworth and Coleridge had been reading, from which only one
man returns to tell the tale, more dead than alive. Throughout most of
the voyage the ship is at the mercy of the conflict of the elements,
driven on its way through the extremes of cold and heat, under the
copper sun or beneath the climbing moon.

> All in a hot and copper sky
> The bloody sun, at noon,

> Right up above the mast did stand,
> No bigger than the moon.

> Day after day, day after day,
> We stuck, nor breath nor motion;
> As idle as a painted ship
> Upon a painted ocean.

Those features of the traditional ballad, repetition and alliteration, which Coleridge imitates so astonishingly accurately, also serve purposes beyond imitation. They contribute to the way in which the verse imposes on our senses as we react to the mood of blank negation of life and purpose that the poem offers at this point. Yet the picture is also graphically present in the mind's eye, sensuous and beautiful. We, like Lamb, are 'stung into high pleasure through sufferings'. Then follow immediately the lines that have passed beyond the literary consciousness into the language of the English people.

> Water, water, every where,
> And all the boards did shrink;
> Water, water, every where,
> Nor any drop to drink.

These lines are deeply embedded in the minds of many people who have only the sketchiest notion of the poem itself because they crystallize a profoundly human experience of the paradox of suffering endured in the sight of plenty. Paradox and reversal, conflict and alternating extremities are the essence of the voyage. The departure by sunlight is an escape.

> With sloping masts and dipping prow,
> As who pursued with yell and blow
> Still treads the shadow of his foe,
> And forward bends his head,
> The ship drove fast, loud roared the blast,
> And southward aye we fled.

The return to a familiar world now transformed by moonlight, is fantom-like and stricken.

> Like one, that on a lonesome road
> Doth walk in fear and dread,
> And having once turned round, walks on,
> And turns no more his head;
> Because he knows, a frightful fiend
> Doth close behind him tread.

The Mariner's return to the known world is that of a man haunted by the compulsive memory of his journey.

At the same time the Mariner's tale is a story of a voyage into the interior. Not only into the unfathomable depths of the sources of human action to be discerned in the unpremeditated shooting of the albatross that causes him his suffering, and the spontaneous blessing of the water snakes that begins his restoration; the story also takes us beyond the human world altogether. Again it is a voyage of extreme contrasts, of suffering and of expiation, of the human and social world and an altogether alien cosmos with its own terrible, yet beautiful order. It is exactly right that the listener should be a wedding guest and that the Mariner denies him his expectations of the natural enjoyment of the music, the celebration and the happiness of the feast. It is also right that the guest should be afraid of the Mariner and feel that he is a being from another world; he is exactly that.

Charles Lamb sees the immensity of the sense of desolation and dereliction that the Mariner suffered:

> O Wedding-guest! this soul hath been
> Alone on a wide, wide sea:
> So lonely 'twas, that God himself
> Scarce seemed there to be.

But he is not the only one to have expressed his impatience with the supernatural apparatus of the poem, to have missed the essential function in the whole experience of the spirits and their part in the Mariner's punishment and restoration. On a famous occasion Coleridge was tasked with having written a poem with no moral. Coleridge's provoking reply is recorded in his *Table Talk* for 31 May 1830. 'I told her that in my own judgment the poem had too much; and that the only, or chief fault, if I might say so, was the obtrusion of the moral sentiment so openly on the reader as a principle or cause of of action in a work of such pure imagination.'

What I take Coleridge to be referring to is the motto-like stanzas near the end of the poem.

> He prayeth best, who loveth best
> All things both great and small;
> For the dear God who loveth us,
> He made and loveth all.

Just as no summary of the poem can ever exhaust the meanings that the poem creates, so no summary of the experience the Mariner undergoes could ever substitute satisfactorily for living through that experience. Further, the experience and the suffering seem immeasurably disproportionate to the 'moral'. But what is it that the Mariner lives through in his unsought encounter with the invisible world? Here I have to turn to what I think Coleridge meant when he described the poem as a work of pure imagination. The clue is given in the Latin epigraph to the poem in its final version which, together with

The ice was here, the ice was there,
The ice was all around:
It crack'd and growl'd, and roar'd and howl'd,
Like noises in a swound!

At length did cross an Albatross,
Thorough the fog it came;
As if it had been a Christian soul,
We hail'd it in God's name.

the prose commentary, was not published until its inclusion in *Sybilline Leaves* of 1817. The quotation is taken from a work by Thomas Burnet, whose connection with Coleridge we have already noted elsewhere (p. 33), on the ancient doctrine of the Origins of Things, the *Archaeologicae Philosophicae* of 1692. A translation of the original reads:

> I can readily believe that there are more invisible than visible natures in the Universe. But who shall describe their family, their orders, relationships, the stations and functions of each? What do they do? Where do they live? The human mind has always sought after knowledge of these things, but has never attained it. Meanwhile I do not deny the pleasure it is to contemplate in thought, as though in a picture, the image of the greater and better world: lest the mind, habituating itself to the minutiae of life, should become too narrow, and subside completely into trivial thoughts only. But, at the same time we must be vigilant for truth, and set a limit, so that we can distinguish the certain from the uncertain and night from day.

Like Burnet, Coleridge believed profoundly in such a world which lay beyond human conception, and his way into it was through poetic or imaginative invention. What he could never *know* he could *imagine* out of the strength of his belief. So the spirit world that the Mariner accidentally reveals by shooting the albatross is only an analogy for the poet's belief in that world. Hence the mixture it presents to us of dream (the skeleton ship was suggested by a friend's dream), of traditional angelology and the exotic world of traveller's tales and accounts. The idea of the albatross came from Wordsworth, who had been reading of such an incident in a book of voyages.

The Mariner forces an accidental entry into this world and his punishment is to be delivered over, not like his ship-mates, to death, but to Life-in-Death who, again accidentally, wins him in the dice-throwing. His journey through and out of suffering and penance is marked by occasional glimpses of the exquisite order of this other world.

> In his loneliness and fixedness he yearneth towards the journeying moon, and the stars that still sojourn, yet still move onward; and every where the blue sky belongs to them and is their appointed rest, and their native country and their own natural homes, which they enter unannounced, as Lords that are certainly expected and yet there is a silent joy at their arrival.

The beauty of that accompanying image of the universe prepares us for the spring of love that gushes from the heart of the Mariner at his new perception of the beauty of the water-snakes.

> Sure my kind saint took pity on me,
> And I blest them unaware.

The unconscious source of the blessing is insisted upon in the repetition of 'unaware'. Appropriately, the next stage of the return journey, begun in the admission of love, is accompanied by music, the expression of all harmony.

> Sometimes a-dropping from the sky
> I heard the sky-lark sing;
> Sometimes all little birds that are,
> How they seemed to fill the sea and air
> With their sweet jargoning!
>
> And now 'twas like all instruments,
> Now like a lonely flute;
> And now it is an angel's song,
> That makes the heavens be mute.
>
> It ceased; yet still the sails made on
> A pleasant noise till noon,
> A noise like of a hidden brook
> In the leafy month of June,
> That to the sleeping woods all night
> Singeth a quiet tune.

The metaphor from Nature and the early summer is completely appropriate and felicitous. Music resumes as the heavenly band, having returned the ship to its harbour, leaves the dead bodies.

> This seraph-band, each waved his hand,
> No voice did they impart—
> No voice; but Oh! the silence sank
> Like music on my heart.

This marvellous phrase echoes that verse earlier in this voyage of discovery:

> Fear at my heart, as at a cup,
> My life-blood seemed to sip.

The rescue and the final death of the ship break rudely into the dream-like atmosphere. Even the Hermit good fears for what sort of thing the Mariner might be. Once he tells his story the Mariner is for a short time at peace but he must continue to live under the compulsion to tell his tale again and again to ordinary mortals who can have had no glimpse of this other world. The Mariner is not fully restored to ordinary life again. That would be an impossibility; there are certain kinds of experience that not merely teach us, but change us utterly whether we will or no, and leave us quite different from what we took ourselves to be. We can never be rid of them. We are both Mariner and the Wedding-Guest who:

> . . . went like one that hath been stunned,
> And is of sense forlorn:
> A sadder and a wiser man,
> He rose the following morn.

'Stunned' and 'forlorn' we may be, yet, at the same time, we are stung with Charles Lamb to 'high pleasure' by the beauty and drama of this unique poem, of which no account can be satisfactory.

NOTES. To attempt anything like a full account of the genesis of this poem and of the references it contains would require another book, but as I have stressed the importance of the close collaboration between Coleridge and Wordsworth at this period of their lives, I must note Wordsworth's involvement in the composition of *The Ancient Mariner*. Much later in his life he dictated a series of comments on his poetry to a Miss Isabella Fenwick and the note which accompanies *We are Seven* illuminates part of the way in which *The Ancient Mariner* and the idea of *Lyrical Ballads* came together.

> I will here mention one of the most remarkable facts in my own poetic history and that of Mr Coleridge. In the spring of the year 1798, he, my Sister, and myself, started from Alfoxden, pretty late in the afternoon, with a view to visit Lynton and the valley of Stones near it; and as our united funds were very small, we agreed to defray the expense of the tour by writing a Poem, to be sent to the *New Monthly Magazine* set up by Phillips the bookseller, and edited by Dr Aikin. Accordingly we set off and proceeded along the Quantock Hills, towards Watchet, and in the course of this walk was planned the Poem of *The Ancient Mariner*, founded on a dream, as Mr Coleridge said, of his friend, Mr Cruikshank. Much the greatest part of the story was Mr Coleridge's invention; but certain parts I myself suggested, for example, some crime was to be committed which should bring upon the Old Navigator, as Coleridge afterwards delighted to call him, the spectral persecution, as a consequence of that crime, and his own wanderings. I had been reading in Shelvock's *Voyages* a day or two before that while doubling Cape Horn they frequently saw Albatrosses in that latitude, the largest sort of sea-fowl, some extending their wings 12 or 13 feet. 'Suppose,' said I, 'you represent him as having killed one of these birds on entering the South Sea, and that the tutelary Spirits of those regions take upon them to avenge the crime.' The incident was thought fit for the purpose and adopted accordingly. I also suggested the navigation of the ship by the dead men, but do not recollect that I had anything more to do with the scheme of the poem. The Gloss with which it was subsequently accompanied was not thought of by either of us at the time; at least, not a hint of it was given to me, and I have no doubt it was a gratuitous after-thought.

We began the composition together on that, to me, memorable evening. I furnished two or three lines at the beginning of the poem, in particular:

> And listened like a three years' child;
> The Mariner had his will.

These trifling contributions, all but one (which Mr C. with unnecessary scrupulosity recorded) slipt out of his mind as they well might. As we endeavoured to proceed conjointly (I speak of the same evening) our respective manners proved so widely different that it would have been quite presumptuous in me to do anything but separate from an undertaking upon which I could only have been a clog. We returned after a few days from a delightful tour, of which I have many pleasant, and some of them droll-enough, recollections. We returned by Dulverton to Alfoxden. *The Ancient Mariner* grew and grew till it became too important for our first object, which was limited to our expectation of five pounds, and we began to talk of a Volume, which was to consist, as Mr Coleridge has told the world, of Poems chiefly on natural subjects taken from common life, but looked at, as much as might be, through an imaginative medium. Accordingly I wrote *The Idiot Boy, Her eyes are wild*, etc., *We are Seven, The Thorn*, and some others.

In the 1817 edition of his poems, *Sybilline Leaves*, Coleridge noted the lines

> And thou art long, and lank, and brown,
> As is the ribbed sea-sand.

as having been suggested by Wordsworth.

Wordsworth also has another, less direct connection with the poem. There is an entry for late 1796 in the Gutch Notebook which contains notes for projected works. One item reads:

> Adventures of CHRISTIAN, the mutineer—

The story of the mutiny led by Fletcher Christian against his captain, Lieutenant Bligh, aboard the HMS *Bounty*, in 1789 is well known. Christian seized the ship in the South Seas and set Bligh and eighteen other crew members adrift in a small boat with inadequate provisions before sailing on to Tahiti. There he left sixteen men who were later arrested by the Royal Navy, and continued to Pitcairn Island where he and the remainder of the mutineers settled. Bligh got back to England in March 1790 and at once published his account of the mutiny. A court-martial and trial were held at Portsmouth in 1792. The story has seized the imagination of all subsequent generations and Coleridge wrote in a letter of December 1796 to Tom Poole: 'I shall again be afloat on the wide sea unpiloted & unprovisioned.'

127

But the connection in Coleridge's case is not merely an imaginative one which finds a parallel in the journey through dereliction of his Mariner. Christian's brother Edward wrote in defence of the mutineers, and Edward Christian was a fellow of St John's College, Cambridge when Wordsworth was an undergraduate there. Furthermore the Christians were in any case known to Wordsworth as they came originally from Cockermouth, his birthplace. He wrote a letter attacking as forgeries the so-called *Letters from Fletcher Christian* when these appeared as a book in 1796. Coleridge would certainly have been aware of Wordsworth's connection with the story and its atmosphere of suffering and guilt. It was on such materials that Coleridge's imagination worked, transmuting them into a poem of inexhaustible richness.

The biblical figure of Cain becomes a Romantic hero of transgression and defiance in the work of Lord Byron. He wrote a drama, *Cain, a Mystery*, in Italy in 1821 and dedicated it to Sir Walter Scott. Coleridge experienced a Cain-like moment in his own childhood when he attacked his tormentor, his older brother Francis, with a knife and then ran away from home and hid outside all night.

Kubla Khan
Or, A Vision in a Dream. A Fragment

In Xanadu did Kubla Khan
A stately pleasure-dome decree:
Where Alph, the sacred river, ran
Through caverns measureless to man
    Down to a sunless sea.
5   So twice five miles of fertile ground
With walls and towers were girdled round:
And there were gardens bright with sinuous rills,
Where blossomed many an incense-bearing tree;
And here were forests ancient as the hills,
10   Enfolding sunny spots of greenery.

But oh! that deep romantic chasm which slanted
Down the green hill athwart a cedarn cover!
A savage place! as holy and enchanted
As e'er beneath a waning moon was haunted
15   By woman wailing for her demon-lover!
And from this chasm, with ceaseless turmoil seething,
As if this earth in fast thick pants were breathing,
A mighty fountain momently was forced:
    Amid whose swift half-intermitted burst
20   Huge fragments vaulted like rebounding hail,
Or chaffy grain beneath the thresher's flail:

And 'mid these dancing rocks at once and ever
It flung up momently the sacred river.
Five miles meandering with a mazy motion
25 Through wood and dale the sacred river ran,
Then reached the caverns measureless to man,
And sank in tumult to a lifeless ocean:
And 'mid this tumult Kubla heard from far
Ancestral voices prophesying war!
30   The shadow of the dome of pleasure
      Floated midway on the waves;
      Where was heard the mingled measure
      From the fountain and the caves.
It was a miracle of rare device,
35 A sunny pleasure-dome with caves of ice!

      A damsel with a dulcimer
      In a vision once I saw:
      It was an Abyssinian maid,
      And on her dulcimer she played,
40   Singing of Mount Abora.
      Could I revive within me
      Her symphony and song,
      To such a deep delight 'twould win me,
That with music loud and long,
45 I would build that dome in air,
That sunny dome! those caves of ice!
And all who heard should see them there,
And all should cry, Beware! Beware!
50 His flashing eyes, his floating hair!
Weave a circle round him thrice,
And close your eyes with holy dread,
For he on honey-dew hath fed,
And drunk the milk of Paradise.

OCCASION. Coleridge did not publish *Kubla Khan* until 1816 and
when he did so he wrote for it the following preface:

The following fragment is here published at the request of a poet of
great and deserved celebrity [Lord Byron], and, as far as the
Author's own opinions are concerned, rather as a psychological
curiosity, than on the ground of any supposed *poetic* merits.

In the summer of the year 1797, the Author, then in ill health,
had retired to a lonely farm-house between Porlock and Lynton, on
the Exmoor confines of Somerset and Devonshire. In consequence
of a slight indisposition, an anodyne had been prescribed, from
the effects of which he fell asleep in his chair at the moment that he
was reading the following sentence, or words of the same substance,

in Purchas's *Pilgrimage*: 'Here the Khan Kubla commanded a palace to be built, and a stately garden thereunto. And thus ten miles of fertile ground were inclosed with a wall.' The Author continued for about three hours in a profound sleep, at least of the external senses, during which time he has the most vivid confidence, that he could not have composed less than from two to three hundred lines; if that indeed can be called composition in which all the images rose up before him as *things*, with a parallel production of the correspondent expressions, without any sensation or consciousness of effort. On awaking he appeared to himself to have a distinct recollection of the whole, and taking his pen, ink, and paper, instantly and eagerly wrote down the lines that are here preserved. At this moment he was unfortunately called out by a person on business from Porlock, and detained by him above an hour, and on his return to his room, found, to his no small surprise and mortification, that though he still retained some vague and dim recollection of the general purport of the vision, yet, with the exception of some eight or ten scattered lines and images, all the rest had passed away like the images on the surface of a stream into which a stone has been cast, but, alas! without the after restoration of the latter!

Neither the dating nor the story of the event and the untraceable person from Porlock has to be absolutely true. More important, the preface has grown into the poem until, in any critical account, the two are inseparable. What Coleridge has done is to compound an already adequate mystery and to give to a very strange incantatory evocation of an exotic and remote past the status of a spectacular kind of *objet trouvé*, an accidental thing that we take to be an art object. In a curious fashion one of the most impressive enquiries ever conducted into Coleridge's poetic method has tended to reinforce this view of the poem. Livingstone Lowes's *The Road to Xanadu* brings to bear on the words of the poem an enormous weight of scholarship starting from that reference to Purchas's *Pilgrimage* of 1613. In tracing out the references that Coleridge gathered from his immensely wide reading of these months, Lowes is attempting to get at the creative process implied in the poem, but by concentrating on the *reading* as opposed to the living and *imagining* that the poet must also have engaged in, he comes to the conclusion that the poem is meaningless. Because the processes of the mind are, as Coleridge himself was acutely conscious, fundamentally mysterious, Lowes excludes them from his consideration and is obliged as a consequence to read the poem as a magnificent collection of accidents. And yet we know that the processes of the mind provided Coleridge with a continuous source of enquiry throughout his poetic and philosophical life. We know further that his elaboration of the poetic faculty of Imagination is a critical resting point in his lifelong enquiry. If we pursue the point even further and ask to what end Coleridge entertained the enquiry then perhaps we could not do better than refer back to the letter to John Thelwall of 14 October 1797 (see p. 33). 'My mind feels as if it ached to behold & know something *great*—something *one* & *indivisible*— and it is only in the faith of this that rocks or waterfalls, mountains or caverns give me the sense of sublimity or majesty!—But in this faith *all things* counterfeit infinity!'

The poetic imagination, the unifying power, is the faculty by which we reach towards and perceive the something one and indivisible. If Coleridge remembered the date of the composition of Kubla Khan accurately, and we have no reason to suppose him to have been more accurate on this than on other occasions, then the mood of sublimity in its relation to the theme of the one and indivisible provides us with at least as important an indication of the area of meaning of the poem as would an enquiry into Coleridge's reading.

'KUBLA KHAN' AND OPIUM.   To such a view of the allegiances of the poem it might be objected that its author directs us specifically to the genesis of the poem in an opium dream and that fact alone would prevent our making the kind of links that we could presume with some confidence in discussing more usual orders of poetic invention. The discussion of the relation between hallucinogenic drugs and literature is complicated in Coleridge's case if only because Coleridge declares himself to be the type of drug poet. The discussion is raised by Coleridge's own case and to turn it back on him might well make our argument circular, in that the evidence for the relation between drugs and poetry in Coleridge's case is—Coleridge's case. Whatever the case is there is no doubt in any one's mind that it is only poets and not other kinds of human beings who produce poetry under the influence of hallucinogenic drugs, and it is an assertion difficult to prove that, whenever one could sufficiently identify the evidence, there exists a kind of similarity between such poems by different poets which (at the same time) makes them dissimilar to other poems written by the same poet.

It is well known that Coleridge took opium and that he only recognized the relation between his drug-taking and his persistent ill-health much later in his life; and it is to this later period of recognition that the preface belongs. At the time of writing he was not aware of the peculiarity of the state of mind during which he, on his own report, composed the poem. He himself calls the poem 'A Vision in a Dream' rather in the same way as he gave the description 'A Poet's Reverie' to *The Ancient Mariner*. Interested as he was in discriminating among states of mind, he would distinguish reverie, vision and dream as certain activities, among others, of the mind. However there is no doubt that the later preface has contributed to the air of mystery that hangs over the fabric of the poem, and so successful an effect is it that I would not like to eliminate it in trying to make clear what I take the poem to be about.

I do not think that the poem was written automatically. It did not write itself in the way some later, especially surrealist, poetry claims to have been written down. Written at great speed it may have been, but then so were many other notable poems. Contrary to such views, the poem seems to me to be a very special yet recognizable kind of poem, and the kind I take it to represent, and to have represented to Coleridge is the irregular or sublime ode.

'KUBLA KHAN' AND THE SUBLIME.   On 26 December 1796, in a letter to Tom Poole, he wrote: 'If it be found to possess that Impetuosity of Transition, and that Precipitation of Fancy and Feeling, which are the *essential* excellences of the sublimer Ode, its deficiency in less important respects will be easily pardoned.' Coleridge is referring to his ode of that month, *Ode on the Departing Year*, which was also written at great speed because it was commissioned at a moment when he was ill with rheumatic pains in the head. What interests me about the reference is the characterization Coleridge offers of the sublimer ode and the readiness with which one might transfer that description to *Kubla Khan* which would then read as a fragment (and so Coleridge describes it) of just such an ode.

Be that as it may, to assert that the poem might have some connection with an inherited theory of poetic genres does not diminish the particular and unique force with which the poem impresses itself on the reader. And yet even here, I feel that Coleridge's preface has helped to mystify the poem unreasonably. Kubla Khan's pleasure dome rises majestically from a paradise garden. The idea of the dome, of the artefact that repeats the shape of the universe is a central Romantic motif, through Shelley's *Ode to the West Wind* to W. B. Yeats's marvellous poem on *Byzantium*. It is also a central feature of the eighteenth-century sublime landscape. There is one at Stourhead in Wiltshire, with a mansion and large landscaped park laid out round an artificially created lake in the style of a painting by Claude. Nature and Art mingled as the grounds were completed during the second half of the century by Henry Hoare, son of the original owner who was a London banker, assisted by Henry Flitcroft. A dome was built by the lake in 1754 and across from it on the other shore is a Paradise Well. Edmund Burke asserts in his *Enquiry* that the dome or rotund is the perfect sublime building.

> Uninterrupted progression . . . alone can stamp on bounded objects the character of infinity. I believe we ought to look for the cause why a rotund has such a noble effect. For in a rotund, whether it be a building or a plantation, you can nowhere fix a boundary;

turn which way you will, the same object seems to continue, and the imagination has no rest. (Part 2, Section IX: Succession and Uniformity)

It is worth noting here that a later section dealing with sublime sounds (Section XIX) opens with the following sentence: 'A low, tremulous, intermitting sound . . . is productive of the sublime.'

The idea of the sublimely imagined landscape also occurs in eighteenth-century poetry. We have already had occasion to signal Akenside's *The Pleasures of the Imagination* as a poem important to Coleridge's beginnings as a poet. In Book Two Akenside tells the story of the sage Harmodius and his encounter with a god-like admonishing spirit called 'Genius of human kind'. The Genius offers him a vision of:

> the primal seat
> Of man, and where the Will Supreme ordain'd
> His mansion, that pavilion fair-diffused
> Along the shady brink.

The passage describing the visionary landscape is worth quoting in full:

> I look'd, and lo! the former scene was changed;
> For verdant alleys and surrounding trees,
> A solitary prospect, wide and wild,
> Rush'd on my senses. 'Twas a horrid pile
> Of hills with many a shaggy forest mix'd,
> With many a sable cliff and glittering stream.
> Aloft, recumbent o'er the hanging ridge,
> The brown woods waved; while ever-trickling springs
> Wash'd from the naked roots of oak and pine
> The crumbling soil; and still at every fall
> Down the steep windings of the channel'd rock,
> Remurmuring rush'd the congregated floods
> With hoarser inundation; till at last
> They reach'd a grassy plain, which from the skirts
> Of that high desert spread her verdant lap,
> And drank the gushing moisture, where confined
> In one smooth current, o'er the lilied vale
> Clearer than glass it flow'd. Autumnal spoils
> Luxuriant spreading to the rays of morn,
> Blush'd o'er the cliffs, whose half-encircling mound
> As in a sylvan theatre enclosed
> That flowery level. On the river's brink
> I spied a fair pavilion, which diffused
> Its floating umbrage 'mid the silver shade
> Of osiers. Now the western sun reveal'd

> Between two parting cliffs his golden orb,
> And pour'd across the shadow of the hills,
> On rocks and floods, a yellow stream of light
> That cheer'd the solemn scene.

It seems difficult to imagine that Coleridge was not reminded of the passage when reading Purchas and of its meaning as a vision of 'the primal seat of Man', that is, of the earthly paradise offered to the poetic imagination.

Again, what has to be noticed about the circumstances of *Kubla Khan* is its orientalism, and its relation to the exotic landscape and reports of travellers. A taste for the oriental was a vogue in England in the second half of the eighteenth century, as may be witnessed by the fashionable portrait painting in oriental costume of the time. Just as with the taste for the medieval world it remained for a long time an eccentric fringe in the tradition of the growth of interest in aesthetics.

THEME. And yet the poem itself remains very much Coleridge's own creation and all I have been attempting to do in the foregoing is to try and render it a little less mysterious an achievement than has sometimes been assumed, and that in writing it, Coleridge's practice is much as it is elsewhere. It would follow from my suggestions that I read the poem as an ode in the sublime manner and that it is only a fragment. It follows further from my placing of it in relation to Akenside's poem that its subject matter is the poetic imagination that strives to know something one and indivisible, and that Kubla's pleasure-dome is the imaginative realization of this knowledge. The most striking feature of the poem is perhaps the insistent music, especially in the opening description of the landscape and the inspired song of the ending. The interplay of vowels and consonants is such as we have noted in other poems but is here realized with such an intensity as to give to the lines an incantatory force. Milton's shadowy presence is again felt, but not, as one might have expected in a poem on the subject of a visionary landscape, the Milton of the epics *Paradise Lost* and *Paradise Regained*, so much as the more lyrical poet of *L'Allegro*, *Il Penseroso* and *Lycidas*. Music is important to Coleridge's vision as it is the type of *harmony*, and harmony and reconciliation are the essential features of the dome.

> It was a miracle of rare device,
> A sunny pleasure-dome with caves of ice!

But music does not play throughout the poem. It has always seemed to me that there is a certain stridency and straining for effect in the opening lines of the second paragraph, or *strophe* as I might have to call it if the poem is a fragment of an ode.

> But oh! that deep romantic chasm which slanted
> Down the green hill athwart a cedarn cover!

Wookey Hole, Somerset by Michael 'Angelo' Rooker painted before 1800

About these lines and the following ones hangs the same air of exclamatory apostrophe that I noted as a disturbance in the texture of *This Lime Tree Bower*. Coleridge seems to reach for a tone of sublime horror not far removed from that of Gray's letter from the Grande Chartreuse, quite unlike the effect of the rest of the poem. The rhyming pentameters are at odds with the variations on the octosyllabic measure in which the rest of the poem is cast. (See p. 29 for Gray's letter and compare its tone with that of Hazlitt describing the Valley of the Rocks on p. 167).

A new change of feeling returns in the last section with the poet's appearance in his own poem. Under the inspiration of an exotic music heard in a vision he would recreate in his poetry the dome and all its qualities. His poem would be a truly Orphic song of such power that it would make of the poet an object of superstitious awe to his listeners. Bearer of such a vision, he would become a magical figure, a demi-god, just as the Ancient Mariner, after his direct experience of the invisible world, can only render his chosen hearers uneasy. Such visions and experiences impose intolerable burdens. They are wild imaginings which, in other moods, Coleridge turned away from deliberately, as in *The Eolian Harp*. If *Kubla Khan* is unfinished then there is a sense in which it is unfinishable, not only by Coleridge, but by any mortal poet. Yet no reader can remain untouched by its power.

NOTES.   Many of the features of the landscape of *Kubla Khan* are referable to specific sources in books of oriental travel and history. One could not, however, even if one wanted to, map out or diagrammatize the relationship of the river, plain and caverns. Yet within the poem they seem to suggest very powerfully a sense of the surging up of the river of life, Alph (or Alpha, the first letter of the Greek alphabet), and the fertilizing of the garden of life before it sinks into an unfathomable sea of death. Consider, too, Wookey Hole here.

Dejection : an ode

I

Well! If the Bard was weather-wise, who made
  The grand old ballad of Sir Patrick Spence,
  This night, so tranquil now, will not go hence
Unroused by winds, that ply a busier trade
5   Than those which mould yon cloud in lazy flakes,
Or the dull sobbing draft, that moans and rakes
Upon the strings of this Aeolian lute,
    Which better far were mute.
    For lo! the New-moon winter-bright!
10   And overspread with phantom light,
    (With swimming phantom light o'erspread

136

But rimmed and circled by a silver thread)
I see the old Moon in her lap, foretelling
   The coming-on of rain and squally blast.
15 And oh! that even now the gust were swelling,
   And the slant night-shower driving loud and fast!
Those sounds which oft have raised me, whilst they awed,
   And sent my soul abroad,
Might now perhaps their wonted impulse give,
20 Might startle this dull pain, and make it move and live!

II

A grief without a pang, void, dark, and drear,
   A stifled, drowsy, unimpassioned grief,
   Which finds no natural outlet, no relief,
     In word, or sigh, or tear—
25 O Lady! in this wan and heartless mood,
To other thoughts by yonder throstle woo'd,
   All this long eve, so balmy and serene,
Have I been gazing on the western sky,
   And its peculiar tint of yellow green:
30 And still I gaze—and with how blank an eye!
And those thin clouds above, in flakes and bars,
That give away their motion to the stars;
Those stars, that glide behind them or between,
Now sparkling, now bedimmed, but always seen:
35 Yon crescent Moon, as fixed as if it grew
In its own cloudless, starless lake of blue;
I see them all so excellently fair,
I see, not feel, how beautiful they are!

III

   My genial spirits fail;
40   And what can these avail
To lift the smothering weight from off my breast?
   It were a vain endeavour,
   Though I should gaze for ever
On that green light that lingers in the west:
45 I may not hope from outward forms to win
The passion and the life, whose fountains are within.

IV

O Lady! we receive but what we give,
And in our life alone does Nature live:
Ours is her wedding garment, ours her shroud!
50   And would we aught behold, of higher worth,

Than that inanimate cold world allowed
To the poor loveless ever-anxious crowd,
   Ah! from the soul itself must issue forth
A light, a glory, a fair luminous cloud
55   Enveloping the Earth—
And from the soul itself must there be sent
   A sweet and potent voice, of its own birth,
Of all sweet sounds the life and element!

V

O pure of heart! thou need'st not ask of me
60   What this strong music in the soul may be!
What, and wherein it doth exist,
This light, this glory, this fair luminous mist,
This beautiful and beauty-making power.
   Joy, virtuous Lady! Joy that ne'er was given,
65   Save to the pure, and in their purest hour,
Life, and Life's effluence, cloud at once and shower,
Joy, Lady! is the spirit and the power,
Which wedding Nature to us gives in dower
   A new Earth and new Heaven,
70   Undreamt of by the sensual and the proud—
Joy is the sweet voice, Joy the luminous cloud—
   We in ourselves rejoice!
And thence flows all that charms or ear or sight,
   All melodies the echoes of that voice,
75   All colours a suffusion from that light.

VI

There was a time when, though my path was rough,
   This joy within me dallied with distress,
And all misfortunes were but as the stuff
   Whence Fancy made me dreams of happiness:
80   For hope grew round me, like the twining vine,
And fruits, and foliage, not my own, seemed mine.
But now afflictions bow me down to earth:
Nor care I that they rob me of my mirth;
   But oh! each visitation
85   Suspends what nature gave me at my birth,
   My shaping spirit of Imagination.
For not to think of what I needs must feel,
   But to be still and patient, all I can;
And haply by abstruse research to steal
90   From my own nature all the natural man—
   This was my sole resource, my only plan:
Till that which suits a part infects the whole,
And now is almost grown the habit of my soul.

VII

Hence, viper thoughts, that coil around my mind,
95   Reality's dark dream!
I turn from you, and listen to the wind,
     Which long has raved unnoticed. What a scream
Of agony by torture lengthened out
That lute sent forth! Thou Wind, that rav'st without,
100   Bare crag, or mountain-tairn, or blasted tree,
Or pine-grove whither woodman never clomb,
Or lonely house, long held the witches' home,
     Methinks were fitter instruments for thee,
Mad Lutanist! who in this month of showers,
105 Of dark-brown gardens, and of peeping flowers,
Mak'st Devils' yule, with worse than wintry song,
The blossoms, buds, and timorous leaves among.
     Thou Actor, perfect in all tragic sounds!
Thou mighty Poet, e'en to frenzy bold!
110   What tell'st thou now about?
     'Tis of the rushing of an host in rout,
     With groans, of trampled men, with smarting wounds—
At once they groan with pain, and shudder with the cold!
But hush! there is a pause of deepest silence!
115   And all that noise, as of a rushing crowd,
With groans, and tremulous shudderings—all is over—
     It tells another tale, with sounds less deep and loud!
     A tale of less affright,
     And tempered with delight,
120 As Otway's self had framed the tender lay,—
     'Tis of a little child
     Upon a lonesome wild,
Not far from home, but she hath lost her way:
And now moans low in bitter grief and fear,
125 And now screams loud, and hopes to make her mother hear.

'Tis midnight, but small thoughts have I of sleep:
Full seldom may my friend such vigils keep!
Visit her, gentle Sleep! with wings of healing,
     And may this storm be but a mountain-birth,
130 May all the stars hang bright above her dwelling,
     Silent as though they watched the sleeping Earth!
     With light heart may she rise,
     Gay fancy, cheerful eyes,
     Joy lift her spirit, joy attune her voice;
135 To her may all things live, from pole to pole,
Their life the eddying of her living soul!

O simple spirit, guided from above,
Dear Lady, friend devoutest of my choice,
Thus mayest thou ever, evermore rejoice.

OCCASION. The poem was first written down as *A Letter to—* dated Sunday evening, 4 April 1802. It was sent to Sara Hutchinson and can be found, in this original version, as an appendix on p. 190. An intermediate version—shortened and with considerable revisions, and this time addressed to Wordsworth, appears in a letter sent to a friend, William Sotheby, on 19 July 1802. Coleridge writes because:

> I wished to force myself out of metaphysical trains of Thought— which, when I trusted myself to my own Ideas, came upon me uncalled—& when I wish to write a poem, beat up Game of far other kind—instead of a covey of poetic Partridges with whirring wings of music, or wild Ducks *shaping* their rapid flight in forms always regular (a still better image of Verse) up came a meta-physical Bustard, urging its slow, heavy, laborious, earth-skimming Flight, over dreary & level Wastes. To have done with poetical Prose. . . . Sickness & some other & worse afflictions, first forced me into *downright metaphysics*, for I believe that by nature I have more of the Poet in me. In a poem written during that dejection to Wordsworth, & the greater part of a private nature—I thus expressed the thought— in language more forcible than harmonious.

The version I have chosen to print is addressed to the other Sara, his wife, and was published in the *Morning Post* for 4 October 1802. The date is doubly significant: it was his seventh wedding anniversary and Wordsworth's wedding day. That is not my reason for choosing this final version. Readers may compare the two and decide that they prefer the original version as more personal and painful and therefore more 'sincere'. It is a matter of emphasis. Nor would I take it as a principle that one's preference among different versions of a poem should be determined by the author's decision in the matter. What I want to direct attention to in the poem is what I take to be its theme following the hints thrown out in the letter to Sotheby, rather than use the poem as evidence of Coleridge's private griefs during these months. In fact he reworked the poem so as to cut out all the associa-tions that had occasioned the poem originally. Coleridge's procedure is justified in that in a very private poem there is a continuous temptation to read beyond it into the poet's life, whereas Coleridge himself, as an aesthetic principle and laying aside the argument about what is revealed in the original *Letter*, continuously asserted that the poet is honoured in his poetry, not the poetry for who wrote it. It is a sound principle and the study of English Romantic poetry has suffered greatly from its neglect.

THEME. *Dejection* is one of a number of poems written in the early months of 1802 by both poets. They include Wordsworth's *Resolution and Independence* (which I have printed as an appendix together with *A Letter to*— for their close connection) and *Intimations of Immortality from Recollections of Early Childhood*. Each of them is a response to a sense of irreparable loss, and the phrase 'There was a time' from *Dejection* becomes the opening line of the *Immortality Ode*. (Coleridge had first employed the phrase in a poem *The Mad Monk* written two years earlier.) Each poet seems to be suffering a crisis of confidence in his poetic gift, fearing the loss of his creative imagination; and each uses the word dejection to describe the accompanying mood. In Coleridge's case the circumstantial explanation is all too readily available, but more difficult to establish for Wordsworth in the middle of a period of great creative energy, and contemplating marriage. His anxieties may have stemmed from the need to settle finally his broken relationship with Annette Vallon and his daughter by her in France before settling into marriage with Mary Hutchinson. They may also have some connection with Hartley's theory of the development of the human mind in early manhood from the imaginative to the philosophical stage of perception. Each poet conceived of and responded to the crisis in his own way and the paradoxical result was the creation of three major Romantic poems on the subject of the loss of the poetic imagination. The paradox is most clearly stated and felt in the final *Dejection* which had by now become a poem about the inability to make poetry.

Although the setting is similar, the mood is the opposite of that created in *Frost at Midnight*. This time the influences of Nature will not work to relieve the dull pain of 'stifled, drowsy, unimpassioned grief'. The mood is peculiarly modern, recognizable as free-floating anxiety to the psychoanalyst or as existential dread to the existentialist philosopher. (Coleridge was to write later in *The Friend* of the contemplation of mere existence as a source of 'sacred horror' in ancient peoples, and that it was this feeling that drove man towards religion.) Its chief characteristic is that it is a generalised and inexplicable feeling which cannot be located in any particular source. The promise of the storm cannot move him to passion, or to life.

> I may not hope from outward forms to win,
> The passion and the life, whose fountains are within.

The metaphor of the fountain is, like the aeolian lute, an important Romantic image. It appears in *Kubla Khan* and in Wordsworth's definition of poetry in the 1800 Preface as 'the spontaneous overflow of powerful feelings'. But we also find it in Akenside's *The Pleasures of Imagination*.

Mind, mind alone (bear witness earth and heaven!)
The living fountains in itself contains
Of beauteous and sublime.

(Book 2)

The parallel is very close although Coleridge's expression of the idea is personal and urgent, while Akenside's is more abstract and generalizing in its appeal to earth and heaven. It is a formal declaration whereas we feel the importance of experience in Coleridge's use of words like 'passion', 'life', and 'within' which contrast sharply with Akenside's placing of 'mind alone' as the container of life.

Fountain and wind-harp as metaphors of creativity are, of course, in conflict, and the mood of dejection suggests very powerfully the shift from one way of conceiving creativity to the other in Coleridge. If we compare *The Eolian Harp* with the present poem, the difference is clear. The place of the lute in *Dejection* is in sharp contrast to the speculations it gives rise to in the earlier poem. Beginning in a 'sobbing moan' the lute sends out a scream of agony by torture lengthened out at the wind's height. The language of strophe VII shows a sense of straining after effect, a falling back on eighteenth-century diction in an effort to match appropriately the mood of the storm. It is a kind of strain we have noticed in other poems and it seems out of key with the rest. The last strophe follows only uneasily on the heels of this outburst. But behind the strident tones of the mad lutanist we feel some stirring of the imagination, through scenes of Alpine loneliness to pictures of public and private distress, the battle cries and groans and the wailing of a lost child. (Thomas Otway was a seventeenth-century playwright who, like Chatterton, the 'marvellous boy' of *Resolution and Independence*, died miserably.) Coleridge is remembering Otway's blank verse tragedy '*The Orphan*', and, although in the poem the child hopes to make her mother hear, one cannot help associating the half-remembrance closely with Coleridge's own sense of being orphaned at an early age.

But the imaginative resolution is noth forthcoming: the poet breaks off at this point to address the Lady of the poem, now his wife. In the final strophe we are reminded of the other polarisation in the poem, that of Dejection and Joy. Joy is the opposite mood.

Joy, Lady! is the spirit and the power
Which wedding Nature to us gives in dower
 A new Earth and a new Heaven,
Undreamt of by the sensual and the proud—
Joy is the sweet voice, Joy the luminous cloud—
 We in ourselves rejoice!
And thence flows all that charms or ear or sight,
 All melodies the echoes of that voice,
All colours a suffusion from that light.

But the poem does not settle the issue since it was created, not out of joy, but out of pain and a sense of desolation. The turning to his wife resolves nothing in imaginative terms and the dilemma was to occupy Coleridge for the next fifteen years of his life until it emerges in the central formulations of *Biographia Literaria*, by which time 'abstruse research' had 'become a habit of the soul'. Yet *Dejection: an Ode* is a remarkable poem; together with *Resolution and Independence* it forms an expression of Romanticism that seems far removed from those views of the meaning of the word that would associate it with mindless optimism and heedless escapism. The Romantic poets are at the same time the discoverers of the dark side of the modern soul.

NOTES. The editor E. H. Coleridge wrote a note on this use of the word 'Joy' by Coleridge. 'He called it joy, meaning thereby not mirth or high spirits, or even happiness, but a consciousness of entire and therefore well being, when the emotional and intellectual faculties are in equipoise.' And yet this definition is not entirely satisfactory, in that it scarcely avoids a passive sense to the word, whereas we know that for Coleridge and Wordsworth it signalled an active mode of attention, and was closely related, in Coleridge's case, to the 'shaping spirit of imagination'. Note also the shaping rapid flight of the wild ducks in the letter to Sotheby above: a very potent and dynamic metaphor for what Coleridge already has in mind in 1802 as a way of conceiving of the poetic imagination.
'The grand old ballad of Sir Patrick Spence', in the version in Percy's *Reliques* appears on Appendix C (p. 202).

Coleridge's Prose

Examples of Coleridge's prose style appear everywhere in this book. Even on the subject of the most intimate details of his private life, it is expansive and fluid, rich in metaphoric invention and restless in the continuous pursuit of the implications of any particular thought or impression. It is perhaps this quality of an insatiable hunting out and exploration of meaning that distinguishes his style from that of his eighteenth-century predecessors, so that the comparison one is driven to make is rather with the great English prose stylists of the seventeenth century. I can make no pretence to have made a selection from his vast output, but would indicate the following extracts to emphasize his continuous flowing response to his material and to the way in which the response is informed and controlled by the dominating idea.

Coleridge's response to Shakespeare's *Hamlet* is well known, especially his characterisation of the Prince: 'He is a man living in meditation, called upon to act by every motive human and divine, but the great object of his life is defeated by continually resolving to do, yet doing nothing but resolve' (Twelfth Lecture, *Lectures on Shakespeare*).

Whether or not Coleridge is imposing on Hamlet his own divided character, the view that he proposes of the tragic prince is one that has survived into our own day. What gives it its peculiar authority is Coleridge's responsiveness to the texture of the play, and it is this quality I have chosen to represent. Here again, what he fastens on in the text we may recognize as being peculiarly Coleridgean; the evocation of the effects of the supernatural on ordinary individuals, the soldiers on guard on the walls of the Castle of Elsinore, but the response is immediate, coherent and utterly persuasive. The passage is taken from the notes of the tragedies which he made in the margins of his own copy of Shakespeare's plays.

> Compare the easy language of common life in which this drama opens, with the wild wayward lyric of the opening of *Macbeth*. The language is familiar: no poetic descriptions of night, no elaborate information conveyed by one speaker to another of what both had before their immediate perceptions (such as the first distich in Addison's *Cato*,[1] which is a translation into poetry of 'Past four o'clock, and a damp morning')—yet nothing bordering on the comic on the one hand, and no striving of the intellect on the other. It is the language of *sensation* among men who feared no charge of effeminacy for feeling what they felt no want of resolution to bear. Yet the armour, the dead silence, the watchfulness that first interrupts it, the welcome relief of guard, the cold, the broken expressions as of a man's compelled attention to bodily feelings allowed no man,—all excellently accord with and prepare for the after gradual rise into tragedy—but above all into a tragedy the interest of which is eminently *ad et apud intra*, as *Macbeth* . . . [?] is *ad extra*.
>
> The preparation *informative* of the audience [is] just as much as was precisely necessary: how gradual first, and with the uncertainty appertaining to a question—
>
> > What, has *this thing* appeared *again* to-night.
>
> Even the word 'again' has its *credibilizing* effect. Then the representative of the ignorance of the audience, Horatio (not himself but [quoted by] Marcellus to Bernardo) anticipates the common solution, ' 'tis but our phantasy.' But Marcellus rises secondly into '[this] dreaded sight.' Then this 'thing' becomes at once an 'apparition,' and that too an intelligent spirit that is to be *spoken* to.
>
> > Tush, tush! 'twill not appear.
>
> [1] *Port* The dawn is over-cast, the morning hours,
> And heavily in clouds brings on the day.'

144

Then the shivery feeling, at such a time, with two eye-witnesses, of sitting down to hear a story of a ghost, and this, too, a ghost that had appeared two nights before [at] about this very time. The effort of the narrator to master his own imaginative terrors; the consequent elevation of the style, itself a continuation of this effort; the turning off to an *outward* object, 'yon same star.' O heaven! words are wasted to those that feel and to those who do not feel the exquisite judgement of Shakespeare.

As the notebooks become available in an authoritative edition so we are enmeshed even more deeply in the web of Coleridge's inexhaustibly inventive mind. Many of them were written in a code only deciphered in our own time which has kept vast areas of his thought hidden to generations of readers and scholars. In the secrecy of the notebooks he turns his intellectual scrutiny against himself, viewing himself ironically and justly at once:

There are two sorts of talkative fellows whom it would be injurious to confound & I, S.T. Coleridge, am the latter. The first sort is of those who use five hundred words more than needs to express an idea—that is not my case—few men, I will be bold to say, put more meaning into their words than I or choose them more deliberately & discriminatingly. The second sort is of those who use five hundred more ideas, images, reasons &c than there is any need of to arrive at their object till the only object arrived at is that the mind's eye of the bye-stander is dazzled with colours succeeding so rapidly as to leave one vague impression that there has been a great Blaze of colours all about something. Now this is my case—& a grievous fault it is my illustrations swallow up my thesis—I feel too intensely the omnipresence of all in each, platonically speaking—or psychologically my brain-fibres, or the spiritual Light which abides in the brain marrow as visible Light appears to do in sundry rotten mackeral & other *smashy* matters, is of too general an affinity with all things and 'tho' it perceives the *difference* of things, yet is eternally pursuing the likeness, or rather that which is common. Bring me two things that seem the very same, & then I am quick enough to shew the difference, even to hair-splitting—but to go on from circle to circle till I break against the shore of my Hearer's patience, or have my Concentricals dashed to nothing by a Snore—that is my ordinary mishap. At Malta however, no one can charge me with one or the other. I have earned the general character of being a quiet well meaning man, rather dull indeed—& who would have thought, that he had been a *Poet*! 'O very wretched Poetaster, Ma'am! As to the reviews, it is well known, he half ruined himself in paying cleverer fellows than himself to write them' &c—25 Dec 1804

In March 1805 there is an entry which throws light on Coleridge's conception of what thought is like. 'Root', 'growth', 'bud' and 'delving' distinguish it from what he takes to be the tradition from Locke to Mackintosh. Priestley we have already noted. William Paley was another theological utilitarian, who in his works *Evidences of Christianity* (1794) and *Natural Theology* (1802) found in the design apparent in natural phenomena proof of the existence of God.

> Cause/Duty.—Now if I say to a Paleyan or Priestleyan my *mist*, my delving & difficulty, & he answers me in a set of parrot words, (quite satisfied, clear as a pike-staff,— nothing *before & nothing behind*— a stupid piece of mock-knowledge, having no *root* for then it would have feelings of dimness from *growth*, having no buds or twigs, for then it would have yearnings & strivings of obscurity from *growing*, but a dry stick of Licorish, sweet tho' mawkish to the palate of self-adulation,) acknowleging no sympathy with this delving, this feeling of a wonder, then I must needs set him down for a Priestleyan, Paleyan, Barbouldian, &c &c &c &c &c— from Locke to Macktintosh.

Finally, from *Anima Poetae* I have chosen a daring speculation dated 1811–2 to display the kind of penetration that Coleridge brings to reflection in order to defeat easy, mechanical explanations of existence:

> What a swarm of thoughts and feelings, endlessly minute fragments, and, as it were, representations of all preceding and embryos of all future thought, lie compact in any one moment! So, in a single drop of water, the microscope discovers what motions, what tumult, what wars, what pursuits, what stratagems, what a circle-dance of death and life, death-hunting life, and life renewed and invigorated by death! The whole world seems here in a many-meaning cypher. What if our existence was but that moment? What an unintelligible affrightful riddle, what a chaos of limbs and trunk, tailless, headless, nothing begun and nothing ended, would it not be? And yet scarcely more than that other moment of fifty or sixty years, were that our all? Each part throughout infinite diminution adapted to some other, and yet the whole a means to nothing—ends everywhere, and yet an end nowhere.

Metaphor and energy jostle and reinforce each other in this pursuit of ultimate questions in the contemplation of the microcosmic moment or water-drop. It is a prose at once thoroughly alive and enlivening.

Part Three

Reference Section

Coleridge's friends
and contemporaries

ALLSTON, WASHINGTON (1779–1843) Allston was an American painter whom Coleridge met in Rome at the beginning of 1806 on his Italian journey. Allston invited him to stay at his country house at Olevano (see p. 177). Whatever ideas Coleridge took from him on the subject of the aesthetics of painting, Allston later made handsome acknowledgement of his debt to the friendship. 'To no other man do I owe so much intellectually, as to Mr Coleridge, with whom I became acquainted in Rome, and who has honoured me with his friendship for more than five and twenty years.' They met frequently in England during the following years until Allston's return to America in 1818. At the beginning of the century he studied in England with Fuseli and Benjamin West and painted subjects in which Coleridge was also interested: illustrations to *Paradise Lost*, Schiller's *The Robbers* and Mrs Radcliffe's tale *The Mysteries of Udolpho*. In Coleridge's notebook for 1806 there is a long analysis of Allston's painting *Diana and her Nymphs in the Chase* which emphasizes its sublime elements. Allston started a portrait of the poet in Rome in 1806 and painted a full portrait in London which now hangs in the National Portrait Gallery in London. (See illustrations of Allston's paintings on pp. ii and 178.)

BALL, SIR ALEXANDER (1757–1809) Ball served with Nelson in the British Navy and was for many years his close friend. As a commander under Nelson during the whole of the naval campaign against the French in the Mediterranean he was responsible for the two-year siege of Malta and the final surrender of the French garrison there in 1802. Against Nelson's wishes and advice Ball remained on the island as Governor until his death. For a short period in 1805 Coleridge was on his staff as public secretary (see under *Mediterranean* in the Gazetteer, p. 173). There is a portrait of him in the National Maritime Museum at Greenwich.

BEAUMONT, SIR GEORGE (1753–1827) Painter and patron of the arts, Beaumont is remembered for his patronage of Coleridge and Wordsworth, and, later, of the great English landscape painter, John Constable. He was taught painting at Eton by Alexander Cozens, a notable landscape artist. Beaumont's sketches of Keswick and Greta Hall appear on p. 175. He illustrated Wordsworth's works and, as President of the Sketching Society, encouraged the illustration of literary works. He was a prime mover in the founding of the National Gallery. Coleridge stayed with him on many occasions, whether at his London house in Grosvenor Square, at Dunmow in Essex or at

Coleorton in Leicestershire, his country seat. Coleridge wrote many letters to Sir George and his wife on the subject of his personal and literary life.

BEDDOES, JOSEPH (1760–1808) Beddoes resigned his Readership in Chemistry at Oxford in 1792, partly on account of his expressed sympathies with the aims of the French Revolution, and partly to pursue his own researches. In the following year he set up an institute at Clifton, near Bristol, in order to experiment in the uses of the inhalation of gases in the cure of disease. Josiah Wedgwood, the great pottery manufacturer, contributed £1,000 to the establishment of the Pneumatic Institute. The young Humphry Davy became his assistant and so made the acquaintance of Coleridge. It was Beddoes's political activities and his anti-Pitt pamphleteering that brought him to Coleridge's attention in Bristol. He was married to the sister of the writer Maria Edgeworth, and his son, Thomas Lovell Beddoes, is remembered as a poet of some quality.

BOWLES, THE REV. WILLIAM LISLE (1762–1850) After graduating from Trinity College, Oxford, Bowles resigned his fellowship to become a country parson at Bromhill in Wiltshire. His chief claim to be remembered is for the effect of his *Fourteen Sonnets* of 1789 on Coleridge and Wordsworth. Coleridge met the older, admired poet while he was living in Somerset, but managed to offend him by attempting to offer friendly criticism and improvements to his later verse. A complete edition of his *Poetical Works* appeared in 1855.

BURKE, EDMUND (1729–1797) Educated at Trinity College, Dublin, where his father was an attorney, Burke, after training as a lawyer in London, entered Parliament in 1765. In his early years in the House of Commons he consistently attacked the government's American policy and was a powerful advocate of free trade and Catholic emancipation. His most notable achievements included his speeches against the conduct of the American war and the impeachment of Warren Hastings, the first Governor-General of British India. As a reformer, he opposed the radicalism and atheism of the French Revolution in his best known work *Reflections on the Revolution in France* in which he rejects the whole notion of 'natural rights'. His view that society is of organic growth is the starting point of Coleridge's own reflections on the nature and development of society. Burke's *Enquiry into the Sublime and the Beautiful* (1756) is an important document in the history of aesthetics.

BYRON, GEORGE GORDON, 6th Baron (1788–1824) Byron's first volume of verse *Hours of Idleness* came out in 1807 while he was still an undergraduate at Trinity College, Cambridge. Just before finally quitting England in 1816 he visited Coleridge and persuaded him to publish *Christabel* and *Kubla Khan*, by offering £50 towards the expenses of printing the pamphlet. The popularity of Byron's later poetry, especially in Europe, was for a long time inseparable from the public myth of his immorality, his defiance of society and his death in Greece where he had gone to join the liberation struggle against the Turkish domination. In *English Bards and Scotch Reviewers* (1809) he attacked Coleridge's early poetry: 'to turgid ode and tumid stanza dear'.

CARLYLE, THOMAS (1795–1881) After entering Edinburgh University at the age of fifteen, Carlyle became a schoolmaster for a short while upon taking his degree, but he soon gave up his post in order to write. His long essays on historical and political subjects began to appear in the *London Magazine* and the *Edinburgh Review*. After his marriage the couple lived in retirement on his wife's farm, but moved to their Chelsea house in London in 1834. Carlyle was as important to his generation, including especially Charles Dickens the novelist, and the next as much for the fiercely declamatory tone of his writing as for his political views. These were extremely reactionary and sharply formulated. Contemptuous of democracy, social hope lay for him in a return to a kind of feudalism and the rule of strong, just men. After his wife's death in 1866 he wrote very little of any importance. Early influenced by Coleridge's philosophical views he wrote a severe attack on him in 1851 (see p. 21).

COLERIDGE, DERWENT (1800–83) Coleridge's third son edited a number of his brother's and his father's works. He was the first Principal of St Mark's College, Chelsea, in London, which he made famous for its performances of Church music.

COLERIDGE, GEORGE (1764–1828) A few years after their father's death Coleridge's brother George became schoolmaster and chaplain-priest at Ottery St Mary in 1794. He became a second father to his younger brother, especially during the period of his scrapes at Cambridge over money and his disastrous few months in the army.

COLERIDGE, HARTLEY (1796–1849) Hartley was Coleridge's eldest son, named after the associationist philosopher. Brought up in the continuous company of Wordsworth and Southey at Keswick (see *Frost at Midnight* on p. 112), he was later educated at Merton College, Oxford. Subsequently he lost his fellowship at Oriel College after being charged with 'intemperance' by the College authorities, and he returned to the Lake District where he earned some kind of living by writing. His poems were published in 1851 and in the same year an edition of his prose works and essays was issued by his brother Derwent. In the following year appeared a long appreciation of his work and character by Walter Bagehot which can be found in Volume One of his *Literary Studies*.

COLERIDGE, HENRY NELSON (1798–1843) Coleridge's nephew by his brother James, H. N. Coleridge married Coleridge's daughter Sara. It was he who took down the major part of Coleridge's *Table Talk* during the last years at Highgate. Two volumes appeared in 1835 and 1836. He was Coleridge's literary executor and continued until his death as editor of his uncle's literary remains. His brother Edward was the assistant master at Eton, and a third brother became a Chief Justice.

COLERIDGE, JOHN (1719–81) A schoolmaster who wrote a Latin Grammar and was Vicar of Ottery St Mary from 1760 until his death, Coleridge's father is described by his son as a man of great learning and extreme simplicity. Coleridge, in one of his autobiographical letters, compares him with Parson Adams in Fielding's *Joseph Andrews*, one of the great comic characters of English fiction. Coleridge writes of him at length in his autobiographical letters to Tom Poole, and De Quincey tells anecdotes about his eccentricity in the early pages of *Recollections of the Lake Poets*.

COLERIDGE, SARA (née Fricker) (1770–1845) Coleridge's wife had much to put up with but, from what little is revealed of her in all the contemporary references, was not a very enlightened or understanding wife. De Quincey's account, in attempting to be fair, is ambiguous and tinged with the need to hide his own dislike of her. He reports: 'What he (Coleridge) had to complain of was simply incompatibility of temper and disposition. Wanting all cordial admiration, or indeed comprehension, of her husband's intellectual powers, Mrs Coleridge wanted the original basis for affectionate patience and candour.' As well as her daughter's memoir of her there is an edition of her letters to Tom Poole edited in 1934 by Stephen Potter, *Minnow among Tritons*.

COLERIDGE, SARA (1802–52) Coleridge's daughter married her cousin Henry Nelson Coleridge and helped him and her brother Derwent to edit her father's works. In 1837 she published a romantic fairy tale and, in 1850, *Essays on his own Times* from *The Friend*. Her memoir of her mother together with a selection of letters appeared in 1873.

COTTLE, JOSEPH (1770–1853) Cottle went into bookselling in Bristol in 1791 on the advice of a school teacher. There he met Southey through Robert Lovell who then introduced Coleridge to him. He undertook to publish the poetry of Southey and Coleridge and also printed *Lyrical Ballads* in 1798. In the following year he sold out to Longman of London and gave the copyright of *Lyrical Ballads* to Wordsworth when Longman refused it. He continued writing and printing his own poetry and put out the first edition of *Early Recollections, chiefly relating to Samuel Taylor Coleridge* in 1837. Southey wrote of the work that 'the confusion in Cottle's *Recollections* is greater than anyone would think possible'. Its unreliability as a source of reference for Coleridge stems from Cottle's aim to justify himself and his role in the poet's early life, feeling that he had not been sufficiently appreciated by any of the group. As a result he shaped the material according to his own ends. It was here that the knowledge of Coleridge's addiction to opium was first made public. A revised edition with additions appeared as *Reminiscences of Coleridge and Southey* in 1847.

COWPER, WILLIAM (1731–1800) Articled to a solicitor, called to the Bar and then a clerk at the House of Lords, Cowper became progressively subject to depression and occasional mania. He retired, first to Huntingdon and then, on the death of his host, with his host's widow Mrs Mary Unwin to Olney in Buckinghamshire. Here he composed a number of evangelical hymns, some satires and, in 1784, *The Task*. As well as his poetry, Coleridge greatly admired Cowper's letters.

DAVY, SIR HUMPHRY (1778–1829) Davy was gifted as a poet as well as being, from an early age, a remarkable scientist. Having begun experiments in chemistry as a boy in Cornwall, he developed rapidly as Beddoes's assistant in the Pneumatic Institute at Clifton, Bristol. It was Count Rumford (one of the founders) who invited him to become an assistant lecturer to the Royal Institution in 1801 where he immediately became Professor of Chemistry. He was knighted in 1812. Coleridge and he were lifelong friends; Coleridge sustaining his interest in poetry, Davy interesting Coleridge in chemistry. At Bristol Davy and Southey experimented on the hallucinogenic effects of the inhalation of nitrous oxide, and Coleridge certainly conducted similar experiments. Southey thought that Davy had invented a new pleasure as a result. Davy later became a close friend of Sir Walter Scott.

DE QUINCEY, THOMAS (1785–1859) It was as an undergraduate at Oxford that De Quincey first began taking opium. He sought out Coleridge in 1807 at Bridgwater in Somerset from where he escorted Coleridge's family back to Keswick. (Coleridge was due in London for a lecture series at the Royal Institute.) He was an early member of the staff of *Blackwood's Magazine* in which his *Confessions of an English Opium Eater* appeared in 1822. He settled in Dove Cottage at Grasmere after the Wordsworths moved and continued as an essayist of brilliance on a large variety of subjects. His *Recollections of the Lake Poets (1834–1840)* is an important and entertaining contribution to our knowledge of Coleridge, Southey and Wordsworth (see p. 19) despite the occasional malicious expression and the frequent recourse to unsupported gossip. His works, together with a *Life*, were first edited by David Masson in 1889–90.

FLOWER, BENJAMIN (1755–1829) Flower was editor of the *Cambridge Intelligencer* in which appeared a number of Coleridge's undergraduate verses. He also printed, in Coleridge's name, *The Fall of Robespierre* in 1794.

FREND, WILLIAM (1757–1841) Frend had been tutor of Jesus College, Cambridge, until 1788 when his Unitarian and libertarian views brought him into dispute with the college authorities. He was still in Cambridge when Coleridge was an undergraduate and was a major influence on him in religion and politics. He resigned his fellowship and later became a successful journalist and political commentator in London.

GILLMAN, DR. JAMES (1782–1839) It was on advice offered by a Bristol connection that Coleridge entered the house of Dr Gillman in Highgate as a patient in search of a cure for his addiction to opium which he had at last recognized as a serious contributing factor to his continuous ill-health. Originally intending his stay to be a short one, Coleridge remained Gillman's house-patient to the end of his life. In 1838 Gillman published *The Life of Samuel Taylor Coleridge* based largely on extracts from Coleridge's own writing.

GODWIN, WILLIAM (1756–1836) Trained as a dissenting minister, Godwin became an atheist and philosopher of anarchy. According to his *Enquiry Concerning Political Justice* of 1793 men are rational creatures who can live together in freedom without suffering under oppressive institutions. In the following year he published a novel, *Adventures of Caleb Williams*. Godwin had a complex relationship with two generations of Romantic poets. He was an early influence on the political views of Wordsworth and Coleridge, with whom he was friendly for a time, and then became an important influence on Shelley who married his first wife's daughter, Mary. Mrs Godwin was Mary Wollstonecraft, an early vindicator of the rights of women. His second wife's daughter (by an earlier marriage) was the mother of Byron's illegitimate daughter Allegra.

GREEN, JOSEPH HENRY (1791–1863) Green had a distinguished career as a surgeon and professor of medicine. When he first knew Coleridge, he was demonstrator of anatomy at St Thomas's Hospital in London. In 1824 he was appointed Professor of Anatomy at the College of Surgeons and then first Professor of Surgery at King's College, London, when it was established in 1830. From 1824 he spent much of his private time in Coleridge's company at Highgate. Coleridge made him his second literary executor, responsible for his philosophical writings. He laid on Green the duty to prepare a systematic account of his philosophy, and *Spiritual Philosophy*, in two volumes, appeared in 1865. Green also wrote a preface for the first publication in 1844 of *Confessions of an Enquiring Spirit*.

HAZLITT, WILLIAM (1778–1830) Hazlitt's first meeting with Coleridge, recorded in *My First Acquaintance with Poets*, appears on p. 16. He inherited strong liberal views from his father, a dissenting minister at Shrewsbury, which he never gave up and which colour his appreciation of Coleridge and Wordsworth, with whom he quarrelled in 1803 during a visit to Grasmere. His is the questioning other voice in Wordsworth's poems *Expostulation and Reply* and *The Tables Turned*. His relations with the Lake poets are described at length in P. P. Howe's *Life of William Hazlitt*. He became the foremost literary critic of his age and was an important influence on the development of John Keats's views on poetry. His essays on Coleridge and Wordsworth in *The Spirit of the Age* (1825) should be read.

HUTCHINSON, SARA (1775–1835) Wordsworth's sister-in-law is addressed in a number of Coleridge's poems, usually as 'Asra'. The original version of *Dejection: an Ode* (see Appendix A) was written to her, and she is continuously mentioned in Coleridge's notebooks while he was staying in Malta. (In 1805 Wordsworth's brother John, who the family were certain would marry Sara, was drowned when his ship, the *Abergavenny*, was lost in a storm off Portland Bill.) After Coleridge's return to Grasmere, Sara helped him prepare the twenty-seven numbers of *The Friend* in 1809. Kathleen Coburn has made an edition of her letters.

KEATS, JOHN (1795–1821) Keats gave up the study of medicine for poetry, publishing his first volume in 1817. In the following year his poems were savagely criticized in *Blackwood's Magazine*. In 1820, now seriously ill with tuberculosis, he sailed to Italy in the hope of improving his health. He died in Rome early in 1821. His meeting on Hampstead Heath with Coleridge, as he recalled it in a letter, appears on p. 21.

LAMB, CHARLES (1775–1834) Lamb is best remembered for his *Essays of Elia* and his work on the Elizabethan dramatists. Coleridge's junior at Christ's Hospital, he remained his closest lifelong admirer and friend, despite the quarrel over Charles Lloyd in 1798 and the subsequent two year estrangement. Lamb is the friend addressed in *This Lime Tree Bower* (see Critical Survey, p. 107) which prompts us to recall his long career in the London Office of the East India Company (like John Stuart Mill after him). He was a friend of many of the literary figures of his day, and Wordsworth wrote a long epitaph on him, *Written after the death of Charles Lamb*. Lamb's recollections of Coleridge at school are on p. 15. The news of Coleridge's death affected him profoundly and threw him into a melancholy from which he never seemed to recover. Less than a month before his own death he wrote the following obituary at the request of a friend.

When I heard of the death of Coleridge, it was without grief. It seemed to me that he long had been on the confines of the next world,—that he had a hunger for eternity. I grieved then that I could not grieve. But since, I feel how great a part he was of me. His great and dear spirit haunts me. I cannot think a thought, I cannot make a criticism on men and books, without an ineffectual turning and reference to him. He was the proof and touchstone of all my cogitations. He was a Grecian (or in the first form) at Christ's Hospital, where I was a Deputy-Grecian; and the same subordination and deference to him I have preserved through a lifelong acquaintance. Great in his writings, he was greatest in his conversation. In him was disproved that old maxim, that we should allow every one his share of talk. He would talk from morn to dewy eve, nor cease till far midnight; yet who ever would interrupt him—who would obstruct that · continuous flow of converse, fetched from Helicon or Zion? He had the tact of making the unintelligible seem plain. Many who read the abstruser parts of his 'Friend' would complain that his works did not answer to his spoken wisdom. They were identical. But he had a tone in oral delivery which seemed to convey sense to those who were otherwise imperfect recipients. He was my fifty-years-old friend without a dissention. Never saw I his likeness, nor probably the world can see again. I seem to love the house he died at more passionately than when he lived. I love the faithful Gillmans more than while they exercised their virtues towards him living. What was his mansion is consecrated to me a chapel.

LLOYD, CHARLES (1775–1839) Lloyd was the son of a Birmingham banker whom Coleridge met early in 1796 on his advertising tour for *The Watchman*. Lloyd came to live with Coleridge, first at Bristol and then again for a few months in 1797 at Nether Stowey. He was subject to epileptic fits and had to be removed to a Bristol doctor's care. His novel, *Edmund Oliver*, shocked Coleridge for its betrayal of confidences when it appeared in April 1798. The hero is a thinly disguised portrait of Coleridge, who later insisted that it was the discovery of Lloyd's treachery that had prevented his finishing *Christabel* at that time. Some years later Lloyd, now married, settled in the Lake District near Ambleside, much to the concern of the Wordsworth household. In later years, however, he seems to have been on good terms with both Wordsworth and Southey (who had perhaps suggested to him in the first place the idea of writing the novel). His *Poems on Various Subjects* appeared in 1795 and he later published prose works, dramas and a final volume of poems (1823).

LOVELL, ROBERT (1770–96) Lovell was a Bristol friend of Robert Southey who married a third of the Fricker sisters (Mary), of whom Southey (Edith) and Coleridge (Sara) each married one. Lovell was an early recruit to Pantisocracy and wrote a sonnet to celebrate its fulfilment. In 1795 he and Southey published a joint volume of verse. After his early death from a fever caught while travelling his widow lived permanently with Southey's family.

MACKINTOSH, SIR JAMES (1765–1832) Educated at Aberdeen University, Mackintosh wrote and lectured on philosophical subjects, Like his brother-in-law Daniel Stuart he became a London Scot and moved in fashionable intellectual circles. It was probably Stuart who first brought Coleridge to his attention. On the death of his first wife he married a sister of the younger Wedgwoods, so it was probably he who mentioned Coleridge's name to them as a possible subject for their philanthropic intentions. Macktintosh wrote a reply to Burke's *Reflections on the Revolution in France*, and in 1830, a much-discussed *Dissertation on the Progress of Ethical Philosophy*. He also wrote on the subject of English history.

MONTAGU, BASIL (1770–1851) A contemporary of Wordsworth's at Cambridge, Montagu became a solicitor. When his first wife died, Wordsworth agreed to take his son as a boarder at Racedown and, later, at Alfoxden. On a visit to Wordsworth in 1810, he invited Coleridge to return with him to London, but, once arrived, told him that Wordsworth had warned him against Coleridge's hopelessly unmanageable way of life. Coleridge was outraged and remained estranged from Wordsworth for two years. It was Henry Crabb Robinson who finally brought them together again.

PITT, WILLIAM (1759–1806) Educated at Pembroke Hall, Cambridge, the son of a Whig prime minister, Pitt became Chancellor of the Exchequer at the age of twenty and prime minister at twenty-four. He held the post from 1783 until 1801 and again from 1804 until his death. Thus his ministry spanned the disturbed period of the French Revolution and it was he who led the way in the formation of the series of grand European coalitions designed to oppose France's military ambitions. At the turn of the century Coleridge spoke and wrote in violent opposition to his domestic and foreign policy. A contemporary caricature of Pitt by James Gillray is reproduced on p. 44.

POOLE, THOMAS (1765–1837) Poole inherited a tannery business at Nether Stowey from his father and became known as a good employer, an enlightened business man and local benefactor. His democratic sympathies led him to befriend Southey and Coleridge and, a little later, Wordsworth. He was the stable centre round whom the rest of the group circulated during their years in Bristol and Somerset. He and Coleridge corresponded continuously, although his family shared neither his friendship with that opinionated young man, as they thought of him, nor his political views. *Thomas Poole and his Circle*, written by a descendant, Mrs M. Sandford, was published in 1888.

PRIESTLEY, JOSEPH (1733–1804) As a scientist, Priestley is remembered for his discovery of oxygen and, as a philosopher, for the phrase 'the greatest happiness of the greatest number' from his *Essay on Government* of 1768 which, in the next generation, became a central tenet of Utilitarian philosophy. Brought up in Yorkshire among strict Calvinist protestants, he was educated at a school for dissenters and became a dissenting minister, settling at Birmingham. He was a prolific and influential writer on theology and politics. He was a founder-member of the Unitarian society; a dissenting sect which opposed belief in the Trinity, and affirmed the single personality of the Christian God. Coleridge came under the influence of Unitarianism at Cambridge. Priestley's *Letters to Burke* (1791) provoked popular demonstrations against him. After escaping the burning down of his house, he lived for a while in London where he was supported by his patrons. In 1793 he followed his sons to America where he lived privately after refusing a number of University posts.

PYE, HENRY JAMES (1745–1813) Pye became Poet Laureate in 1790 and, at the same time, a figure of ridicule. He was succeeded by Robert Southey, on whose death Wordsworth accepted the Laureateship. As appropriate illustration of Pye's style, I have chosen the last verse of his Birthday *Ode to George III* for the disturbed year of 1795, but in fact the variations in the theme, mood, language and rhymes of the addresses of different years are scarcely perceptible.

> Yet if the stern vindictive foe,
> Insulting, aim the hostile blow,
> Britain, in martial terrors dight,
> Lifts high the avenging sword, and courts the fight.
> On every side behold her swains
> Crowd eager from her fertile plains!
> With breasts undaunted, lo, they stand
> Firm bulwarks of their native land,
> And proud her floating castles round,
>   The guardians of her happy coast,
> Bid their terrific thunder sound
>   Dismay to Gallia's scatter'd host,
> While still Britannia's navies reign
> Triumphant o'er the subject main.

ROBINSON, HENRY CRABB (1775–1867) Robinson kept a series of thirty-five diaries of his acquaintance with many of the leading literary figures of his day, including Wordsworth and Coleridge, Lamb, Southey and William Blake. For a time during the Napoleonic Wars he was foreign news editor of *The Times* and was the first ever accredited foreign correspondent for an English newspaper. Several selections from his Diaries have been made since his death.

SCOTT, SIR WALTER (1771–1832) Born and educated in Edinburgh, Scott was trained as a lawyer but turned more and more to literature. Inspired by his reading of Percy's *Reliques* he published three volumes of *Border Minstrelsy* in 1802 and 1803. *Marmion* and *The Lady of the Lake* followed and were widely read. In 1814 the first of his enormously popular *Waverley* novels appeared anonymously. Despite financial difficulties in later life his novels written on themes of recent Scottish history and the medieval world swept the reading public for many years. He met the Wordsworths when they called on him during their 1803 tour of Scotland and, in his turn, stayed with them at Grasmere in 1807. Although he had heard *Christabel* recited and had used its metre in *The Lay of the Last Minstrel* (see Appendix C), he seems not to have met Coleridge until the Highgate period. J. G. Lockhart's *Life of Scott* records his opinion of Coleridge's genius. 'No man has all the resources of poetry in such profusion, but he cannot manage them so to bring out anything of his own on a large scale at all worthy of his genius. He is like a lump of coal rich with gas, which lies expending itself in puffs and gleams, unless some shrewd body will clap it into a cast-iron box, and compel the compressed element to do itself justice.'

SHERIDAN, RICHARD BRINSLEY (1751–1816) From his first successful comedy *The Rivals*, written when he was twenty-four, Sheridan was the first man of the theatre of his day. He acquired a share in Drury Lane Theatre in London in 1776 and produced *The School for Scandal* there in the following year. In 1780 he became a member of parliament and was a supporter of reforming causes. In 1797 he invited Coleridge to write a play for him, but, at the time, nothing came of plans to perform either *Osorio* or Wordsworth's tragedy *The Borderers* which Coleridge also offered him. The theatre was burned down and rebuilt in 1812. Coleridge's rewritten version of his play, now called *Remorse*, was given a successful production there in the next year.

SOUTHEY, ROBERT (1774–1843) Expelled from Westminster School, and educated at Balliol College, Oxford, where he met Coleridge in the summer of 1794, Southey is at once the least attractive and, on his own terms, the most successful of the group of Lake Poets. Bearing in mind his dominant part in the marriage of Coleridge to the sister of his own wife-to-be, the following extract from a letter to Joseph Cottle, written in February 1797, illustrates the least likeable side of his character. 'You may know that I neither lightly undertake any scheme, nor lightly abandon what I have undertaken. I am happy because this independence I labour to obtain, and of attaining which my expectations can hardly be disappointed, will leave me nothing to wish.' At the same time as appearing quite ruthless and overbearing, he was utterly dependable and took over without complaint the responsibility for Coleridge's family from 1803 on. In 1807 he received a government pension and, in 1813, at the suggestion of Sir Walter Scott who had refused the offer, became Poet Laureate in succession to Henry James Pye whose verse had made the laureateship an object of ridicule. From being a founder of Pantisocracy he became the panegyrist of George III in *A Vision of Judgement* (1821), which suggests a political reversal much more extreme than that of either Wordsworth or Coleridge. The poem was cruelly parodied by Byron. Southey was an excellent letter writer and his voluminous correspondence should be looked at for the light it sheds on his close collaboration and association with Coleridge.

STODDARD, SIR JOHN (1773–1856) Stoddard was Hazlitt's brother-in-law. He reviewed the second edition of *Lyrical Ballads* favourably in the *British Critic* for February 1801 under the impression that Coleridge was the sole author. It was he, reported to have a 'wicked memory', who recited *Christabel* to Scott in 1800. In 1803 he was appointed Advocate in the Admiralty Court at Malta and invited Coleridge to come and stay there with him. He later became a leader-writer on *The Times*, but founded his own newspaper, *The New Times* after a disagreement in 1817. He was later knighted. On his qualities as a critic, Coleridge made the following comment in a notebook entry of 1806, shortly after his return from Malta. 'Stoddard passes over a poem as one of those tiniest of night-flies runs over a leaf, casting its shadow, three times as long as itself yet only just shading one or at most two letters at a time. Minute Criticism.'

STUART, DANIEL (1766–1846) Born in Edinburgh, Stuart early joined his brothers' printing firm in London. Between them in 1795 they bought the *Morning Post* after having been its printers for a number of years. Stuart used the paper to promote the policy of parliamentary reform, but was at the same time anti-Jacobin. In 1799 he engaged both Coleridge and Southey to write for him regularly at a fee of one guinea a week, and took lodgings in King Street, Covent Garden for Coleridge. In 1800 he offered Coleridge a half-share in both the *Morning Post* and the *Courier* which he had acquired in 1796. The offer was refused, but Coleridge continued the association. He stayed in the *Courier* office in 1807 according to De Quincey, and Stuart certainly helped pay for the publication of *The Friend*. Wordsworth and Lamb also contributed to the *Morning Post* until Stuart sold it in 1803 for £25,000. Afterwards he expanded the *Courier* to two or three daily editions. He wrote a memoir of Coleridge for the *Gentleman's Magazine* and his *Letters from the Lake Poets to Daniel Stuart* were edited by E. H. Coleridge, and printed privately in 1889.

THELWALL, JOHN (1764–1834) Very independent-minded from an early age, Thelwall rejected the Church and the Law as possible careers and, in the early 1790s, made a name for himself as a radical speaker and writer. He became a prominent member of the Corresponding Society and was sent to the Tower of London on a charge of treason in May 1794 along with Horne Tooke (1736–1812) and Thomas Hardy (1752–1832) who were also important members of the Society. Defended brilliantly by the advocate Thomas Erskine (to whom Coleridge addressed one of his *Sonnets on Eminent Personages*) they were acquitted. Following the passage through Parliament of Pitt's Bills against sedition in 1795 he left London and, after thinking of joining Coleridge in Somerset, settled down for a few years in Wales as a farmer. Back in London in the early years of the new century he was in close touch with Coleridge and Charles Lamb and established an institution for the cure of stammering from which he himself had been a sufferer. He returned to editing a journal called *The Champion*, champion, that is, of parliamentary reform. A portrait of him, which is attributed to William Hazlitt, hangs in the National Portrait Gallery in London.

WEDGWOOD, THOMAS (1771–1805) and his brother JOSIAH the younger (1776–1843) were the sons of the great manufacturing potter who wanted to use their inherited wealth to support the arts of learning. Just as Coleridge was considering becoming a dissenting minister early in 1798 they offered him an annuity of £150 a year to be free instead to write. A third brother lived about this time at Westbury near Bristol, and it was probably while on a visit there that Thomas made Coleridge's acquaintance. The brothers paid the expenses of Coleridge's first German tour of 1798–99 and in November 1802 Thomas and Coleridge toured North Wales together. This was probably the origin of Coleridge's plan to go abroad, as Thomas Wedgwood was also in continuous bad health (for which he had recourse to opium and may have become an addict) and suggested they go together. Although he died young, Thomas Wedgwood had already made his mark as a scientist. At the age of twenty he read papers on the subject of the perception of distances to the Royal Society and is remembered as the first experimenter in photography. In 1811 Josiah Wedgwood withdrew his half of the legacy, disappointed that Coleridge had never fulfilled his early promise.

WORDSWORTH, CHRISTOPHER (1774–1846) Wordsworth's younger brother was a contemporary of Coleridge's at Cambridge where he was an undergraduate at Trinity College. While there he kept a diary which records several meetings with Coleridge and discussions of poetry during the Michaelmas Term of 1794. After a distinguished career in the Church he became Master of his old college.

WORDSWORTH, DOROTHY (1771–1855) Dorothy must be remembered not only as Wordsworth's sister and early companion, but in her own right as author of the *Journals* which she kept in Somerset, in Germany and at Grasmere. She also wrote *Recollections* of their tours to Scotland together, primarily for the entertainment of family and friends. Her writing is an invaluable and moving introduction to the world of Wordsworth and Coleridge, and provides rich source material for a study of her brother's poetry. She became seriously ill in 1829 from which date she began to deteriorate mentally until her death. She is addressed by both poets in a number of poems.

WORDSWORTH, WILLIAM (1770–1850) Coleridge never ceased to celebrate the poetry of his close friend and collaborator. Born in Cockermouth, Cumberland, son of a land-agent, he was educated at Hawkshead Grammar School and St John's College, Cambridge. After experiencing the French Revolution at first hand, he was cut off by the war between England and France from contact with Annette Vallon, the French girl who bore him a daughter. Disillusioned by the progress of the Revolution and the betrayal of its early ideals he retired to the country and dedicated himself to poetry. Coleridge read, and quoted from in a poem of his own, *Descriptive Sketches*, when the volume first appeared in 1794. The poets probably met in Bristol in the following year; a meeting which led to the writing in Somerset of *Lyrical Ballads*. After their visit to Germany together, Wordsworth settled finally in the Lake District, the very names of which have ever since been inseparably linked to his. The collaboration is most powerfully celebrated in the *Prelude*, an epic poem in thirteen books relating the growth of his poetic powers. It was published only after his death.

Coleridge's poetic tribute to the poem is *To William Wordsworth, composed on the night of his recitation of a poem on the growth of an individual mind* of 1806.

> . . . that prophetic Lay
> Wherein (high theme by thee first sung aright)
> Of the foundations and the building up
> Of a Human Spirit thou hast dared to tell
> What may be told, to the understanding mind
> Revealable; and what within the mind
> By vital breathings secret as the soul
> Of vernal growth, oft quickens in the heart
> Thoughts all too deep for words!—

Wordsworth's recollection of Coleridge as he was in 1798 appears in his *Stanzas written in imitation of the Castle of Indolence* (by James Thomson).

> With him there often walked in friendly guise,
> Or lay upon the moss by brook or tree,
> A noticeable Man with large grey eyes,

And a pale face that seemed undoubtedly
As if a blooming face it might to be;
Heavy his low-hung lip did oft appear,
Deprest by weight of nursing Phantasy;
Profound his forehead was, though not severe;
Yet some did think that he had little
business here:

Although Wordsworth wrote no formal epitaph to Coleridge, in the year after Coleridge's death he wrote the following lines in an *Extempore Effusion upon the death of James Hogg:*

Nor has the rolling year twice measured,
From sign to sign, its stedfast course,
Since every mortal power of Coleridge
Was frozen at its marvellous source;

The rapt One, of the godlike forehead,
The heaven-eyed creature sleeps in earth:
And Lamb, the frolic and the gentle,
Has vanished from his lonely hearth.

Like clouds that rake the mountain-summit,
Or waves that own no curbing hand,
How fast has brother followed brother,
From sunshine to the sunless land!

In 1843, on the death of Robert Southey, Wordsworth accepted the Laureateship. His last years he passed peacefully as the sage of Rydal.

A Coleridge Gazetteer

NOTE.   I have chosen to treat this account in historical sequence, as a way of supplementing the information outlined in the Biographical Sketch to which this is complementary.

Devonshire

Ottery St Mary lies on the River Otter in South Devon. Coleridge was born in the school house which was pulled down in 1844. His father came from South Molton as the schoolmaster and in 1760, became vicar of the collegiate church of St Mary, founded in 1337. It is a splendid medieval building with a fine fan-vaulted arch built about 1520. The Coleridge family still live there in the Chanter's House, much enlarged in the nineteenth century, which stands in a park at the north-east corner of the churchyard. The school house stood facing the walled walk that flanks the south side of the church, part of the original church college.

There is a small hill overlooking the river two miles to the south of the town called The Pixies' Parlour. It is signposted from the road and is still much visited by local people. It is the scene of an early poem by Coleridge, *Songs of the Pixies*, of 1793.

For later visits to Lynton, on the North Devon coast, see the entry under *Somerset*.

London

Whether he intended to be or not, Coleridge was a metropolitan in a way that Wordsworth chose deliberately not to be. Following his father's death he was sent to Christ's Hospital, of which the original buildings stood in Newgate Street, not far from St Paul's Cathedral. The school was modernized in the 1840s and rebuilt at the beginning of this century at Horsham in Sussex. The original site is now occupied by a Post Office building. The autobiographical letter of 19 February 1798 to Tom Poole describes his recollection of his first year (1781–82) at the school. See contemporary picture on p. 117.

From here Coleridge went swimming in the River Lea with his companions or 'walked the wards' of the London Hospital with his elder brother Luke who was a medical student there. Near the school in Newgate Street was the Angel Inn, frequented by old Christ's Hospital boys. Nearby also stood the Salutation and Cat celebrated in Charles Lamb's essay as the scene of many later encounters with Coleridge. The landlord of the Salutation was so charmed with Coleridge's conversation as the story goes, that he offered him free board and lodging in return for the entertainment that his talk afforded other customers. In his middle years Coleridge lodged for short periods in many parts of London. According to De Quincey's account, Daniel Stuart even had a bed made up in a room of the offices of the *Courier* at one time.

But it is as the 'sage of Highgate' that Coleridge established his firmest connection with London (see p. 22–25 for Carlyle's and J. G. Lockhart's accounts of him there). There is a plaque on the Gillmans'

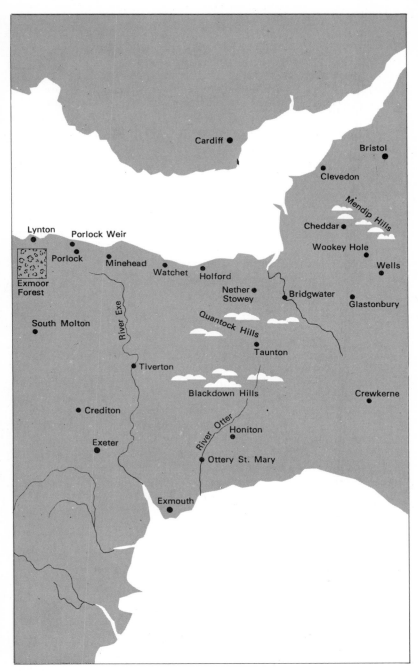

Map of Parts of Devon and Somerset

house in Highgate Grove at the top of Highgate Hill where he had a room at the back overlooking Hampstead Heath. He walked often on the Heath, once at least with Wordsworth in 1820. It was on the Heath that he met Keats (see Sketches from Life, p. 21). He died in the house and was buried in the neighbouring churchyard of Highgate Parish Church. Apart from these vestiges of Coleridge's presence, Highgate today shelters a small private publishing house called The Lime Tree Bower Press which publishes reprints of writings contemporary with Coleridge, Wordsworth and their circle.

Cambridge

Coleridge was an undergraduate at Jesus College from October 1791 to December 1794. The College authorities made a minimal fuss over readmitting him after his escapade in the Army, and even kept his name on the College books for another four months after he finally went down without a degree. His portrait by C. J. Northcote hangs in the College Hall. It was commissioned by Sir George Beaumont in 1804 before Coleridge's departure for Malta, for fear he might not return alive.

Somerset

BRISTOL. From Robert Southey's lodgings in College Street, Coleridge was married to Sara Fricker at the Church of St Mary Redcliffe in Bristol. This same church had been closely connected with Chatterton's family for generations. His father was the sexton there. From Bristol the newly-weds moved to a cottage in Church Street, Clevedon-on-the-sea on the coast a few miles west of Bristol. One of these cottages carries a plaque, although the accuracy of the identification has been questioned on the grounds that the description of it in *The Eolian Harp* and *Reflections on having left a place of retirement* does not tally with the actual cottage. It seems to me rather to be a question of the uses to which description is put in romantic verse and the ends, in the poem, towards which the description is aimed. There is no guaranteed and *direct* cross reference ever possible between a poet's life and his poetry.

NETHER STOWEY. The cottage in Lime Street is now a National Trust Museum. The Inn sign which still hangs outside bearing a portrait of Coleridge, is witness to the fact that the cottage, slightly extended on the north side, became an inn later in the nineteenth century—the 'Coleridge Cottage Inn'. The name argues a certain local popularity beyond the expected audience for imaginative literature. Only the parlour on the righthand side of the narrow entrance passage is open to view, and the disparate collection of items often only tenuously connected with this period of the poet's life does not stir the visitor readily to imagining the great presences that once crowded within its narrow walls and below its ungenerous ceilings. It must have been a very cramped dwelling only relieved (and then for Mrs. Coleridge not often) by the path into Tom Poole's adjoining garden. Poole's house on Castle Street is still a well-proportioned prosperous looking building, even though the south corner of it has long been reshaped as a shop-front. The outbuildings behind still show traces of their use in the processes of tanning. Tom Poole is buried in a family grave in the churchyard. Inside the very simple village church with its Saxon tower is a memorial tablet erected by friends. Near the church is the old dog pound, set into the wall of the neighbouring farm, which at the end of the eighteenth century was kept by the original of Simon Lee, the old huntsman in Wordsworth's poem of that name.

Unfortunately, the new A39 bypass cuts off the church from the rest of the village, but it is still possible to walk over to the village of Holford, to Alfoxton House, without using the main road. Alfoxton stands, facing uphill, in a spacious wooded park and is today a comfortable private hotel.

From Stowey the poets and their friends often walked along the coast from Porlock to Lynton in North Devon. Near Lynton lies the Valley of the Rocks to which all visitors were taken. Here is Hazlitt's account.

> There is a place called the *Valley of the Rocks* (I suppose this was only the poetical name for it) bedded among precipices overhanging the sea, with rocky caverns beneath, into which the waves dash, and where the sea-gull for ever wheels its screaming flight. On the tops of these are huge stones thrown transverse, as if an earthquake had tossed them there, and behind these is a fretwork of perpendicular rocks, something like the Giant's Causeway. A thunder-storm came on while we were at the inn, and Coleridge was running out bare-headed to enjoy the commotion of the elements in the Valley of Rocks, but as if in spite, the clouds only muttered a few angry sounds, and let fall a few refreshing drops. Coleridge told me that he and Wordsworth were to have made this place the scene of a prose-tale, in the manner of, but far superior to the *Death of Abel*, but they had relinquished the design.

About a mile west of Porlock Weir lies Culbone Coombe with its tiny church nestling near the water. According to the preface of *Kubla Khan* it was in a farmhouse up the coombe that Coleridge wrote the poem. Ash Farm does lie up the coombe in a shallow hollow, but there is a local tradition that Coleridge retired, not to Ash Farm, but to the old Culbone Parsonage on the toll road that crosses the top of the coombe. This house has been extensively and elegantly modernized by its present owners but is still today almost as isolated as the farm a little way below it. A number of local landmarks and houses can still be identified from Dorothy Wordsworth's *Alfoxden Journal*.

Another long excursion that the friends made from Stowey was to the Cheddar Gorge and Wookey Hole, a vast limestone cave at the foot of the Mendip Hills. It has sometimes been suggested that this well-known sightseeing spot is the original of 'that deep romantic chasm' of *Kubla Khan*. (The illustration by Michael 'Angelo' Rooker is reproduced on p. 135).

Germany

Wordsworth, his sister and Coleridge, accompanied by young John Chester of Nether Stowey sailed from Yarmouth to Hamburg on 18 September 1798. The journey is recorded in a letter to his wife and in the notebook Coleridge took with him. *Satyranes Letters*, interpolated in *Biographia Literaria*, recall their stay in Hamburg and meetings with F. G. Klopstock, the 'father of German poetry'. After Hamburg the Wordsworths settled at Goslar for what turned out to be the coldest winter of the century, while Coleridge went a little further south to the university town of Göttingen. At this time there were no university buildings proper and the professors taught in their own homes. In May of the following year Coleridge interrupted his successful studies in German language, literature and thought to make a walking tour through the Harz mountains with some German and English acquaintances. The climax was a climb up the Brocken famous for its phenomenon of the giant Spectre. The Spectre of the Brocken, which is an effect of the sun throwing the spectator's vastly enlarged shadow on to the clouds ahead of him, provided Coleridge with a rich metaphor for the workings of the human mind. It came back to him when he wrote the poem *Constancy to an ideal object*. The poem has been tentatively dated 1825 but my feeling is that it was composed much earlier. In the final lines he questions the ideal.

> And art thou nothing? Such thou art, as when
> The woodman winding westward up the glen
> At Wintry dawn, where o'er the sheep track's maze
> The viewless snow-mist weaves a glist'ning haze,
> Sees full before him, gliding without tread,
> An image with a glory round its head;
> The enamoured rustic worships its fair hues,
> Nor knows he makes the shadow, he pursues!

A full report of the tour is made in a long letter to Tom Poole.

Coleridge was in Germany in the summer of 1828, again with Wordsworth. Their companion this time was Wordsworth's daughter

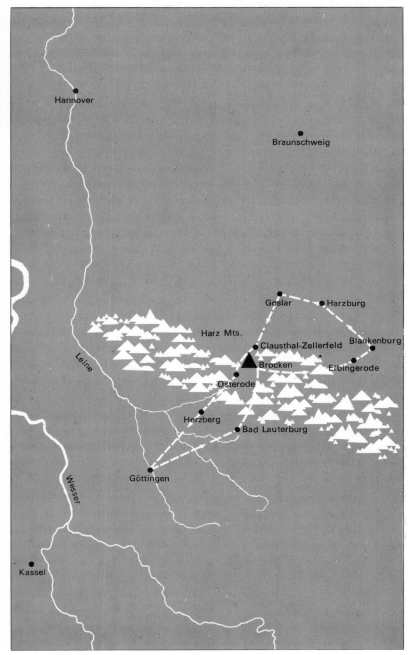

Map of the Harz District of Germany, showing Coleridge's walking tour of 1799

Dora who wrote a lively account of the journey through Belgium, down the Meuse by boat, up the Rhine for a fortnight and then back to England by way of Holland. In her journal (which is preserved in manuscript at Dove Cottage) Dora wrote: 'They get on famously, but Mr C. sometimes detains us with his fiddle-faddling, and he likes prosing to the folks better than exerting himself to see the face of the country and Father with his few half-dozen words of German makes himself much better understood than Mr C. with all his weight of German literature.' Wordsworth reported the tour in a letter to Sir Walter Scott noting that 'the countries were not new to me, but were revisited with great interest in such pleasant company. You would have enjoyed floating down the Meuse and the Rhine with us.'

The Lake District

On his return from Germany in 1799 Coleridge first looked to settle permanently in Somerset near Tom Poole before he went North to join Wordsworth, who had already fixed on Grasmere as his home for the foreseeable future. In the summer of 1800 Coleridge took a lease on half of Greta Hall, Keswick, thirteen miles to the north, for his growing family. The house stands high up above the river Derwent (it now belongs to Keswick School) 'with such a prospect, that if, according to you (Coleridge is addressing William Godwin) & Hume, impressions & ideas *constitute* our Being, I shall have a tendency to become a God—so sublime & beautiful will be the series of my visual existence' (see Sir George Beaumont's sketch on p. 173). In the autumn there was an 'unwelcome addition' to the small circle, as Dorothy expressed it. Charles Lloyd, now with a wife and child, took a house at Brathay, near Ambleside.

Most of the last months of 1800 were spent in preparing the second edition of *Lyrical Ballads* for the press and it is not until 1802 that Coleridge begins to write in detail of his experience of the Lake District. His notebooks for the period from May to August of that year are full of details of walks and climbs he made, alone or in company with Wordsworth or other friends. The descriptions are often accompanied by rough maps or outline sketches of the area, and he is at pains to collect from local people and shepherds the names of individual features of the landscape. Some idea of what these walks meant to him can be gathered from the long journal-letter he wrote to Sara Hutchinson in August; the one dated 6 August describes the gamble he took on getting down Sca Fell with only a walking stick to help him.

My limbs were all in a tremble—I lay upon my Back to rest myself, & was beginning according to my Custom to laugh at myself for a Madman, when the sight of the Crags above me on each side, & the impetuous Clouds just over them, posting so

Late eighteenth-century German etching of the Brocken

St John's Valley, Keswick *by Francis Towne*

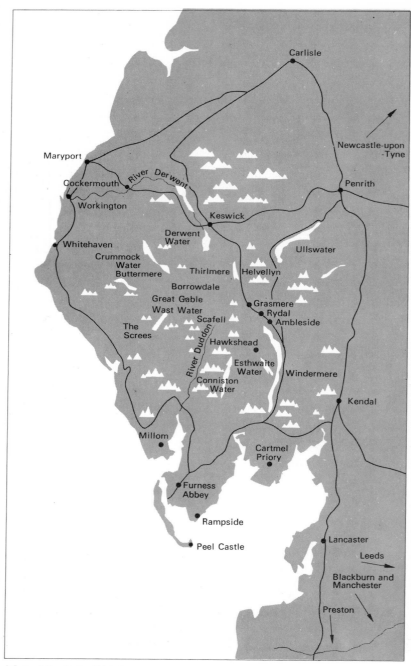

Map of the Lake District

Pencil sketches by Sir George Beaumont of Keswick and Greta Hall 1816

luridly & so rapidly northward, overawed me. I lay in a state of almost prophetic Trance & Delight—& blessed God aloud, for the powers of Reason & the Will, which remaining no Danger can overpower us! O God, I exclaimed aloud—how calm, how blessed am I now. I know not how to proceed, how to return, but I am calm & fearless & confident. If this Reality were a Dream, if I were asleep, What agonies had I suffered.

In the poem that grew out of this experience, Coleridge transferred the scene to a more sublime spot, the Vale of Chamonix below Mont Blanc in the French High Alps. *Hymn before Sunrise* is also, in part, an expansion of an original German poem addressed by a lady to F. G. Klopstock. In the original long note to the poem Coleridge exclaims, 'Who would be, who could be an Atheist in this valley of wonders!'

Robert Southey and his family joined the Coleridges at Greta Hall in 1803, but in continuous ill-health and increasingly estranged from his own wife, Coleridge separated from his family and the Lake District early in 1804. He did not return until September 1809, when he stayed with the Wordsworths in their new house, Allan Bank. His family visited him regularly on Sundays, and from here, with Sara Hutchinson's help, he undertook the editing of *The Friend*. Twelve months later he accompanied Wordsworth's friend Basil Montagu and his wife to their London house where Montagu's report of Wordsworth's opinion of Coleridge led to the break between the two poets. Coleridge thereafter paid only rare, brief visits.

Scotland

On 25 August 1803 Coleridge's wife wrote to Southey. 'Last Monday (15 August) my husband, W. Wordsworth, and D. W. set off for Scotland in an Irish-car and one horse—W. is to drive all the way, for poor Samuel is too weak to undertake the fatigue of driving—he was very unwell when he went off, and, was to return in the *Mail* if he grew worse.' She makes only a small complaint of him. 'My husband is a good man—his prejudices—and his prepossessions sometimes give me pain, but we have all a somewhat to encounter in this life—I should be a very, very happy Woman if it were not for a few things—and my husband's ill-health stands at the head of these evils.'

Wordsworth's son John had just been born; Daniel Stuart had loaned money for the trip which was to be justified as a tonic. Dorothy wrote a journal of the tour, not so much for herself as for friends. The three companions got as far north together as Tarbet, by way of Glasgow and Loch Lomond. After visiting Loch Katrine and the Trossachs, Coleridge decided he was too ill to stay in the cart and, after dividing the money, he took six guineas and went off on foot on 29 August. From Arrochar he walked to Glen Coe and Fort William,

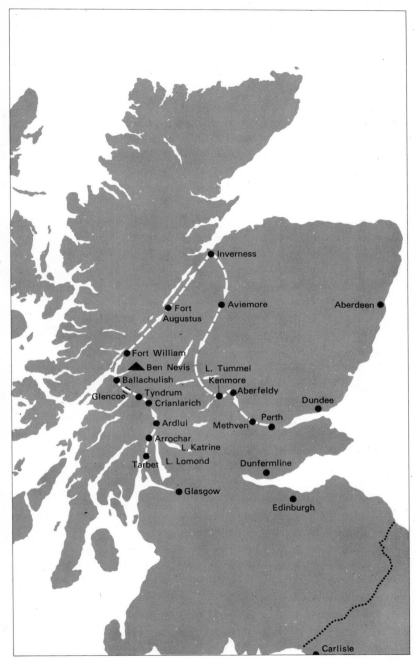

Coleridge's Scottish walk of 1803

where he suffered a severe attack of what he took to be a kind of gout. He then made his way to Fort Augustus where he was arrested as a spy. After breakfasting with the Governor the following morning, and unable to buy a new pair of shoes, he walked the length of Loch Ness to Inverness, and then turned south, walking from Inverness to Aviemore in a day. Continuing south he noted the bank of the River Tummel on his way to Kenmore which lies at the head of Loch Tay. From there via Aberfeldy and Amalree to Glen Almond where he cut across country to Methven and Perth. He writes in a letter to Southey that it was at Perth that he composed *The Pains of Sleep*. What appears to have kept him going during this astonishing endurance test was a steady intake of camphor and ether. At Perth he took the coach to Edinburgh. He reckoned that, despite bouts of vomiting and dizziness, he covered 263 miles on foot in eight days and he was still sufficiently alive to react with his imaginative energy unimpaired to his first sight of Edinburgh. 'What a wonderful City Edinburgh is!' he wrote to Southey from there on 13 September.

—What alternation of Height & Depth!—a city looked at in the polish'd back of a Brobdingnag Spoon, held lengthways—so enormously stretched-up are the Houses!—when I first looked down on it, as the Coach drove in on the higher Street, I cannot express what I felt—such a section of a wasp's nest, striking you with a sort of bastard Sublimity from the enormity & infinity of its littleness— the infinity swelling out of the mind, the enormity striking it with wonder.

He arrived home at Greta Hall having taken the Carlisle coach to find the Southeys there mourning the death of their only daughter.

The Mediterranean

Persuaded that what his health required was a warm climate after the cold and damp of the Lakes which aggravated his rheumatic condition, Coleridge thought for a long time of going to Madeira, perhaps with Tom Wedgwood. It was the Wedgwoods' brother-in-law Mackintosh who suggested Malta for which Coleridge finally sailed in the *Speedwell* from Portsmouth on 9 April 1804. The ship lay in Gibraltar harbour for a week where Coleridge climbed the Rock to see the apes. He finally arrived at Valetta, the capital of the island, on 18 May. His host there was Hazlitt's brother-in-law, John Stoddard. By 5 July he was already working for the Governor of the island, Sir Alexander Ball, as a secretary. To his wife he wrote: 'Sir A. Ball is a very extraordinary man—indeed a great man. And he is really the abstract Idea of a wise & good Governor.' After the death of the eighty-year-old encumbent he became Ball's Public Secretary in January 1805 until the September of that year. From August to early November he paid

a visit to Sicily, where he climbed Mount Etna and stayed at Taormina.

Coleridge's health, however, did not improve and he felt himself confined by the amount of official business he was employed in, and he came to describe Malta as 'a barren Rock'. His mood of this time was also one of despair that he would ever again be able to rouse himself hopefully to any scheme of work or appearance of natural beauty.

The two main features of Coleridge's journey through Italy until his arrival back in London in August 1806 are the descent of Napoleon's armies on Rome and his meeting there with Washington Allston. The capture of Rome put him in fear for both his safety and his eventual return to England. However, he was able to stay with Allston in his house at Olevano, thirty miles east and a little south of Rome, of which he gives the following luxuriating description in his notebook.

To conceive an idea of Olevano you must first imagine a round basin formed by a circle of mountains, the diameter of the Valley about 15 or 16 miles. These mountains all connected and one; but of very various heights, and the lines in which they sink and rise of various Sweep and Form, sometimes so high as to have no visible superior behind, sometimes letting in upon the Plain one Step above them from behind, sometimes two, and three; and in one place behind a third a bald bright Skull of a mountain (for the Snow that wholly covered it lay so smooth & shone so bright in the Sun, that the whole suggested the idea of a polished Skull, and the Snow seeming rather a property or attribute than an accident or adjunct rendered the baldness more intense rather than diminished it.)

The other higher mountains that looked in from behind on the basin with more or less command were lit up with snow-relicts, scarcely distinguishable from Sunshine on bare and moist rock opposed to deep Shade, save when (as often happened) both the one and the other were seen at the same time, when they formed one of the gentlest diversities possible, and yet the distinction evident and almost obvious—How exquisitely *picturesque* this effect is (in the strictest sense of the word) Mr Allston has proved in his Swiss Landscape, of which it is not to much to say—quam qui non amat, illum omnes et Musae et Veneres odere.—The Vale itself is diversified with a multitude of Rises, from Hillocks to Hills, and the Eastern Side of the (circular) mountain Boundary vaults down into the vale in Leaps, forming Steps.—(The first) Hills sink to rise into a higher Hill that sinks to rise into a yet higher and the mountain boundary itself is the fifth Step.—On the third Step, which is broad and heaves in many Hillocks, some bare & like Cairns, some green, stands Olevano, its old ruinous Castle with church-like Tower cresting the height of this third Step. The town runs—down the Ridge in one narrow Line almost like a Torrent of Houses; and where the last House ends, more than half of the whole ridge, a narrow back of

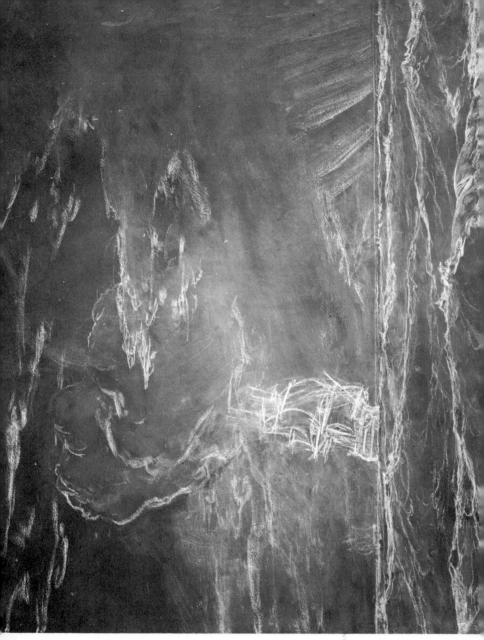

Ship in a Squall *by Washington Allston*

bare jagged grey rock commences, looking like the ruins of a Town. A green field finishes the ridge, which passes into the vale by a Copse of young Oaks. On different heights, on other Steps or other Hills, the towns of Civitella, Pagliano, Avita, Santo Spirito stick like Eagle-nests, or seem as if the rock had chrystallized into those forms. But how shall I describe the beauty of the roads, winding up the different Hills, now lost & now re-appearing in different arcs & segments of Circles—how call up before you those different masses of Smoke over the vale—I count 10 from this one point of view (for they are burning weeds) in different distances, now faint now vivid, now in shade & now their exquisite blue glittering in Sunshine. Our House stands by itself, about a quarter of a mile from the Town and its steep Ridge, on a level Ridge a little lower than it.—This description I have written, standing or sitting on the breast of the fourth Step, or that height which immediately commands Olevano. —But from our House we look down into the Vale of Valleys—for so it may well be called, for the whole Vale heaves and swells like a Plate of cut and knobby Glass, or a Spread of wood knotty and at the same time blistered; for the higher & larger Ranges of Hills include as in a plain a multitude of smaller elevations, swells, and ridges, which from a great Height appear as one expanse—even as a stormy Sea might appear from a Balloon; but lower down you see the Land-billows—&, when in the Vale, you are in a Labyrinth of sweet Walks, glens, green Lanes, with Hillsides for Hedges—some of the Hills & Hillocks wooded, some bare & pastured, several with white Cottages on their sides or summits, & one & sometimes two or three pines by the Cottage Garden Gate.

With Allston Coleridge undertook an exploration of pictorial aesthetics and in his notebook of the journey recorded analyses of paintings by Allston and the art of Rome. It is very likely that much of the material covering these journeys and visits has been lost, as there remains uncharacteristically scanty evidence from surviving letters and notes of his activities and reflections at this interesting moment in his life.

After visiting Florence and Pisa Coleridge sailed for England from Leghorn on 23 June, anxious for his trunks of papers left behind with an acquaintance at Naples. He had also left papers at Malta: most of this material has never come to light again. It is difficult, therefore, to judge the effect of Coleridge's Mediterranean stay on his later development, other than that it greatly improved his knowledge of French and Italian. On his health and mood of isolation and dejection there seems to have been no effect at all.

Coleridge's influence: readers and critics, 1834 to the present day

> The time is yet far distant when, in the estimation of Coleridge, and of his influence upon the intellect of our time, anything like unanimity can be looked for . . . As a philosopher, the class of thinkers has scarcely yet arisen by whom he is to be judged.
>
> J. S. MILL, Coleridge (1840)

Readers will find recorded almost everywhere else in this book those aspects of Coleridge's character and work which captured the attention, admiring or critical, of his friends and contemporaries. In the section on Coleridge's friends occur the necessary references to their written works relevant to our subject. What I am concerned with under this heading is to signal the fate of Coleridge's position and reputation after his death. The task obliges me to face a number of contradictions. These are not only the obvious ones that existed in his character or in the particular characteristics in his life and work that later writers have chosen to emphasize. Rather the contradictions I mean are those that confront one whenever one tries to reconstruct the history of a reputation. Such history, perhaps all histroy, is continually being rewritten by its historians. There is very little agreement about what Coleridge was or what his work, taken as a whole (so far as this has been possible), might mean.

Although I have not dealt with the later religious philosophy, it has been part of my thesis in this book that Coleridge the poet, critic, literary thinker and philosopher, hang together in a way that can be made comprehensible, even when the task is not an easy one. For later writers in the nineteenth century this was certainly not so. After its limited reception by the reviewers, Coleridge's poetry, or his major poems at least, have been continuously admired by poets and literary critics. *Kubla Khan* and *Christabel* were published at the insistence of Lord Byron and the metre of *Christabel* led to Sir Walter Scott's *Lay of the Last Minstrel*. Through the writings of Hazlitt, Swinburne and Pater, the poetic reputation was secured, even though in the twentieth century there has been considerable disagreement about what it all means.

On the other hand, his position as a thinker has been treated much less certainly. Undoubtedly his immediate major influence was as a philosopher of religion. The subject falls outside my present scope, but his importance to men of the next generation, such as Dr Thomas Arnold of Rugby School, or F. D. Maurice cannot be overstated. Maurice, who became Professor of Literature and History in King's

College, London, and later Professor of Moral Philosophy at Cambridge, dedicated his most important popular work *The Kingdom of Christ* (1838) to Derwent Coleridge. In the dedication he writes not only of Coleridge the philosopher but also of the literary critic of *Biographia Literaria* as a guide to any young man who wants, not a system of the 'laws' of art, but an articulation of the vital connection between life and books.

Coleridge also stands behind the most considerable literary critic of the Romantic Age in England, William Hazlitt. Hazlitt wrote at length on Wordsworth and Coleridge, whose impression on him while he was yet still a boy, is recorded in *My First Acquaintance with Poets* (see Sketches from Life on p. 16 for an account of their first meeting). Later in the essay Hazlitt wrote: 'My soul has indeed remained . . . dark, obscure, with longings infinite and unsatisfied; my heart, shut up in the prison-house of this rude clay, has never found, nor will it ever find, a heart to speak to: but that my understanding also did not remain dumb and brutish, or at length found a language to express itself, I owe to Coleridge.'

By the time Hazlitt came to write his essay on Coleridge in *The Spirit of the Age* (1825), they had quarrelled, and Hazlitt propounds the view of Coleridge's fascination and failure, a betrayer of the spirit of liberty and a defender of legitimacy. The essay is, nonetheless, a witty and spirited performance, very characteristic of Hazlitt's ironic intelligence. It is through Hazlitt that Coleridge's influence is transmitted to John Keats. Although he wrote in a letter to his brother of December 1817, 'Coleridge, for instance would let go by a fine isolated verisimilitude caught from the Penetralium of mystery, from being incapable of remaining Content with half knowledge', the principle of *Negative Capability* announced in the letter ('that is when man is capable of being in uncertainties, Mysteries, doubts, without any irritable reaching after fact and reason') must remind us of that willing suspension of disbelief that constitutes poetic faith. Furthermore, like Shelley equally, Keats continuously employs the term 'imagination' with a full Coleridgean power.

The contradictions we face become clearer with the voices of the next generation. If two figures dominate the discussion of political philosophy in the early Victorian period, then they are those of Thomas Carlyle and John Stuart Mill. Carlyle's attack on Coleridge in his *Life of John Sterling* also betrays a fascination with his subject. But that Carlyle did not always reject Coleridge's teaching is made very clear in his 1829 essay *Signs of the Times* in which he makes a very bold distinction between the various forces at work in modern society.

Nay, our whole Metaphysics itself, from Locke's time downwards, has been physical; not a spiritual philosophy, but a material one. The singular estimation in which his *Essay* was so long held as a scientific work (an estimation grounded, indeed, on the estimable character of the man) will one day be thought a curious indication of the spirit of these times. His whole doctrine is mechanical, in its aim and origin, in its method and results. It is not a philosophy of the mind: it is a mere discussion concerning the origin of our consciousness, or ideas, or whatever else they are called; a genetic history of what we see *in* the mind. The grand secrets of Necessity and Freewill, of the Mind's vital or non-vital dependence on Matter, of our mysterious relations to Time and Space, to God, to the Universe, are not, in the faintest degree, touched on in these enquiries; and seem not to have the smallest connection with them.

He describes concisely Coleridge's major concerns and, in a passage which follows a little later, seems to draw heavily on a close and evaluative reading of Coleridge's metaphysics.

To speak a little pedantically, there is a science of *Dynamics* in man's fortunes and nature, as well as of *Mechanics*. There is a science which treats of, and practically addresses, the primary, unmodified forces and energies of man, the mysterious springs of Love, and Fear, and Wonder, of Enthusiasm, Poetry, Religion, all which have a truly vital and *infinite* character; as well as a science which practically addresses the finite, modified developments of these, when they take the shape of immediate 'motives,' as hope of reward, or as fear of punishment.

Now it is certain, that in former times the wise men, the en-lightened lovers of their kind, who appeared generally as Moralists, Poets or Priests, did, without neglecting the Mechanical province, deal chiefly with the Dynamical; applying themselves chiefly to regulate, increase and purify the inward primary powers of man; and fancying that herein lay the main difficulty, and the best service they could undertake. But a wide difference is manifest in our age. For the wise men, who now appear as Political Philosophers, deal exclusively with the Mechanical province; and occupying them-selves in counting-up and estimating men's motives, strive by curious checking and balancing, and other adjustments of Profit and Loss, to guide them to their true advantage: while, unfortu-nately, those same 'motives' are so innumerable, and so variable in every individual, that no really useful conclusion can ever be drawn from their enumeration. But though Mechanism, wisely contrived, has done much for man in a social and moral point of view, we cannot be persuaded that it has ever been the chief source of his worth or happiness. Consider the great elements of human enjoy-ment, the attainments and possessions that exalt man's life to its present height, and see what part of these he owes to institutions, to Mechanism of any kind; and what to the instinctive, unbounded force, which Nature herself lent him, and still continues to him.

Shall we say, for example, that Science and Art are indebted principally to the founders of Schools and Universities? Did not Science originate rather, and gain advancement, in the obscure closets of the Roger Bacons, Keplers, Newtons; in the workshops of the Fausts and the Watts; wherever, and in what guise soever Nature, from the first times downwards, had sent a gifted spirit upon the earth? Again, were Homer and Shakespeare members of any beneficed guild, or made Poets by means of it? Were Painting and Sculpture created by forethought, brought into the world by institutions for that end? No; Science and Art have, from first to last, been the free gift of Nature; an unsolicited, unexpected gift; often even a fatal one. These things rose up, as it were, by spontaneous growth, in the free soil and sunshine of Nature. They were not planted or grafted, nor even greatly multiplied or improved by the culture or manuring of institutions. Generally speaking, they have derived only partial help from these; often enough have suffered damage. They made constitutions for themselves. They originated in the Dynamical nature of man, not in his Mechanical nature.

It seems to me that in the confident declamatory tone of Carlyle there is a sharpening and concentration of Coleridge's views. The centre of Carlyle's complaint is that Coleridge was not more *effective*, but a consequence of the sharpening that has been achieved in the passage of ideas between the two men, there has also been a loss. Carlyle's writing is shriller, narrower and coarser than that of Coleridge in, say, *The Friend* when he is writing on similar themes. The ground of Carlyle's complaint against Coleridge is that he seduced into all kinds of mystical vagaries younger, sensitive and intelligent thinkers like Sterling. But the contrary view is expressed by Julius Charles Hare who edited Sterling's works after his death. In his edition of *Sterling's Essays and Tales* (1848) he wrote that, after the publication of *Aids to Reflection*: 'It was beginning to be acknowledged by more than a few that Coleridge is the true sovereign of modern English thought.... Few felt this obligation more than Sterling. "To Coleridge (he wrote to me in 1836) I owe *education*. He taught me to believe that an empirical philosophy is none, that Faith is the highest Reason." '

In complete contrast is the tone of John Stuart Mill's memorial essay on Coleridge, which appeared in *The Westminster Review* in 1840, the journal founded in 1824 by Jeremy Bentham, with the help of Mill's father, as the organ of philosophical radicalism. Mill's is altogether a more serious attempt than the later Carlyle's to come at Coleridge's position in political philosophy. But his strategy is clear: in epistemology he is a convinced Lockeian and he attempts to reconcile the views of Coleridge to the exposition of the opposite or utilitarian view in a dialectic of progress. What he aims at is a balancing of idealism and materialism that Coleridge himself would have rejected. Nevertheless, his essay is still a memorably readable contribution to Coleridge studies.

This is more than can be said for Walter Pater's essay, *Coleridge's Writings*, which appeared first as a review of Thomas Allsop's *Conversations, Letters and Recollections of S. T. Coleridge* in 1864. The essay was revised with additions for the volume of *Appreciations* of 1889. For Pater, Coleridge's failure was to seek for an outmoded religious truth at a time when religious truth had already succumbed to the combined spirit of criticism and scientific relativism. After the splendid promise and poetry of his early years, he broke himself on this restless search instead of being content with the appreciation of 'culture'. By culture Pater means the cultivation of precious states of mind for their own sake: what religion contributes to these is nothing more than a subtle sacred perfume. Coleridge, that is, failed to be Pater.

Pater's essay marks the beginning of the emergence of modern literary studies in the Universities. Since the end of the nineteenth century the continuous reappraisal of Coleridge has been a professional enquiry, based on ever more exacting scholarly requirements. Professor George Saintsbury's essay of 1895 accepts the nineteenth-century biographical view of Coleridge the 'damaged archangel', the poet ruined by metaphysics, whereas the informing spirit of twentieth-century academic approaches, however much they may disagree amongst themselves, has been rather a wonder that he managed to do as much as he did than regret that he did not do more. The change can be accounted for in part by the increasing amount of Coleridge material that has become available to the twentieth-century scholar. It is also the case, however, that, under the influence of Freud's theories of psychoanalysis, our view of what it means to be a human being has changed, and in a direction more sympathetic to Coleridge.

A nineteenth-century biography designed with love and sympathy for its subject is that of J. Dykes Campbell, *Samuel Taylor Coleridge: A Narrative of the events of his life*, 1895. It is still a standard work of Coleridge reference. The major twentieth-century biography is that of E. K. Chambers which grew out of the occasion of the centenary of Coleridge's death. Finally published in 1938, it is an encyclopaedic work flawed, perhaps, by the author's inability sufficiently to sympathize with the mazy motions of his subject's character.

Two further fictionalized portraits of Coleridge, other than Charles Lloyd's *Edmund Oliver*, should also be noted here. Thomas Love Peacock wrote a number of satirical novels in the early years of the nineteenth century. *Nightmare Abbey*, first published in 1818, is a satirical portrait of his close friend Shelley, but it also contains a philosopher figure, Mr Flosky (the name is a corruption of the Greek for 'lover of shadows') who is described as:

a very lachrymose and morbid gentleman, of some note in the literary world, but in his own estimation of much more merit than name. The part of his character which recommended him to Mr Glowry, was his very fine sense of the grim and the tearful. No one could relate a dismal story with so many minutiae of supererogatory wretchedness. No one could call up a *rawhead and bloody bones* with so many adjuncts and circumstances of ghastliness. Mystery was his mental element. He lived in the midst of that visionary world in which nothing is but what is not. He dreamed with his eyes open, and saw ghosts dancing round him at noontide. He had been in his youth an enthusiast for liberty, and had hailed the dawn of the French Revolution as the promise of a day that was to banish war and slavery, and every form of vice and misery, from the face of the earth. Because all this was not done, he deduced that nothing was done; and from this deduction, according to his system of logic, he drew a conclusion that worse than nothing was done; that the overthrow of the feudal fortresses of tyranny and superstition was the greatest calamity that had ever befallen mankind; and that their only hope now was to rake the rubbish together, and rebuild it without any of those loopholes by which the light had originally crept in. To qualify himself for a coadjutor in this laudable task, he plunged into the central opacity of Kantian metaphysics, and lay *perdu* several years in transcendental darkness, till the common daylight of common sense became intolerable to his eyes. He called the sun an *ignis fatuus*; and exhorted all who would listen to his friendly voice, which were about as many as called 'God save King Richard,' to shelter themselves, from its delusive radiance in the obscure haunt of Old Philosophy. This word Old had great charms for him. The good old times were always on his lips; meaning the days when polemic theology was in its prime, and rival prelates beat the drum ecclesiastic with Herculean vigour, till the one wound up his series of syllogisms with the very orthodox conclusion of roasting the other.

The travesty is not so extreme as to obliterate the original of the description. It is still recognizably Coleridge in the pose of the sage of Highgate.

At the end of the century, the novelist Henry James, after reading the Dykes Campbell biography, wrote in his notebook that he was struck with:

> the suggestiveness of S.T.C.'s figure—wonderful, admirable figure —for pictorial treatment. What a subject some particular cluster of its relations would make for a little story, a small vivid picture. There was a point, as I read, at which I seemed to see a little story— to have a quick glimpse of the possible drama. Would not such a drama necessarily be the question of the acceptance by someone—

someone with something important at stake—of the general *responsibility* of rising to the height of accepting him for what he is, recognizing his rare, anomalous, magnificent, interesting, curious, tremendously suggestive character, vices and all, with all its imperfections on its head, and *not* being guilty of the pedantry, the stupidity, the want of imagination, of fighting him, deploring him in the details—failing to recognize that one *must* pay for him and that on the whole he is magnificently worth it.

Out of this complex and just evaluation of Coleridge the man, James drew the theme of the story he called *The Coxon Fund*.

In 1875 Gustave Doré published his illustrated version of *The Ancient Mariner*. The most famous illustrator of his age, Doré spent many of his later years in London where he opened a gallery for the sale of his works. He illustrated some of the greatest works of literature including Dante's *Divine Comedy*, Rabelais's *Gargantua and Pantagruel* and Milton's epics. He thought of the *Ancient Mariner* illustrations as being among his best and most original work, although many of them suffer from a too precise attempt to localize the period of the poem in the world of medieval France. There is no doubt, however, that the studies of the voyage itself, the immensity and isolation of the scene, are marvellously realized (see p. 123). The work was most successful in America where it was a universal household possession and helped to bring Coleridge's name to an even wider audience.

In the section 'Further Reading', I have noted some of the most valuable twentieth-century critical studies by means of which the reader can extend his reading of Coleridge, but I must mention finally one twentieth-century academic literary critic whose studies are informed by the Coleridgean spirit of resistance to the mechanization of the human world and human values in our culture and society. The best work of F. R. Leavis on the relations between the study of literature in the university and the culture of our society insist repeatedly on the creative quality of that living relationship which has continuously to be remade and restated in the face of the continuous pressure of easily graspable mechanical explanations of human and cultural life.

Further Reading

Primary Sources

POEMS. The standard edition is still that of E. H. Coleridge *The Complete Poetical Works of Samuel Taylor Coleridge* (Oxford University Press, 1912), vol. 1; vol. 2 contains the drama and drama translations. *Biographia Literaria*, edited with an introduction by J. Shawcross (Oxford University Press, 1907).

CORRESPONDENCE. *Letters of Samuel Taylor Coleridge* in six volumes, edited by Earl Leslie Griggs (Oxford University Press, 1956–1972).

THE NOTEBOOKS. A complete edition in five double volumes of some sixty notebooks dating from 1794 is being edited by Kathleen Coburn for the Bollingen Foundation. The first two double volumes (Text and Notes) appeared in 1957 (published in England by Routledge & Kegan Paul) and 1961 (by the Bollingen Foundation, New York). (*Anima Poetae* is a selection made by E. H. Coleridge in 1895.) The Bollingen Foundation is preparing to publish for the first time the whole of Coleridge's writings, under the general editorship of Professor Coburn. A number of valuable volumes, exhaustively annotated, has already appeared in the series. They include *The Watchman* (edited by Lewis Patton) and *The Friend* (edited by Barbara Rooke).

COLERIDGE'S CRITICISM. There are two collections by T. M. Raysor: *Shakespearean Criticism* (1930) anA *Miscellaneous Criticism* (1936); they were revised in 1960 and are available in Dent's Everyman's Library.

Secondary Sources

Coleridge, edited by Kathleen Coburn in the series *Twentieth Century Views* (Prentice-Hall, 1967). This series of essays by different critics covers a wide range of Coleridge's life and thought. It also contains an extended critical bibliography.

Coleridge by Humphry House (Hart-Davis, 1953). An important unified account of Coleridge's personality, poems, criticism and critical theory.

English Romantic Poets edited by M. H. Abrams (Oxford University Press, 1960). This volume contains some very valuable essays on Coleridge's poetry and on Romantic Poetry in general.

Many books have been written on, or around, *The Ancient Mariner* and *Kubla Khan*. The best known is *The Road to Xanadu*, by J. Livingstone Lowes (Constable, 1927). Others include *Coleridge, Opium and Kubla Khan*, by Elisabeth Schneider (N.Y., Octagon, 1966) which proposes 1799 or even 1800 as the most suitable date of composition for the poem. Readers may like, at the same time, to refer to *Opium and the Romantic Imagination*, by Alethea Hayter (Faber, 1968) and *Coleridge the Visionary*, by John Beer (Chatto, 1959) for its close study of Coleridge's debt to the hermetic and cabalistic traditions of thought.

Coleridge's Thought

The standard work on the philosophy is still *Coleridge as a Philosopher* by J. Muirhead (Allen & Unwin, 1930). On his critical theory and its relation to his philosophy there is *Coleridge on Imagination*, by I. A. Richards (Kegan Paul, 1934), in which 'a materialist looks at an idealist'. A recent valuable addition to this area of enquiry is *Coleridge's Philosophy of Literature 1791–1819*, by J. A. Appleyard (Harvard University Press, 1965). Coleridge's relation to the larger movement in England and Europe of Romantic Aesthetics is dealt with in great detail in *The Mirror and The Lamp* by M. H. Abrams (Oxford University Press, 1953). None of these titles is easy to read, but then the whole area of Coleridge's thought is a particularly difficult one to approach. Its value and relevance, however, are stated very explicitly in *Coleridge: The Work and the Relevance* by William Walsh (Chatto & Windus, 1967). See also Basil Willey, *Samuel Taylor Coleridge* (Chatto, 1972). Coleridge's religious thought is dealt with in *Coleridge to Gore*, by B. M. G. Reardon (Longman, 1971).

Wordsworth and Coleridge

Wordsworth and Coleridge 1795–1834 by H. M. Margoliouth (Oxford University Press, Home University Library, 1953) is a short and excellent account of their long association. A recent book on their poetic collaboration is *Coleridge and Wordsworth: The Poetry of Growth*, by Stephen Prickett (Cambridge University Press, 1969). Volume 1 of Mary Moorman's two-volume *William Wordsworth: a biography* (Oxford University Press, 1957; paperback 1968) also traces their relationship in detail. P. P. Howe's *The Life of William Hazlitt* (1922; Penguin edition 1949), gives in its early chapters a graphic insight into the lives of the whole group, first in Somerset and later at Grasmere, in Hazlitt's own words.

The Intellectual Background

Readers should refer to the chapter on Coleridge in *Nineteenth Century Studies* (chapter 1) by Basil Willey (Chatto & Windus, 1944). The later chapters of *The Eighteenth-Century Background* (Chatto & Windus, 1946) are an important introduction to Hartley, Priestley and Godwin. An extremely useful book on the aesthetic movement from Neo Classicism to Romanticism is *Classic to Romantic: Premises of Taste in the Eighteenth Century*, by W. J. Bate (Harvard University Press, 1946). On eighteenth and early nineteenth century philosophy there is no better modern account than Volume 6 of F. Copleston's *History of Philosophy* (Burns & Oates, 8 vols, 1952–66).

Appendices

A *The original version of 'Dejection: an Ode', addressed to Sara Hutchinson*

A Letter to —

Well! if the Bard was weatherwise, who made
The grand old Ballad of Sir Patrick Spence,
This Night, so tranquil now, will not go hence
Unrous'd by winds, that ply a busier trade
5   Than that, which moulds yon clouds in lazy flakes,
Or the dull sobbing Draft, that drones and rakes
Upon the Strings of this Eolian Lute,
Which better far were mute.
For, lo! the New Moon, winter-bright!
10 And overspread with phantom Light
(With swimming phantom Light o'erspread
But rimmed and circled with a silver Thread)
I see the Old Moon in her Lap, foretelling
The coming-on of Rain and squally Blast—
15 O! Sara! that the gust ev'n now were swelling,
And the slant Night-shower driving loud and fast!

A Grief without a pang, void, dark and drear,
A stifling, drowsy, unimpassion'd Grief
That finds no natural outlet, no Relief
20 In word, or sigh, or tear—
This, Sara! well thou know'st,
Is that sore Evil, which I dread the most,
And oft'nest suffer! In this heartless Mood,
To other thoughts by yonder Throstle woo'd,
25 That pipes within the Larch tree, not unseen,
(The Larch, which pushes out in tassels green
Its bundled Leafits) woo'd to mild Delights
By all the tender Sounds and gentle Sights
Of this sweet Primrose-month—and *vainly* woo'd
30 O dearest Sara! in this heartless Mood
All this long Eve, so balmy and serene,
Have I been gazing on the western Sky
And its peculiar Tint of Yellow Green—
And still I gaze—and with how blank an eye!
35 And those thin Clouds above, in flakes and bars,
That give away their Motion to the Stars;
Those Stars, that glide behind them, or between,
Now sparkling, now bedimm'd, but always seen;
Yon crescent Moon, as fix'd as if it grew
40 In its own cloudless, starless Lake of Blue—

A boat becalm'd! dear William's Sky Canoe!
—I see them all, so excellently fair!
I see, not feel, how beautiful they are.

My genial spirits fail—
45 And what can these avail
To lift the smoth'ring Weight from off my Breast?
It were a vain Endeavour,
Tho' I should gaze for ever
On that Green Light that lingers in the West!
50 I may not hope from outward Forms to win
The Passion and the Life, whose Fountains are within!

These lifeless Shapes, around, below, Above,
    O what can they impart?
When even the gentle Thought, that thou, my Love!
55 Art gazing, now, like me,
And see'st the Heaven, I see—
Sweet Thought it is—yet feebly stirs my Heart!
Feebly! O feebly!—Yet   ·
(I well remember it)
60 In my first Dawn of Youth that Fancy stole
With many secret yearnings on my Soul.
At eve, sky-gazing in 'ecstatic fit'
(Alas! for cloister'd in a city School
The Sky was all, I knew, of Beautiful)
65 At the barr'd window often did I sit,
And oft upon the leaded School-roof lay,
And to myself would say—
There does not live the Man so stripp'd of good affections
As not to love to see a Maiden's quiet Eyes
70 Uprais'd, and linking on sweet Dreams by dim Connections
To Moon, or Evening Star, or glorious western Skies—
While yet a Boy, this Thought would so pursue me,
That often it became a kind of Vision to me!

Sweet Thought! and dear of old
75 To Hearts of finer Mould!
Ten thousand times by Friends and Lovers blest!
I spake with rash Despair,
And ere I was aware,
The Weight was somewhat lifted from my Breast!
80 O Sara! in the weather-fended Wood,
Thy lov'd haunt! where the Stock-doves coo at Noon
I·guess, that thou hast stood
And watch'd yon Crescent, and its ghost-like Moon.

And yet, far rather in my present Mood
85 I would, that thou'dst been sitting all this while
Upon the sod-built Seat of Camomile—
And tho' thy Robin may have ceas'd to sing,
Yet needs for *my* sake must thou love to hear
The Bee-hive murmuring near,
90 That ever-busy and most quiet Thing
Which I have heard at Midnight murmuring.

I feel my spirit moved.
And whereso'er thou be,
O Sister! O Beloved!
95 Those dear mild Eyes, that see
Even now the Heaven, *I* see—
There is a Prayer in them! It is for *me*—
And I, dear Sara, *I* am blessing *thee*!

It was as calm as this, that happy night
100 When Mary, thou, and I together were,
The low decaying Fire our only Light,
And listen'd to the Stillness of the Air!
O that affectionate and blameless Maid
Dear Mary! on her Lap my head she lay'd—
105 Her Hand was on my Brow,
Even as my own is now;
And on my Cheek I felt the eye-lash play.
Such joy I had, that I may truly say,
My spirit was awe-stricken with the Excess
110 And trance-like Depth of its brief Happiness.
Ah fair Remembrances, that so revive
The Heart, and fill it with a living Power,
Where were they, Sara?—or did I not strive
To win them to me?—on the fretting Hour
115 Then when I wrote thee that complaining Scroll,
Which even to bodily Sickness bruis'd thy Soul!
And yet thou blam'st thyself alone! And yet
Forbidd'st me all Regret!

And must I not regret, that I distress'd
120 Thee, best belov'd, who lovest me the best?
My better mind had fled, I know not whither,
For O! was this an absent Friend's Employ
To send from far both Pain and Sorrow thither
Where still his Blessings should have call'd down Joy!
125 I read thy guileless Letter o'er again—
I hear thee of thy blameless Self complain—

And only this I learn—and this, alas! I know—
That thou art weak and pale with Sickness, Grief, and Pain—
And *I*,—*I* made thee so!

130 O for my own sake I regret perforce
Whatever turns thee, Sara! from the course
Of calm Well-being and a Heart at rest!
When thou, and with thee those, whom thou lov'st best,
Shall dwell together in one happy Home,
135 One House, the dear *abiding* Home of All,
I too will crown me with a Coronal—
Nor shall this Heart in idle Wishes roam
    Morbidly soft!
No! let me trust, that I shall wear away
140 In no inglorious Toils the manly Day,
And only now and then, and not too oft,
Some dear and memorable Eve will bless
Dreaming of all your Loves and Quietness.
Be happy, and I need thee not in sight.
145 Peace in thy Heart, and Quiet in thy Dwelling,
Health in thy Limbs, and in thine eyes the Light
Of Love and Hope and honorable Feeling—
Where e'er I am, I shall be well content!
Not near thee, haply shall be more content!
150 To all things I prefer the Permanent.
And better seems it, for a Heart, like mine,
Always to *know*, than sometimes to behold,
    Their Happiness and thine—
For Change doth trouble me with pangs untold!
155 To see thee, hear thee, feel thee—then to part
    Oh! it weighs down the heart!
To *visit* those, I love, as I love thee,
Mary, and William, and dear Dorothy,
It is but a temptation to repine—
160 The transientness is Poison in the Wine,
Eats out the pith of Joy, makes all Joy hollow,
All Pleasure a dim Dream of Pain to follow!
My own peculiar Lot, my house-hold Life
It is, and will remain, Indifference or Strife.
165 While *Ye* are *well* and *happy*, 'twould but wrong you
If I should fondly yearn to be among you—
Wherefore, O wherefore! should I wish to be
A wither'd branch upon a blossoming Tree?

But (let me say it! for I vainly strive
170 To beat away the Thought), but if thou pin'd
Whate'er the Cause, in body or in mind,

I were the miserablest Man alive
To know it and be absent! Thy Delights
Far off, or near, alike I may partake—
175 But O! to mourn for thee, and to forsake
All power, all hope, of giving comfort to thee—
To know that thou art weak and worn with pain,
And not to hear thee, Sara! not to view thee—
Not sit beside thy Bed,
180 Not press thy aching Head,
Not bring thee Health again—
At least to hope, to try—
By this Voice, which thou lov'st, and by this earnest Eye—
Nay, wherefore did I let it haunt my Mind
185 The dark distressful Dream!
I turn from it, and listen to the Wind
Which long has rav'd unnotic'd! What a Scream
Of agony, by Torture lengthen'd out
That Lute sent forth! O thou wild Storm without!
190 Jagg'd Rock, or mountain Pond, or blasted Tree,
Or Pine-Grove, whither Woodman never clomb,
Or lonely House, long held the Witches' Home,
Methinks were fitter Instruments for Thee,
Mad Lutanist! that in this month of Showers,
195 Of dark brown Gardens and of peeping Flowers,
Mak'st Devil's Yule with worse than wintry Song
The Blossoms, Buds, and timorous Leaves among!
Thou Actor, perfect in all tragic Sounds!
Thou mighty Poet, even to frenzy bold!
200 What tell'st thou now about?
'Tis of the Rushing of an Host in Rout
And many groans for men with smarting Wounds—
At once they groan with smart, and shudder with the cold!
'Tis hush'd! there is a Trance of deepest Silence,
205 Again! but all that Sound, as of a rushing Crowd,
And Groans and tremulous Shudderings, all are over.
And it has other Sounds, and all less deep, less loud! . .
A Tale of less Affright,
And tempered with Delight,
210 As William's self had made the tender Lay—
'Tis of a little Child
Upon a heathy Wild,
Not far from home, but it has lost its way—
And now moans low in utter grief and fear—
215 And now screams loud, and hopes to make its Mother hear!

'Tis Midnight! and small Thoughts have I of Sleep.
Full seldom may my Friend such Vigils keep—
O breathe She softly in her gentle Sleep!
Cover her, gentle sleep! with wings of Healing.
220 And be this Tempest but a Mountain Birth!
May all the Stars hang bright above her Dwelling,
Silent, as though they *watch'd* the sleeping Earth!
Healthful and light, my Darling! may'st thou rise
With clear and chearful Eyes—
225 And of the same good Tidings to me send!
For oh! beloved Friend!
I am the buoyant Thing I was of yore
When like an own Child, I to Joy belong'd:
For others mourning oft, myself oft sorely wrong'd
230 Yet bearing all things then, as if I nothing bore!

Yes, dearest Sara, yes!
There *was* a time when tho' my path was rough,
The Joy within me dallied with Distress;
And all Misfortunes were but as the Stuff
235 Whence Fancy made me Dreams of Happiness;
For Hope grew round me, like the climbing Vine,
And Leaves and Fruitage, not my own, seem'd mine!
But now Ill Tidings bow me down to earth,
Nor care I that they rob me of my Mirth—
240 But Oh! each Visitation
Suspends what nature gave me at my Birth,
My shaping spirit of Imagination!

I speak not now of those habitual Ills
That wear out Life, when two unequal Minds
245 Meet in one House and two discordant Wills—
    This leaves me, where it finds,
Past Cure, and past Complaint,—a fate austere
Too fix'd and hopeless to partake of Fear!
But thou, dear Sara! (dear indeed thou art,
250 My Comforter, a Heart within my Heart!)
Thou, and the Few, we love, tho' few ye be,
Make up a World of Hopes and Fears for me.
And if Affliction, or distemp'ring Pain,
Or wayward Chance befall you, I complain
255 Not that I mourn—O Friends, most dear! most true!
    Methinks to weep with you
Were better far than to rejoice alone—
But that my coarse domestic Life has known

No Habits of heart-nursing Sympathy,
260 No Griefs but such as dull and deaden me,
No Mutual mild Enjoyments of its own,
No Hopes of its own Vintage, None O! none—
Whence when I mourn'd for you, my Heart might borrow
Fair forms and living Motions for its Sorrow.
265 For not to think of what I needs must feel,
But to be still and patient all I can;
And haply by abstruse Research to steal
From my own Nature, all the Natural man—
This was my sole Resource, my wisest plan!
270 And that, which suits a part, infects the whole,
And now is almost grown the Temper of my Soul.

My little Children are a Joy, a Love,
    A good Gift from above!
But what is Bliss, that still calls up a Woe,
275   And makes it doubly keen
Compelling me to *feel*, as well as *know*,
What a most blessed Lot mine might have been.
Those little Angel Children (woe is me!)
There have been hours when feeling how they bind
280 And pluck out the Wing-feathers of my Mind,
Turning my Error to Necessity,
I have half-wish'd they never had been born!
That seldom! but sad Thoughts they always bring,
And like the Poet's Philomel, I sing
285 My Love-song, with my breast against a Thorn.

With no unthankful Spirit I confess,
This clinging Grief, too, in its turn awakes
That Love, and Father's Joy; but O! it makes
The Love the greater, and the Joy far less.
290 These Mountains too, these Vales, these Woods, these Lakes,
Scenes full of Beauty and of Loftiness
Where all my Life I fondly hop'd to live—
I were sunk low indeed, did they *no* solace give;
But oft I seem to feel, and evermore I fear,
295 They are not to me now the Things, which once they were.

O Sara! we receive but what we give,
And in *our* life alone does Nature live.
Our's is her Wedding Garment, our's her Shroud—

And would we aught behold of higher Worth
300 Than that inanimate cold World allow'd
To the poor loveless ever anxious Crowd,
Ah! from the Soul itself must issue forth
A Light, a Glory, and a luminous Cloud
Enveloping the Earth!
305 And from the Soul itself must there be sent
A sweet and potent Voice, of its own Birth,
Of all sweet Sounds, the Life and Element.
O pure of Heart! thou need'st not ask of me
What this strong music in the Soul may be,
310 What and wherein it doth exist,
This Light, this Glory, this fair luminous Mist,
This beautiful and beauty-making Power!
Joy, innocent Sara! Joy, that ne'er was given
Save to the pure, and in their purest Hour,
315 *Joy*, Sara! is the Spirit and the Power,
That wedding Nature to us gives in Dower
        A new Earth and a new Heaven,
Undreamt of by the Sensual and the Proud!
Joy is that strong Voice, Joy that luminous Cloud—
320   We, we ourselves rejoice!
And thence flows all that charms or ear or sight,
All melodies, the Echoes of that Voice,
All Colors a Suffusion of that Light.
Sister and Friend of my devoutest Choice
325 Thou being innocent and full of love,
And nested with the Darlings of thy Love,
And feeling in thy Soul, Heart, Lips, and Arms
Even what the conjugal and mother Dove,
That borrows genial Warmth from those, she warms,
330 Feels in the thrill'd wings, blessedly outspread—
Thou free'd awhile from Cares and human Dread
By the Immenseness of the Good and Fair
        Which thou seest everywhere—
Thus, thus, should'st thou rejoice!
335 To thee would all things live from Pole to Pole;
Their Life the Eddying of thy living Soul—
O dear! O Innocent! O full of Love!
A very Friend! A Sister of my Choice—
O dear, as Light and Impulse from above,
Thus may'st thou ever, evermore rejoice!

                                    S.T.C.

B 'Resolution and Independence' by William Wordsworth

I have already noted, in two contexts, the close connection between Coleridge's preoccupations in poetry and Wordsworth's *Resolution and Independence*, which is printed here for comparison. (Composed between 3 May and 4 July 1802 it was first published in 1807.) Chatterton, with other 'mighty poets in their misery dead' is not only mentioned by name, the poem itself, unusually for Wordsworth, is written in formal Chattertonian stanzas. Its subject is similar to Coleridge's; Wordsworth fears the loss of his natural creative gift. It is the figure of the leech-gatherer that suggests how he must respond to the possibility. Just as the leeches dwindle and the old man must suffer and endure accordingly, so must Wordsworth. He feels admonished, not so much by the old man's example, as by the dreamlike atmosphere of bleakness of the entire natural scene.

Resolution and Independence

I

There was a roaring in the wind all night;
The rain came heavily and fell in floods;
But now the sun is rising calm and bright;
The birds are singing in the distant woods;
Over his own sweet voice the Stock-dove broods;
The Jay makes answer as the Magpie chatters;
And all the air is filled with pleasant noise of waters.

II

All things that love the sun are out of doors;
The sky rejoices in the morning's birth;
The grass is bright with rain-drops;—on the moors
The hare is running races in her mirth;
And with her feet she from the plashy earth
Raises a mist; that, glittering in the sun
Runs with her all the way, wherever she doth run.

III

I was a Traveller then upon the moor;
I saw the hare that raced about with joy;
I heard the woods and distant waters roar;
Or heard them not, as happy as a boy:
The pleasant season did my heart employ:
My old remembrances went from me wholly;
And all the ways of men, so vain and melancholy.

IV

But, as it sometimes chanceth, from the might
Of joy in minds that can no further go,
As high as we have mounted in delight
In our dejection do we sink as low;
To me that morning did it happen so;
And fears and fancies thick upon me came;
Dim sadness—and blind thoughts, I knew not, nor could name.

V

I heard the sky-lark warbling in the sky;
And I bethought me of the playful hare:
Even such a happy Child of earth am I;
Even as these blissful creatures do I fare;
Far from the world I walk, and from all care;
But there may come another day to me—
Solitude, pain of heart, distress, and poverty.

VI

My whole life I have lived in pleasant thought,
As if life's business were a summer mood;
As if all needful things would come unsought
To genial faith, still rich in genial good;
But how can He expect that others should
Build for him, sow for him, and at his call
Love him, who for himself will take no heed at all?

VII

I thought of Chatterton, the marvellous Boy,
The sleepless Soul that perished in his pride;
Of Him who walked in glory and in joy .
Following his plough, along the mountain-side:
By our own spirits are we deified:
We Poets in our youth begin in gladness;
But thereof come in the end despondency and madness.

VIII

Now, whether it were by peculiar grace,
A leading from above, a something given,
Yet it befell that, in this lonely place,
When I with these untoward thoughts had striven,
Beside a pool bare to the eye of heaven
I saw a Man before me unawares:
The oldest man he seemed that ever wore grey hairs.

As a huge stone is sometimes seen to lie
Couched on the bald top of an eminence;
Wonder to all who do the same espy,
By what means it could thither come, and whence;
So that it seems a thing endued with sense:
Like a sea-beast crawled forth, that on a shelf
Of rock or sand reposeth, there to sun itself;

X

Such seemed this Man, not all alive nor dead,
Nor all asleep—in his extreme old age:
His body was bent double, feet and head
Coming together in life's pilgrimage;
As if some dire constraint of pain, or rage
Of sickness felt by him in times long past,
A more than human weight upon his frame had cast.

XI

Himself he propped, limbs, body, and pale face,
Upon a long grey staff of shaven wood:
And, still as I drew near with gentle pace,
Upon the margin of that moorish flood
Motionless as a cloud the old Man stood,
That heareth not the loud winds when they call;
And moveth all together, if it move at all.

XII

At length, himself unsettling, he the pond
Stirred with his staff, and fixedly did look
Upon the muddy water, which he conned,
As if he had been reading in a book:
And now a stranger's privilege I took;
And, drawing to his side, to him did say,
'This morning gives us promise of a glorious day.'

XIII

A gentle answer did the old Man make,
In courteous speech which forth he slowly drew:
And him with further words I thus bespake,
'What occupation do you there pursue?
This is a lonesome place for one like you.'
Ere he replied, a flash of mild surprise
Broke from the sable orbs of his yet-vivid eyes.